To Connie + Jim Calaway!
Warmest Greetings!
Marilyn —
12/83

# MARILYN HORNE
*My Life*

# MARILYN HORNE
## *My Life*

BY

# MARILYN HORNE

*with Jane Scovell*

*New York*

ATHENEUM

1983

*Library of Congress Cataloging in Publication Data*

Horne, Marilyn.
  Marilyn Horne, my life.

  Discography: p.
  Includes index.
    1. Horne, Marilyn.  2.  Singers—United States—
Biography.  I.  Appleton, Jane, 1934–    .  II.  Title.
ML420.H66A3  1983        782.1'092'4  [B]        83-45075
ISBN 0-689-11401-X

*Published simultaneously in Canada by McClelland and Stewart Ltd.*
*Composition by Heritage Printers, Inc., Charlotte, North Carolina*
*Manufactured by Fairfield Graphics, Fairfield, Pennsylvania*
*Designed by Kathleen Carey*
*First Printing October 1983*
*Second Printing October 1983*

*To Mom & Dad*
AND
*Angela*

# Introduction

IT WAS 1967. I had recently been elected to the Board of Trustees of the Opera Company of Boston when Sarah Caldwell announced that the following February Marilyn Horne would sing Carmen, with her husband, Henry Lewis, conducting. I was elated. Though Horne was not as well known in Boston as in New York, I knew her from her recordings and played them constantly in my opera class at Newton College of the Sacred Heart. My students thought her name was "Lena" Horne—but then again they also believed that Verdi's *La Traviata* derived from Dumas' *"Our" Lady of the Camellias.*

Traditionally, opening-night parties were given by the trustees, but as the time grew shorter and no invitation appeared in the mail, I asked the Opera Company's Artistic Director, Miss Sarah Caldwell, who would be giving the *Carmen* party.

"No one," replied Miss Caldwell.

"You're kidding," I said. "Somebody's got to give a party for Marilyn Horne."

"You give it," she suggested.

The opening was barely a week away—little time to create a big party—nevertheless, I agreed to do it for a select group of directors and trustees, and Sarah promised to invite Mr. and Mrs. Lewis. I quickly called the Boston restaurateur Jacques Noé, another Horne devotee, and he promised to prepare a post-opera buffet.

On opening night, Jacques delivered a celebratory cake dazzlingly decorated with scenes from *Carmen*—truly a baked masterpiece—set up the food preliminaries and went off to his restaurant as I set out for the opera. Jacques planned to return before the party to get everything ready, ably assisted by a few Newton College students hastily pressed into service and cautioned not to refer to Miss Horne as "Lena."

I found Sarah Caldwell patrolling the theatre lobby and proudly announced to her that all systems were go for the big celebration.

"Well, honey," she replied in sepulchral tones, "that's nice, but Miss Horne isn't coming."

"What do you mean?"

"She said she can't come," answered Sarah, shrugging her shoulders and moving off.

Fearlessly, with no thought for my own safety, I blocked Miss Caldwell's exit. "When did you ask her?" I questioned suspiciously.

"Oh, ah . . . let's see . . . ah . . . I guess I mentioned it . . . ah . . . well, honey, I just dropped backstage and told her a few minutes ago."

"No wonder she won't come," I fumed. "It's insulting! You can't ask the guest of honor at the last minute, you were supposed to ask her days ago."

"Well, honey, I just forgot."

"Sarah, I've gone to a lot of trouble. My friend Jacques is working overtime, so are my students. She's got to come!"

"Okay, honey, you tell her."

And that's exactly what I did.

After the final curtain, Miss Caldwell ushered me into Miss Horne's dressing room, then disappeared quicker than you could say Georges Bizet. Backstage at the Opera House (formerly the Loew's State Theatre) was a setting worthy of Dante's Inferno. Peeling, crumbling walls and dank dressing rooms frequented by indigenous rodents as well as visiting singers created an inappropriate ambiance for a trustee resplendently arrayed in a Sarmi evening dress with yards and yards of white tulle cascading down from an Empire waist (a Filene's Basement bargain I had bought for $79.99, with an original price tag of $600). Marilyn Horne sat in front of a large mirror that was encircled by light bulbs, most of which were out. Her dark, close-cropped hair, wringing wet from the weight of a heavy wig worn for four acts, was pulled back tightly by a wide white band, her face glistened with Albolene cream and she was draped in a makeup-smeared robe.

"Excuse me, Miss Horne," I began quickly. "I'm going to level with you. The minute I found out there was no party scheduled, I told Sarah and she told me to do it. Believe me, it's a privilege and an honor, but there wasn't time to send a formal invitation and Sarah promised to ask you right away and . . ."

The diva stood up, turned around and interrupted my plaintive recitative. A look in her eyes and a distance in her attitude told me "no" before she opened her mouth. "Thank you, it's very kind of you, but I really have made other plans. I have friends with me and we're going back to the hotel, I'm sorry."

"Bring your friends," I squeaked impetuously. I could see Jacques' *Carmen* cake moldering like the centerpiece at Miss Havisham's feast.

"I'm sorry," repeated the singer emphatically. "I just can't."

I moved toward her. "Isn't there anything I can do to make you change your mind?"

The mezzo shook her head, still courteous, still cold as ice.

*"No,"* she said, raising her right arm and bringing it down in a gesture of finality. Her hand struck a coffee cup on the dresser and the cup flipped up off the saucer, splattering its contents down the front of my splendid white skirt.

"Shit!" cried Marilyn Horne before I had time to react. "I'm so sorry, I'm so sorry," she keened, leaning over and brushing furtively at the stains. This was no longer a prima donna giving the brushoff to a dressing-room pest; this was one woman who had messed up another woman's dress. "I'm so sorry, forgive me," she implored. "What can I do?"

"Come to the party," I said unhesitatingly.

Horne looked up, stared at me for a second, then threw her head back, laughing aloud. She had a marvelous laugh, deep, hearty and totally infectious. "Okay, okay," she agreed, "but it's a helluva way to invite someone!"

Thus my dress was ruined and our friendship began, a friendship which led to this book.

Over the years, I've learned a lot about the life of an opera singer. If you want to be the best, it's unrelieved toil. "You know," she sighed to me once, "at the most, it's fun maybe twice a year. The rest is just plain work." Horne wasn't kidding when she said she didn't want to go to the *Carmen* party. I naïvely thought that going to fancy soirees, and at far swankier quarters than mine, was part of the fun in being a celebrity. The truth is that, exhausted after a performance, Horne likes nothing better than to go home or to her hotel room, have a snack and perhaps watch a late movie on TV. Glamorous? Hardly, yet I've seen her be the life of parties she never wanted to attend, simply because some person or cause she cared about needed her. Despite an incredible work load, her energy rarely flags. I marvel at the level of performance she maintains on and off the stage as her energy is tested and retested. Hers is also a life filled with sudden pitfalls and alarms—concerns that most of us never dream of. I'll give one brief example.

In the summer of 1982, I accompanied her to Ottawa, Canada, where she was to appear in Handel's *Rinaldo.* It was a very important occasion, since this same production would be taken to New York in January 1984, not only the first Handel opera ever to appear on the Metropolitan stage, but a major offering of the opera house's centennial celebration as well. What's more, the performance would mark the occasion of Marilyn Horne's fiftieth birthday *and* the thirtieth anniversary of her operatic debut. There was a lot riding on the Ottawa "dry run"—which made it a particularly inappropriate time for her wisdom tooth to start acting up. No matter that she was in the middle of rehearsals—the tooth had to come out.

On the dread morning, we took a cab to the clinic and waited in an anteroom filled with people, none of whom were smiling. After what seemed an eternity, a nurse beckoned from the back hall—"Horne"—and Marilyn disappeared into the offices.

Ninety minutes later, the receptionist took me to the recovering patient. In a small back room, on a couch against the wall, lay the international opera star Marilyn Horne, and on a cot opposite her lay the supine figure of an acned teen-age boy, as comatose as the prima donna: extractions make for strange bedfellows. I went to Marilyn's side and leaned over. Her mouth was plugged with gauze and her eyes were closed.

"Congratulations," I whispered, "it's a boy."

Her eyes opened slowly. "Very funny," she said, "very funny."

It wouldn't be funny, though, if the extraction knocked Marilyn out of the opera. She spent a miserable afternoon and survived the night only with a hefty dose of Percodan. The next day wasn't much better: constant pain relieved by medication. The administration of the Ottawa Opera kept calling to see when she would be available for rehearsal and, though sympathetic, were obviously concerned about their big attraction. Lots of people have teeth pulled and go through the agony of recovery, but lots of people aren't opera singers worried about every nook and cranny of their oral cavities. One "solicitous" cast member actually phoned to ask if Marilyn despaired at losing a "resonator." Marilyn laughed it off, but, how did I know? Could the resulting hole somehow adversely affect her voice?

After three days of hotel-room confinement, Marilyn returned to rehearsals. We marched through the labyrinthine backstage area to her dressing room, to the tinny sounds of the orchestra tuning up over the intercom. A stream of well-wishers poured into the cramped quarters filled with letters and bouquets, until it began to resemble the stateroom scene from *A Night at the Opera*.

"Miss Horne onstage, please," squeaked the intercom.

"Wish me luck," said Marilyn as she walked out of the room. Her words were nonchalant, but she was worried. "Resonator" or not, after any crisis involving the voice or its production, the question always is, "Will it be okay when I open my mouth?" It's like a pilot pulling back on the stick and expecting his plane to take off. Of course it's going to lift up, but . . . what if it doesn't? As I waited in the dressing room, I heard muffled applause coming over the wall machine, members of the orchestra welcoming the diva back to the fold. It wasn't as easy to hear the conductor, Mario Bernardi, giving instructions, but soon came the tap-tap of his baton. Then, after a momentary silence and a short orchestral prelude, the inimitable voice of Marilyn Horne surged forth triumphantly from the intercom. The crisis was over.

Or was it? Days away at the time of the dental visit, the night of the premiere suddenly came upon us. We ate in the hotel room the evening of the performance, a light dinner marked by silence. Believe me, opera singers are not scintillating company before performances. They like to save their voices and store up energy by keeping to themselves, and what abbreviated chatter there is is liberally punctuated by sudden scales and ear-splitting throat-clearings.

After the dinner, I cleared the table and did the dishes in the kitchenette as she washed up in the bathroom. I was just stepping across the hall to ask if I should call for a taxi when suddenly she screamed and slammed the door in my face.

"Jesus, Jesus!" she cried. There was real terror in her voice and, frightened myself, I began banging on the door.

"What's the matter, what's happened?" I cried, but for the longest time she didn't answer. I could hear the water running furiously, and the sounds of gargling and spitting made a hideous parody of the usual noises emanating from that golden throat. At last, she opened the door and motioned for me to keep quiet as she continued to scoop up water from the tap and rinse out her mouth over and over again.

"Oh God, Jane, what am I going to do?" she implored.

"What *did* you do?" I asked urgently. It turned out she'd been using a glass inhaler to wash a mild saline solution through her mouth and nasal cavities in preparation for the performance. A plastic jar containing the solution stood right next to a similar container filled with alcohol, and by mistake she had poured the latter's contents into the inhaler and, for one brief, awful second, swirled it through her nose and mouth.

"I think I've burned my vocal cords," she said in a hoarse whisper.

"Don't be silly," I reassured her, "it's just the same as getting whiskey in your nose. It burns, but I'm sure there's no permanent damage." I spoke authoritatively, but was I right? What if she *had* burned her throat? Would she be able to sing that night? Would she be able to sing ever?

"I washed my nose and mouth out with saline," she said tearfully, "but it still stings." I helped her over to a chair in the sitting room. She sat down, put her head back and closed her eyes. The setting sun poured light into the room as we sat in silence. Every so often, Marilyn would clear her throat and wipe away the result with tissues. I got a wastebasket from the bedroom and put it beside her; soon it was filled with Kleenex.

"Do you think I can sing tonight?" she asked, opening her moistened eyes.

I shrugged my shoulders.

"Maybe I'll damage the cords," she continued despondently.

Finally, I said, "The opera company must have a doctor on call. Why don't you arrange to have him look at you? At least, then you'll *know* if there's been any damage."

"Good idea," she said, and though the news of her latest mishap must have staggered administrative officials still reeling from the tooth escapade, Marilyn was assured that a throat doctor would be at the auditorium. We dressed quickly and hurried to the concert hall. A little while later, as she sat in her dressing room applying makeup, an assistant stage manager peeked in and said a doctor was waiting in another room. I crossed my fingers and listened to the noise from the wall box. The minutes ticked by, stretching on endlessly. Nobody else had been told about the accident—how would they react when they heard? What if the production had to be canceled? The questions buzzed around in my head until finally the door opened and there was Marilyn, a triumphant smile on her face. Not only was there nothing wrong, but "You know what else?" she added proudly. "He told me I did just the right thing by washing out my mouth and nose." Like many performers, Miss Horne fancies herself a Dr. Kildare and is thrilled when her own assessment or treatment is verified by a *bona fide* physician. Nothing could have capped her pleasure more.

The performance that night was great and grueling. Rinaldo, one of those baroque roles of unrelenting *fioritura*, demands a Marilyn Horne to sing it. After the final curtain, she wanted to head straight back to the hotel and collapse in front of the TV, but there was the inevitable reception and she was the guest of honor. Matthew Epstein, an energetic young opera entrepreneur and erstwhile protégé of Horne's, was in Ottawa for the premiere and he urged her to attend the party.

"Come on," insisted Matthew, "it's a big night for Canada. You've got to show up."

She did. Despite the tooth, the alcohol and the weeks and weeks of work, she spent the rest of the evening chatting, smiling, signing autographs and being gracious—and on an empty stomach. The main buffet dish was shrimp and Marilyn Horne is allergic to shellfish. After all that effort, she couldn't even eat!

These tales are the merest suggestion both of the perils and of the day-to-day grind of her life. No words of mine can do justice to the constant pressure an artist like Marilyn Horne faces. Singing one role, preparing others, recording albums, making business arrangements, making personal appearances, constantly traveling from city to city, country to country, climate to climate, living out of hotels and—hardest of all, for Marilyn—being away from her daughter, Angela. For two years, I was part of this operatic mayhem and it left me ragged, and *I* didn't have to sing.

The *Rinaldo* incidents are still fresh in my memory; there are many, many more. I'd love to go on writing in *my* words, but this is *her* story, the story of a woman whose warmth, vitality, intelli-

gence, humor and generous spirit match in every respect her glorious voice. No one could better celebrate herself or sing herself than
Marilyn Horne.

JANE SCOVELL
*January, 1983*

# ACKNOWLEDGMENTS

Thanks to relatives, friends, associates and colleagues, especially Steve Rubin, Larry Tucker, Herbert Breslin, Shelley Welton, Cynthia Robbins, Bruce and Enid Beal, Norma Wasserman, Virginia Harris, Claire Montecalvo, Mikki Ansin, Joyce Arbib, Jay Siegel, Charles Beye, Polly Drinkwater, Neil Nyren, Gertrude Ginsburg, Fran Zaslow and my family. Finally, no collaborator could have a better subject and friend than Jackie Horne.

J.S.

# CONTENTS

# ILLUSTRATIONS

My La Scala debut as Jocasta, 1969
*L'Assedio di Corinto* with Beverly Sills at La Scala, 1969
With Angela, almost four


*(following page* 168)

My Met debut role, Adalgisa, in 1970
With Joan Sutherland in *Semiramide*, Chicago, 1971
A special role: Rosina
*Orfeo ed Euridice* at the Met
Marilyn Horne singing, Henry Lewis conducting
With Angela after *L'Italiana* at the Met
*Mignon* with Nicola Zaccaria at the Dallas Opera
On tour with the Met in Japan, 1975
*L'Italiana*, La Scala, 1975
Fides in *Le Prophète.*
Recording *Mignon* with Frederica von Stade, 1978
Dick, Gloria, me, and Jay—our last picture together
*Orlando Furioso*, Verona, 1978
Amneris in *Aïda*, Salzburg, 1979
Princess Eboli in *Don Carlo* at the Met, 1979
With Nico at a *Tancredi* rehearsal, 1979
*Semiramide*, Aix-en-Provence, 1980
Joan, Luciano and I, live from Lincoln Center, 1981
*Tancredi* with Katia Ricciarelli
"Coming home" to Venice twenty-five years after my debut there
With Angela in Venice
One more time: Sutherland and Horne in *Norma*, 1982
*Cenerentola*, 1982
With Martin Katz
With Angela at an autographing
With Francisco Araiza, Montserrat Caballé and Samuel Ramey in
    Hamburg
With James Levine and Leontyne Price at Lincoln Center, 1982
General Horne strikes again: *Rinaldo*

# MARILYN HORNE
*My Life*

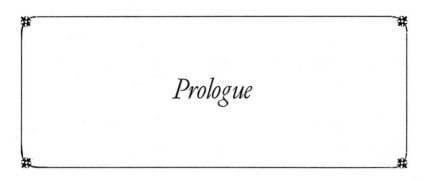

# *Prologue*

CALL ME JACKIE. My brother Dick gave me that nickname when I was born. He wanted a kid brother so badly he had the name ready, and my gender didn't alter his plan. So it's been "Jackie" ever since for family and friends.

My dad had a pet name for me, too. He called me "Peanut," and this is what he told me when I was a very little girl.

"Don't ever forget, Peanut. Whenever you think you're getting too big for the guy sitting next to you, remember the only thing that separates you from the rest of the world, what makes you special, is a little piece of gristle in your throat."

Isn't it inspirational to be told your claim to fame rests on a bit of cartilage? That's the way my dad talked, though—matter-of-fact, straight out, with no embellishments. He made no bones about the fact that my gift was an anatomical quirk, and was just as direct in telling me what he expected me to do with it. I was to go to the top, and in order to reach the pinnacle, I had to work—hard! From the beginning, there simply was no other way, and the result is that I'm an international opera star still bound to the Protestant work ethic of her youth. I've always had a purpose around which my life revolved, and that was to sing. Sure, I fought against it. As a kid, I sometimes wanted to play, go to the movies, parties, baseball games, *anything* rather than practice—and I did do those things—but my singing came first, and I learned early how to sacrifice. It's rough for a kid to know she's got responsibilities beyond the simple enjoyment of life, but the lessons my dad taught me have stood me in good stead for nearly half a century. Fifty years— I can't believe it myself, yet I know for sure that I wouldn't be singing today if I hadn't stuck to the principles established by my father.

My father was a pivotal figure in my life. A semi-professional singer with a fine voice, he was named Bentz Horne, and his middle name easily could have been Determination. I've inherited those two characteristics from him, the determination and the musicality, especially the former. Some people who don't know me well think of me as a bit tough, a bit brassy, someone who really speaks her mind. Well, to a certain extent that *is* part of me, but I don't always speak my mind and sometimes I'm not as tough as I should be. It's because I'm not only a singer, I'm a woman.

As a singer, I've gone from Hollywood soundstages to grand-opera houses, from genteel poverty to genteel riches, from boarding-houses to palaces, from choruses to center stage. Nobody ever handed me anything; I had to study, work and sing my heart out. I've been lucky, too—J. M. Barrie said of charm that if you didn't have it, nothing else mattered, and the same can be said of luck— but you have to take advantage of good fortune, and that I've done.

As a woman, my struggles have been more arduous.

In 1960, before Selma and Freedom Rides, before desegregation, before black became beautiful, I married a Negro, and America's unwritten apartheid threatened to stop my career before it began. The man was Henry Lewis, a brilliant musician and conductor. I loved him and had a child by him, a child who is everything to me.

My daughter, Angela, is eighteen, of mixed blood, and a talented and beautiful human being. Because her parents were celebrities, she led a sheltered life surrounded by friends in the entertainment world. It is only recently that she has had to come to grips with other people's reality. A little while ago, she spent an evening at home, waiting to hear from two school friends who were to meet her at the Plaza, along with one of the girls' mothers. They never phoned. The next day, one of the girls called in tears to say that the mother hadn't wanted to include Angela because of my daughter's heritage. I called that woman, and though she denied everything, she didn't fool me. Angela didn't whimper about the situation, she simply got mad at the stupidity of prejudice. It's a battle my daughter will have to learn to wage. I'll be there to back her up, but she was born to it.

Her father is there to help her, too, and though we are united in loving and caring for our child, we are no longer married. At the height of my career, my marriage failed. Like so many women of my generation, I had to learn to face life alone. I was lucky, I had a career, but even that couldn't protect me from the torture of divorce, the pain of finding and creating a place for myself as a single woman. I came out of it, though, and that's part of my story. I want to tell you all about it, and I'll open in Venice.

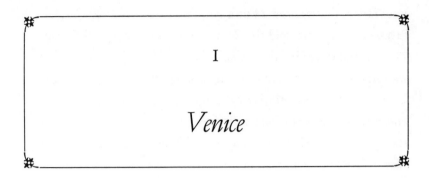

I

*Venice*

"*Venetia, Venetia,*
*Chi non ti vede non ti pretia.*"
"Venice, Venice,
Who doesn't know you doesn't appreciate you."
OLD PROVERB

ON DECEMBER 9, 1981, I arrived in Venice, Italy, to make my debut at La Fenice, the most beautiful opera house in the world, on whose stage Rossini's *Semiramide* and *Tancredi*, Bellini's *I Capuleti e i Montecchi*, Verdi's *Ernani, Attila, Rigoletto, La Traviata* and *Simon Boccanegra*, Stravinsky's *Rake's Progress* and Britten's *Turn of the Screw* all had had their premieres. I had been engaged to sing the title role in *Tancredi* one hundred and sixty-eight years after its premiere here and a quarter of a century after my first visit to the city of liquid streets. In 1956, Igor Stravinsky had chosen me to perform in the International Festival of Music in Venice. I had been a twenty-two-year-old unknown singer, alone in a foreign country, an ambitious, sassy, somewhat idealistic, single young woman, sure of her talent and determined to succeed.

6

Twenty-five years later, I was still blessed with my voice, still ambitious and sassy, and single again, but I was no longer unknown. Ten months before, in *Opera News* magazine, editor Robert Jacobson had declared, "It's that simple. Marilyn Horne is probably the greatest singer in the world." (If only it were that simple!) In a few months, the Rossini Foundation would present me with its very first Golden Plaque, calling me *"il più grande Rossini cantante del mondo"*—"the greatest Rossini singer in the world." Some might dispute that phrase, but who was I to argue with Italy? In fact, that was what made it all the more special. The very idea of a non-Italian receiving such an honor would once have been inconceivable.

*Tancredi* had already proven a spectacular vehicle for me in Houston, San Francisco, Aix-en-Provence, New York City and Rome, but the Venice engagement was especially meaningful for me. Because the opera—Rossini's first big triumph—had been born there, as had my international career, it felt, in a sense, as if both *Tancredi* and I were coming home.

Ironically, though, for all my success with *Tancredi*, my association with this opera almost never began. Until a scant two decades ago, Rossini had been known primarily for his comic operas such as *Il Barbiere di Siviglia*; few people appreciated the greater number of serious operas this prolific, versatile genius had also composed—elaborate, formal works such as *Semiramide*, *L'Assedio di Corinto* and *Tancredi*, all of which I've performed many times now. Indeed, my efforts to revive his serious works had much to do with the Rossini medal I'd be receiving.

Reviving *Tancredi* had posed some problems, however. There were at least two versions of the opera in existence, one with a happy ending and one that was much more somber and downbeat. The plot of *Tancredi*, set in Syracuse in the ninth century, has the daughter of the lord of Syracuse promised to one man, Orbazzano,

7

while in love with another, Tancredi, the son of the *deposed* lord of Syracuse. (One thing is certain in opera: if a daughter's hand is promised to one man, she has to be in love with another.) The daughter, Amenaide, sends a message to Tancredi, telling him to come take both the city and her heart, but it's intercepted by Orbazzano and misinterpreted as a letter to the leader of the enemy Saracens, and Amenaide is forthwith condemned to death as a traitor. Tancredi challenges Orbazzano to a duel to prove Amenaide's innocence—even though the young warrior believes she's guilty. Orbazzano is killed, Tancredi goes off to fight the Saracens, the notorious message is revealed to have been written to Tancredi and, in the happy ending created by a librettist catering to public taste, the young lovers are reunited at the victory celebration.

That ending didn't sit right with me, though. Musically, dramatically and every other way, it just seemed wrong, and though I knew that another version existed in which Tancredi in fact died in battle, I had no idea where to locate it. When the Houston Opera presented plans to stage a revival of the opera with me as Tancredi, I told them flat out that I would not do it unless they *found* that other ending. Happily, Philip Gossett, a renowned musicologist, had searched and searched—and finally unearthed it. When it was shown to me, I *knew* my instincts had been correct. Tancredi's death scene, mournful, noble and moving, was in keeping with the opera's prevailing mood, and that was the version we did, and would be doing in Venice.

Those unfamiliar with opera may wonder when I say that the part I played was Tancredi, the young warrior himself. Tancredi is a "trouser role," meaning that a woman plays the man, and it's not unusual for me—indeed, my career has been given quite a boost by my proficiency in such roles. A good portion of them are a legacy from the legendary castrati: promising boy singers mutilated at puberty, thus calling a halt to certain primary and secondary sexual developments, and producing a freak voice with a female timbre and range supported by the more powerful male physique. Such voices were capable of incredible vocal pyrotechnics, and castrati dominated the musical world from the mid-seventeenth century to the early nineteenth.

Rossini wrote for one castrato, a man named Velluti, but Tancredi was not a castrato role. It was a male character actually written for a female to sing, thus carrying on the tradition of the treble voice for the leading male role. Such parts were usually young men, often aristocratic and just on or over the brink of manhood, but already commanders of armies—hence the gallery nickname for me, "General Horne." The essence of this delicate stage in development is best represented by women rather than by full-grown tenors or baritones, and the vocal range, as a rule, calls for the low female register, contralto or mezzo.

Well, mezzo, that's me, and here I was in Venice and I couldn't wait to begin.

On a sunny Wednesday afternoon, representatives from La Fenice met me at the Marco Polo airport and escorted me to the waiting "taxi"—a motor boat—and we sped across the lagoon into *"La Serenissima,"* the city of Venice. Rehearsals began the next day.

Opera rehearsals always include a *Sitzprobe* or, as the Americans call it, the *ala Italiana.* All the principals in the opera sit down and go through the score, providing themselves and the director with a basic musical run-through. Among the others with me at the *Sitzprobe* that day were Ernesto Palacio as Argirio, Lella Cuberli as Amenaide and Nicola Zaccaria as Orbazzano. This was quite unusual. Ernesto was Peruvian, Lella was Texan, Nicola was Greek and, besides me, there was yet a third American, and a Yugoslavian! Such a lineup would have been unheard of a few years ago. It says a lot for the state of opera today that more and more "foreigners," particularly Americans, are performing in Italy. Once upon a time, you almost *had* to be Italian to sing opera, not only in the mother country but here at home. Singers even changed their names to sound Italian: Lily Norton from Farmington, Maine, went to Milan in the late nineteenth century and returned to sing at the Metropolitan Opera as Lillian Nordica. If I'd been performing in those days, my name would probably have ended up something like Mafalda Corno!

Anyway, that day went well enough, but putting on an opera often involves as much drama offstage as on, and *Tancredi* proved to be no exception.

First, there was the flooding. Venice seems constantly on the verge of being permanently engulfed, and during rehearsal the *"aqua alta"* (high water) actually lapped its way into part of the opera house. My stage entrance as Tancredi was to be on the prow of a boat, and from the way the canals were overflowing, I feared I might really be sailing in! The cast and crew alike had to garb themselves in waterproof boots and slosh around during high tides like fishermen rather than musicians and technicians.

Then came the Roggiero crisis. When the opera had been revived in Aix-en-Provence one year before, many cuts had been made, including an aria for Roggiero, another pants role. The Venice production was supposed to be definitive, but the complete opera is very, very long, and a tribunal of Rossini authorities, desperate to preserve and at the same time slim down the work, had decided to eliminate Roggiero's big aria. The young American mezzo essaying the role was understandably upset and came to me.

"Please, please, Miss Horne," she pleaded. "This is my big chance, but it's all tied up in that aria. If they take it away, then I have nothing to show. Please, my career is in your hands!"

Suddenly, her career was in *my* hands? And she was a mezzo, to boot! I decided to help her anyway. The next day, I spoke to the tribunal, assuring them that in order to honor Rossini rightly, Roggiero's aria should be included. "After all, gentlemen," I purred, "the *Tancredi* in Aix-en-Provence was a 'provincial' production. Are you going to follow the lead of the provinces here in the Big City, in the very house where *Tancredi* premiered? Are you going to butcher the master's work?" The tribunal relented and the aria was restored.

Length posed another problem for me during those rehearsals, but in a very different way. During the first week, I was presented with a splendid gold-trimmed royal-blue cloak for Tancredi. Alas, when I donned it for the run-through, it proved to be way too long and I kept tripping over my feet. To my complaints, the dresser responded,

"Ah, but, Signora, it is only long because it makes you look so grand and gives you the noble line."

"Garbage," I rejoined (or words to that effect), "it's long because my understudy takes over the part when I leave and she's a foot taller than I am!" I flung the cape to the floor and walked out of the dressing room. The next time I assumed the mantle, the hemline was just right.

Let me make myself clear about that cloak. I didn't make a fuss about it because I wanted to act the prima donna, but because singing on an opera stage is such hard work that it is absolutely necessary to feel completely in command when you're out there. If you have to worry about the length of a cloak or the reliability of a prop or a cramp in your leg, it can take the edge right off your concentration, and that will affect the performance.

For the same reason, it's important to try to keep in shape physically. Singing is a strain on the entire physical being, not just the vocal cords and diaphragm. My woes come from my legs, not my lungs—I'm more worried about my knees giving out than my breath and have a whole set of exercises designed to keep them supple and my muscles from cramping up. When I neglect to do them, I suffer the consequences on stage. It's hard to move with ease, and you *have* to move onstage; you can't just stand there if you're going to be Arsace or Tancredi. When Stendhal spoke of Giuditta Pasta as Tancredi, he said she presented the "aspect of the warrior." A real artist *must* give this "aspect."

Again, the role of costuming is important. When I'm doing a young warrior, I like to stride like a soldier, and I need the proper footwear to capture the movement. For *Tancredi*, I brought a special pair of boots with me, the most comfortable ones I owned, which allowed me the freedom of movement necessary to create the character. Besides three-inch heels, they were built up inside, and not just for comfort—I need the height. My dad nicknamed me "Peanut" because I was short, and my size is especially evident when I'm playing trouser roles. Adalgisa, Carmen, Rosina, Isabella, Cenerentola—all those gals can be five foot two, but Arsace, Orlando, Orfeo, Neocle, Rinaldo and Tancredi need elevation. When I'm playing the part of a man, I like to be as high as the heroine and, thanks to my special boots, can reach some sort of altitudinal compromise with my innamorata. There are exceptions, though. I could pile up boxes and stand on them tiptoe, and I'd still be looking at Joan Sutherland's neck.

While all these rehearsal dramas were playing themselves out, eventfully but at least more or less normally for opera, another crisis was brewing—one of a distinctly more personal nature.

I've mentioned that Nicola Zaccaria, a Greek basso, was also appearing in *Tancredi*. I knew Nico very well. He was a friend, a close friend—in fact, my love. Our relationship had begun after my breakup with Henry Lewis and had endured despite certain difficulties, namely ( 1 ) my daughter, Angela; ( 2 ) Nico's estranged wife; and (3) my own feelings about whether or not I wanted a permanent alliance.

Two weeks after our arrival, Angela would be joining us in Venice to spend Christmas, and though I was eager to see my baby, her presence would be a mixed blessing. From the very beginning, she'd been openly hostile to Nico. Although he doesn't speak English, he's fluent in four other languages including French, which Angela speaks, but she wouldn't talk to him. It's understandable for a child not to want anyone to take her father's place, but I'd never asked her to "accept" Nico, just to be civil to him. It may be true that Hell hath no fury like a woman scorned, but second place has to go to a teen-age girl whose mother has taken another man.

Nevertheless, Nico was always understanding and took Angela's barbs with incredible equanimity. The Greek male gives new meaning to the word "macho," yet he was consistently kind, turning the other cheek so often I was surprised his head didn't screw right off his neck. As far as Angela, Nico and I were concerned, I was desperately hoping for "peace on earth" that Christmas—but I wasn't banking on it.

The problem with Nico's wife was equally perplexing. They'd been married for thirty-five years and estranged for many of those, but they still were not legally divorced. Being with a "married" man bothered me, because I didn't want to be cast in the role of the "other woman." Luckily, my work kept me from thinking too much about the problem, but that didn't mean it was going to go away—a fact which was driven home to me quite forcefully one day, about two weeks into rehearsal.

In its own destructive way, the floods that were battering Venice were quite exciting, and one afternoon, after a rehearsal, I decided to brave the waves and visit San Marco. Nico was off somewhere and I walked alone down the Calle Seconda de l'Ascension and into a little corner where the designer Roberta de Camerino had a shop. Who could walk by without looking in the window? I was standing there, checking the display, when I felt my sleeve being tugged. I'm used to being tugged, pushed, pulled and even mauled, so I don't pay much attention when I'm accosted. Most of the time, I smile and move on, and that's what I tried to do then, but the person caught me by the sleeve. I turned around to face my admirer and knew right away that this was no ordinary fan.

She was about my height and nearly my size. She had a strong Mediterranean face, a wig on her head, and her face was lined— wrinkles had gathered at the corners of her eyes and mouth. I guessed her to be in her late fifties, still handsome, yet a spark seemed to be missing in those eyes.

"You are *la Signora* Horne?" she asked in Italian.

"Yes," I replied.

"I must talk to you," she said. "I am Elefteria Zaccaria."

Now, I may be from Bradford, Pennsylvania, out of Long Beach, California, but I know how to be civilized in the European manner. It means that when you meet your boyfriend's wife, much as you would like to, you don't turn and run, you stand and talk. I hope my mouth didn't fall open when Mrs. Zaccaria introduced herself. It was quite a jolt, though; as far as I knew, she was supposed to be in Athens. Though she'd refused to give Nico a divorce, she had never tried to contact me in all the years I'd been with her husband . . . and now here she was in person. I suggested that we not remain in the street, but repair to the nearby Bauer Grunwald Hotel. As we walked, she linked elbows with me in the cozy European style. Anyone seeing us would have thought we were two old chums out for a stroll.

We sat at a table in the nearly empty lobby. I could feel her staring at me as I removed my coat and draped it over the chair, and remember wishing I looked a little snappier. I was wearing a tight-fitting turban and no makeup—perfect for rehearsal but a bit lacking in style for a personal drama. Worse, I'd put on weight. Isn't it ridiculous! I wanted to "look my best." We ordered tea and indulged in small talk about opera and Venice until the main topic finally surfaced. She was staying for my entire run in *Tancredi* and had taken a room at the Hotel Ala. The Ala is in the Campo Santa Maria del Giglio, directly across the square from the Gritti Palace apartments where we were staying. It wasn't a coincidence. Though she didn't come out and say it, she'd obviously checked our itinerary and carefully chosen her vantage point.

Her choice was made all the more obvious by the fact that her room at the Hotel Ala had no television, radio or even telephone, deprivations she pointed out tellingly, perhaps to contrast her sparse surroundings with my deluxe quarters—quarters in which Nico was ensconced. I've been through separation and divorce and understand the torments they can bring, and in many ways I sympathized with this woman. Nevertheless, I didn't like the way she had followed me, nor did I like having to explain what I didn't feel had to be explained.

"You, Signora Horne, have everything—a great career, fame, money, a child. Why did you take my husband?" she said.

Very carefully, I pointed out that I had not taken away her husband, that in fact they'd been separated before I'd ever appeared. Furthermore, I was letting no cats out of the bag when I commented that I was not the first nor the only woman with whom Nico had had a relationship (personally, I knew of at least two sopranos and a mezzo, but didn't mention them to her). None of it had any effect. When I finished, Mrs. Zaccaria asked me to give him up.

"Even if I gave him up," I replied as gently as possible, "do you think he'd go back to you?"

She was silent for a moment. "Signora Horne, I have nothing in my life besides Nico. What can I do? What shall I do?"

Again, I was being asked for help, but it wasn't a question of restoring an aria this time. This was real life and there was nothing I could do. Her marriage had soured, but not because of me, and all I could do was try to convince her that I was not an adversary. I succeeded, at least partially, when I said quite frankly that I had told Nico not to get a divorce on my account, because I couldn't promise to marry him. The statement seemed to relieve her.

It was some tea party that afternoon in Venice, almost as dizzy as the Mad Hatter's. I was used to playing prima donna or even the girl next door, not the other woman, so when an opportune moment arrived, I suggested we part. When we reached the street, Mrs. Zaccaria and I embraced, kissed and wished each other well.

Nico was aghast when I told him of my experience. "How could she? How could she?" he kept saying, and I had to explain it all to him. Under similar circumstances, it was possible I might have done the same thing—who could say? I didn't blame Elefteria Zaccaria. What really concerned me was her proximity. Angela was due to arrive the next day, and I didn't want my daughter mixed up in this affair.

My life was not grand opera, it was soap opera.

The following afternoon, busy with rehearsal, I arranged for a launch to meet Angela at the airport. When I returned to the Gritti apartments in the early evening, I found my teen-ager settled in, the Who blasting from the tape recorder and assorted clothing strewn from the rafters. We hugged and kissed, but the frost was on my little pumpkin. Though Nico had discreetly stayed away from the initial mother-daughter meeting, his presence was obvious and Angela visibly stiffened at the telltale signs of his occupancy. She knew he was going to be there and, though we each had a separate room in the four-room suite, regarded the evidence of his presence with customary disdain. When he arrived later and warmly welcomed Angela, she sneered and went into her room. Nico shrugged his shoulders and smiled at me; I sighed and began to prepare dinner. Playing "mother" was far more difficult than playing Tancredi. Despite my hopes, the prospects for a truly merry Christmas didn't look rosy.

Nico stayed out of the picture for the next few days. He was always up and out early in the morning, while Angela and I arose around noon or later. We'd brunch together, then go our separate ways, my route always the same: to the Fenice. Rehearsals took place in the afternoon and as the strains of *Tancredi* filled the Fenice, the sounds of the Who, the Police and the Beatles reverberated in the Gritti. Angela didn't go out much without me and was cautioned, when she did, not to talk to strangers, especially, I wanted to add, to middle-aged Mediterranean ladies. I needn't have worried. Signora Zaccaria never crossed our paths, though Nico took her out a few times and unsuccessfully tried to persuade her to leave. She stayed, but at a judicious distance. Occasionally, I'd catch a glimpse of her walking in the piazza, but that was all. What a situation! Opera is full of good guys and bad guys, but life isn't so clearly divided. Mrs. Zaccaria was just an unhappy woman —and because of my alliance with her "husband," I couldn't classify myself as a thoroughly wonderful human being either. All I could do was hope all would be for the best.

Meanwhile, as my domestic drama surged on, my operatic drama continued to take shape. Tancredi is a marvelous part, marvelous to sing, that is, and very difficult, especially the aria *"Ah, che scordar."* It is a slow-moving piece which requires me to measure the exact flow of my breath, because the notes go into the worst part of the female voice. Tancredi is the kind of part that gives the singer a run for her money. Some operatic roles are naturals; you shine no matter what you do—Arsace in *Semiramide* is one of those. Tancredi is a hero of a different color. He has three big arias and three big duets and the hero must be "up" for the entire evening, especially at the end when the dying warrior is carried onstage to sing the final aria horizontally! Lella said to me after the first full run-through, "How do you do it, Jackie, how do you keep it up? I'm ready to collapse after the prison scene!" Obviously, Lella didn't have Bentz Horne for a father! I *had* to keep it up.

On opening night, the city was covered by an Adriatic mist. It was positively eerie, and as we set out for the theatre, I couldn't help thinking how many times my important appearances had been accompanied by bad weather. Always before, it had brought luck; I certainly hoped this time would be no exception.

La Fenice has a tradition: before every performance, a cat is let in and sent down the center aisle. I don't know where the tradition came from, but it's charming, a kind of good-luck token for us all. That night, as usual, the audience assembled, the house lights dimmed, the cat came in on little fog feet—and the overture to *Tancredi* began. Backstage, I climbed into the prow of Tancredi's ship and sailed into my Fenice debut.

Everything went well—splendidly, in fact—but I've rarely known a production where *something* didn't go wrong. In this case, it didn't happen until the last scene, in which the dying hero (me) is brought in on a bier and remains supine during the final aria. Amenaide goes to her lover and stands beside him, falling to her knees as he bids her farewell. I was carried in, saw Lella Cuberli as Amenaide approaching, and raised my head to acknowledge her. When I did so, one of the pillows propping me up was dislodged and began to slide down my face. A heavy cloth had been draped over my body, pinning down my arms—I was helpless. As Lella bent over, I whispered frantically, "Get the pillow out of my mouth!" Lella stepped between me and the audience, knocked the pillow to the floor and started to sing. I joined her, and the opera finished to thunderous applause. One hundred and sixty-eight years later, *Tancredi* was still a hit!

Even the critics, distrustful of such a predominantly foreign cast, agreed. The Communist newspaper went so far as to say, gritting its teeth, "If we're going to do Rossini, then we must hire Marilyn Horne and pay her whatever she wants. She's the only one who can do it."

The second performance, on the 23rd, went even more smoothly —no pillow in the mouth this time—and it finally looked like I could stop worrying about the opera and just enjoy it. Now if only I could do the same for my home life. I so much wanted our Christmas together to be happy, but the ice maiden hadn't melted and things looked chilly indeed.

At last, it was the night before Christmas. A small group was due to gather in my apartment, including Ernesto; Lella and her husband, Luigi; Nico, Angela, me and two or three others. Earlier in the evening, Angela and I had gone shopping at Standa, the Woolworth's of Italy, and bought decorations. Then, we'd picked up a sweet little tree near the Rialto and loaded up with cold cuts, cheeses, bread, cakes and wine at the local grocery. Venice was clear, chilly and sparkling with lights. A huge Christmas tree aglow with red, green and yellow bulbs stood in front of the Accademia. The setting was perfect, outside and in.

Back at the apartment, Angela and I trimmed the tree together, laughing and arguing over what should go where, just as we had at home for so many years. Once the tree was decorated, we placed the presents at the base, and then dressed for the celebration.

Our guests arrived and Angela was a perfect hostess, chatting and giggling—but not in Nico's direction. I sighed inwardly. We ate, sang Christmas carols and watched the Mass from St. Peter's on television. Then it was time to open the presents. Angela gave me a delicate gold pin with a white coral rose in the center. I gave her a sledful of goodies from Paris, including enough clothes, accessories and makeup kits to take her into middle age. (I have a tendency to go overboard in gift-giving. Marty Katz, my accompanist, says I buy everything in bulk.) Then Angela unwrapped another present. It was from Nico, a handsome wallet from Balenciaga. She looked at it, held it in her hands for a moment and then looked over at Nico. "Thanks," she said. It was the most beautiful word I'd ever heard. And I was in for another surprise. A minute later, Nico retrieved a package from under the tree marked with his name. Inside was a package of assorted liqueurs and a card reading, "To Nico, Merry Christmas, from Angela." It was the first time she'd given him anything and I don't know who was more pleased, Nico or me. Angela had called a truce for the holiday and it was my nicest present. I knew she hadn't made a complete turnabout and wasn't about to become best friends with Nico, but I wasn't asking for big miracles. The mini-miracle was enough to make it a very happy Christmas Eve.

Angela left Venice on December 30. It had been a good time for us. We'd gotten along with a minimum of mother-daughter outbursts, and having her with me had made my Christmas perfect. Now only four more performances remained before the cloak would have to be let down for the next *Tancredi*. After that, I would go to Milan to record a new *Barber* with La Scala, then Nico and I would return to New York City and a new production of the *Barber* at the Met.

My last performance, on January 11, 1982, was non-subscription and opera lovers came from all over—not a seat could be had. The house was so packed, even the cat must have had difficulty getting in. Once more, I stepped into the boat and, along with the audience, enjoyed the magic of Rossini. The spell was so great I even had to repeat the opening aria, a rare and very special moment for me.

At times, I get a spiritual, mystical feeling when singing. It's difficult to put into words, because it is so tied to the music, but I can only say I experience a sublime peace. Usually, it happens when I'm in recital, since in opera there's so much going on that you can't fully give yourself over to the music, whereas in concert one brief song can bring rapture. However, at the end of *Tancredi*, as I lay dying, all need for worry about stage directions past, I looked up and out into the jewel-box theatre and that ethereal feeling came over me. I was here in the Fenice, surrounded by Rossini's glorious music, singing a role first heard nearly two centuries ago. I was a part of history, part of an unbroken tradition of song which I'd served all my life. There was something sacred about this moment, and as the curtain fell on the final hushed chords, I thought to myself, "If you're up there listening, Gioacchino Rossini, thank you and I hope you liked it."

I'd come a long, long way to be where I was now. Like Tancredi and other heroes I'd portrayed, I'd had a quest in life . . . and for me it had begun in Bradford, Pennsylvania.

## I I

# *Bradford*

I WAS born in Bradford at the height of the Great Depression. The town itself lies four miles below the New York State line in the Appalachian Plateau region of Pennsylvania, not far from the Allegheny River. The plateau, a land of great divides, covers almost the entire northern and western portions of the state. Its terrain of deep valleys, broad flattop plateaus and glacial rocks is most beautiful in the fall when colors burst over the rolling hills. Bradford was right out of Middle America, a backlot version of Small Town, U.S.A. Judge Hardy could have lived there, though perhaps not on our street—we weren't as affluent as the Judge's family.

The Hornes and Mother's family, the Hokansons, had been around for a long, long time. My father's ancestors came from Germany in the early nineteenth century, but Mother's went way back to 1610 when the Van Hoorn brothers arrived from Holland. Later, they were joined by my great-grandparents, Wilhelm and Hulda Hokanson, who, along with their five-year-old son, Emil, sailed from Smoland, Sweden, in the late 1800's. Plenty of relatives were here in Colonial times—an ancestor even fought at Bunker Hill. That's the plus side. Then there's my grandmother, Sadie Hokanson. Though nobody knew it until after her death, she was a card-carrying member of the Ku Klux Klan. While going through her effects, they found it, big as life and twice as ugly— a genuine membership card proclaiming Grandma a KKK member in good standing. Lucky for her she died before my marriage!

David Horn, my great-grandfather, fought with the Union Army at Antietam, Fredericksburg and Chancellorsville, then, when the war was over, returned to York, Pennsylvania, married Sarah A. Morningstar and had eleven children, four of whom survived. Samuel H. assisted his father in his prosperous plumbing business. James B., my grandfather, a musician by profession, moved to Bradford, Pennsylvania. Luther P., a businessman in Hanover, Pennsylvania, patented and manufactured something called the Laraphone. Arthur H., also a talented musician, studied piano at the Stuart Gipes Academy of Music and Languages in York. Both Luther and James taught piano.

Bentz Horne, my dad, was born on November 7, 1906, in Pittsburgh, the son of James Bentz Horn and Ada Mae Prunkard Horn. His only sister, Adelaide, was born on January 20, 1909. Most immigrant families lop off letters or syllables from their names; not my dad—for some reason, he added a final "e" to Horn before his marriage. Later, in high school, I would do my own brief version of ornamentation by adding a final "n" to Marilyn, making it "Marilynn." It was lopped off when I went to Germany in 1956 and it's been back to Marilyn ever since.

My mother, Berneice, the daughter of Emil Hokanson and Sarah

"Sadie" Huff Hokanson, was one of six children: Ernest, Kenneth, Violet, Florence and Genevieve were the others. I have twelve first cousins on my mother's side.

Bentz and Berneice were married on June 2, 1926; neither graduated from high school. Their first child, Richard, arrived on February 27, 1927—Mom swore he was conceived on her wedding night, but she was always a bit embarrassed about the proximity of those dates. Dick was followed by Gloria on May 23, 1931, and yours truly, Marilyn Berneice, made her debut at 3:20 p.m. EST on January 16, 1934. That looked to be it as far as Hornes went, but there turned out to be a sibling codicil. On October 18, 1949, sixteen years after me and all the way across the country in California, my baby brother, Jay, was born. It's strange that the first decade and a half of my life doesn't include Jay, who knows about Bradford only through story and two sad visits to bury parents, and is himself a child of the West Coast.

Our household was, with a few exceptions, American Normal. I was baptized in the United Brethren Church, but later joined the Methodist Church because we all sang in its choir. Later still, Mother, Gloria and I became confirmed Episcopalians and attended the Church of the Ascension and St. Luke's Episcopal Church in California. Dad and Dick stayed Methodists. I was a regular churchgoer until I went to Europe, when I became a practicing Christian humanist. I still go to church on holidays and occasionally drop in to sit with my thoughts, but, after being a Protestant magpie for so long, I've finally settled down into agnosticism.

In typical Depression fashion, Dad went from job to job and made a barely living wage, while Mother both worked and raised the family. The worst came when she had to leave baby Richard with Grandma Horne and travel thirty-five miles away to work in Warren, Pennsylvania. The separation was financially necessary but emotionally devastating. Years later, when career demands forced me to leave my daughter in the care of others, I recalled mother's distress with added understanding.

When I was a baby, we lived in a house with a small store in front. I don't remember those days, but I gather that Mom and Dad ran a grocery to help get us through the Depression years. I'm sure Mom was the driving force in this operation. The store and house were on Elm Street, and when the Hornes became more secure financially and moved to number 9 Avenue B around the corner, it was a real step up. Number 9 was the best house on the block. During my childhood, Nanny Horne was the official baby-sitter and looked after Dick, Gloria and me. She was there when we came home from school for lunch and after school let out. Nanny Horne fixed meals for us, ironed and cleaned, mended clothes, applied bandages and did anything else that was necessary. She herself had only gone as far as the eighth grade, but what she lacked in education she made up for in humanity. Though argumentative as all get-out, Ada Prunkard Horne gave us nothing but love.

My father's love—indeed, his passion—was music, a natural affinity since his family was so thoroughly musical, and on a professional level. His father and uncles taught piano, and all my uncles sang in barber-shop quartets. On the other side, Aunt Maybelle, Mother's sister-in-law, was a fine pianist and some of my happiest childhood recollections are of her at the keyboard. Dad was a tenor and had a lovely voice. Music, particularly church music, was what got him around. He sang everywhere, from the Methodist Church to the United Brethren Church to the High Holy Days at the Jewish Temple. Music got me around, too; through church work, I got to know kids outside of my district and made friends all over the city. Dad should have been a professional singer, but the Depression was hardly the setting for such career chances. A job was a job, the steadier the better, and Bentz Horne had to provide for his family. Though he did pick up money as a church soloist, trying to make a living as a singer was simply too risky. Ironically, the five dollars a week he made as soloist in the church choir kept us going through those lean years.

My father was either an optimistic pessimist or a pessimistic optimist, and if I had to settle for one definition, I'd go for the latter. He wasn't a bitter man, and certainly not a stage mother in the show-biz sense. Though Gloria and I were both trained in music from infancy, we entered it naturally; Dad encouraged us, but never pushed us. If Dad was frustrated or looking to live artistically through his children, I never noticed. I felt he simply wanted us to do our best. He set a very high standard, though, and I've spent a lifetime trying to reach and maintain it. My training bears witness to his expert guidance. "It's not good to start singing too young, unless you really know what you're doing," Dad cautioned, and it's true. If you begin singing early and without proper instruction, you can ruin the throat muscles. When a singer's voice goes, it's not because the vocal cords have given out, but because the muscles of the larynx have lost their elasticity, and that can be a direct result of improper training. You've probably heard a lot about Maria Callas "losing" her voice. I believe she was a victim of laryngeal muscle deterioration (and lost as well that "great will" it takes to get out on stage).

The only thing I sometimes disagreed with my father about at the time was his rule that "singers have to sing, no matter what!" He made me sing even when I was ill with a cold or worse. In principle, Dad was right, but in practice I've found that necessary cancellations are a wiser course. I've made the mistake of going on when I shouldn't have, with a few near-disastrous results.

My earliest recollections of our household are of song—not the phonograph, but living sound. Oddly enough, it was Mother who first brought such melody into my life. Mother sang in church choirs with Dad and had taught herself to play the piano, so every day she played and sang, warbling melodies from Stephen Foster to pop tunes—not, however, operatic arias. We weren't exactly the Osmond family, but the Horne family did have a reputation for musicality. Lack of real music in the home is one of the great sadnesses of modern times. Stacks of music books have been replaced by piles of cassettes, and instead of gathering around the piano, we huddle in front of the small screen. How much people are missing!

My debut as a chanteuse—meaning I got through a whole number—occurred at around eighteen months, when I delighted my parents with a garbled rendition of "Walking in a Winter Wonderland." My musical precocity wasn't surprising, since I'd been talking for some time. According to family lore, my first word, uttered at six months, pertained to food. It figures! "Apple," gurgled little Jackie, and perhaps this was the beginning of my lifelong romance with nourishment.

By the age of two, I could sing my mother's repertoire, and did at the drop of a hat. I was the Shirley Temple of the Appalachian Plateau, a dimpled, singing darling, and it wasn't long before I made my first public appearance at, of all places, a political rally for Franklin Delano Roosevelt.

Though Bradford was a Republican bastion, the Hornes were on the Democratic roster. Dad later transferred his allegiance to FDR's successor, Truman, but during the Depression it was FDR who fired Bentz Horne's political fervor. At that Roosevelt rally, Bentz's four-year-old, Marilyn, sang, "Believe Me, If All Those Endearing Young Charms," a lyric I thought had something to do with a popular nickel candy of the day. As far as FDR was concerned, though, some sacred melody might have been appropriate, because I didn't say a prayer but that I didn't see the wise, good FDR enthroned up there in heaven. FDR *was* God to my generation, the one and only President of my childhood. My daughter was born in

1965 and within eleven years had Johnson, Nixon, Ford and Carter! We may have lived through a Depression and a war, but there was a stability in this country then that the generations since haven't known. It may have been a false sense of security, but it was security all the same.

Not long ago, FDR's centennial was celebrated. Ill with a virus, I spent the evening watching a television special on his life. He looked handsome and winning, still like a god, and, as always, it was a shock to see he was a cripple. Children of the Thirties and Forties were not aware of FDR's affliction, nor were many adults. The press observed an unwritten law and only photographed him seated or standing unaided. Never was there a hint that he was struggling to walk. What a wonderful subject he'd be for an opera, a real Verdian baritone role.

The television special started me thinking, and afterward I composed a letter to Sara Wilford, the wife of my longtime manager, Ronald Wilford. Sara, FDR's granddaughter, was adopted at an early age by her staunch Republican stepfather, Jock Whitney, so I figured she might have had conflicting reports about her grandparent. I had positive things to say:

January 28, 1982

Dear Sara,

We were certainly raised differently and I thought maybe you'd like to know from a child of the Depression and the War what he meant to my family. He was a saint, if not God, and my parents were not uninformed people, though without funds, especially my father who read and listened to anything he could get his hands on and ear to. My mother opened the first Social Security office in Bradford along with a couple of other people. She had some ridiculously low number like one or two or something like that. FDR was the hope and the light and gave just that, along with concrete programs to help these young people find their way. He was our constant, right? and he represented everything to us. Who cares about the foibles, who cares that he was the consummate politician and well he should have been. He did it, and as history goes on he can only get better and better. I had chills (not my fever), tears and smiles during all these hours of his life. What an appealing man he was, he was surely to be hugged. I can well imagine that you must have experienced doubts growing up in a strongly Republican household, but make no mistake, in Bradford, PA, strongly Republican, there were those whose lives he literally saved and led on to the great middle class. I'm one of those children and it fills me with great pride. My mother and father worked furiously for his elections each time, and when all of Bradford went Republican, the Fifth Ward District always went Democratic. I've so many memories of the polling place, the FDR buttons, just so much, but that's not why I'm writing to you, it's just to let you know what he meant to my family, those unemployed millions and what he still means to me now. I did meet your grandmother when I was 13, in Los Angeles, a great thrill, I shall never forget it. It was the Jackson Day Dinner and she spoke, oh how she spoke! I had sung with the Roger Wagner Chorale that evening and stayed on to hear her, sitting on the stairs to the kitchen listening to her along with my father and my sister. Never having lacked courage, I went up and spoke to her afterwards.

Bless them, they tried, they gave, they succeeded.

Love,<br>Jackie

Yes, it was a privilege to sing for FDR's sake and I'm thrilled my public debut was linked to him.

* * *

Once I was started on my "career," Dad set to work in earnest. After his marriage, he'd studied singing with Arthur King Barnes in Buffalo, and it was because of his late start that my father realized the importance of proper vocal schooling early. The minute his daughters opened their mouths in song, he coached them. When I was five, my outside studies began with Hazel Bittenbender. Ramrod-backed, prim, her hair cut short as a man's, Miss Bittenbender sang out of the side of her mouth. She made me stand in the middle of the room and do vocal exercises, "Ba bee bi bo boo," over and over until I thought I'd go mad. The most I can say for her method is, she didn't do me any harm. My next instructor, Clayton Brennaman, was choir director of the Catholic church. I was about seven. Mr. Brennaman kept my head tones going and didn't interfere with my vocal progress. At around eight, I began study with Edna Luce, a local singer who had had a small career in Buffalo. Mrs. Luce was probably in her seventies when she taught me, and this time Dad had picked a winner. Edna Luce showed me the basic technique of breath support, which I have never forgotten and is, in fact, the very basis of how I breathe.

The principle of support is simple: you stand erect—like those cartoons of the prima donna with the big chest and straight spine —and as you inhale air and the muscle across your diaphragm expands, you push out and shove to keep it there. Breathing in is really breathing out, in singing—a yoga principle as well. As a result, the muscles of the diaphragm and the back become very strong, like a brick wall. Every good singer knows that support is the key, the foundation. When Luciano Pavarotti, Joan Sutherland and I did our televised concert at Lincoln Center in March 1981, we filmed an intermission discussion during which each of us divulged what we considered the secret of singing: breath support. Ironically, in order to fit the interview into the allotted television time-block, someone chose *that* moment to cut. Here was advice straight from the horses' mouths—three of the biggest singers in the business—and out it went to fit the exigencies of prime time!

Whatever Miss Bittenbender and Mr. Brennaman taught me has long since flown out the window, but Mrs. Luce's instruction has remained, as have the things my dad had to say, especially a little piece of advice he gave when I started my lessons: "Peanut, if you want to get people's attention and hold it, sing softly." Nearly four decades later, I heeded those words with significant results at my Metropolitan debut.

I honestly don't know what life would have been like without singing. This may sound contradictory, but singing did and didn't interfere with my childhood. Though I didn't want to do it, I enjoyed doing it—especially when Gloria and I were appearing on bandstands! Singing in the children's choir of the Church of the Ascension where Dad was a paid soloist and Mom a chorister was okay, but even then I leaned to the secular life. By the time I was seven and she was nine, my sister and I were already "on the road" with our duets, and Dad, Gloria and I appeared for a variety of events, including bond rallies, regular dates at the service club and school programs. My first formal recital took place at the Kane High School when I was eleven, and it was a gala occasion, but I loved those bond rallies more. Were we ever patriotic during World War II! Gloria and I had a ball at those rallies, performing all over the city with the Citizens Band. Dad had been the featured soloist until he introduced his progeny; then the singing Horne sisters took the spotlight from their father. The bandleader was embarrassed, but Dad was pleased as punch. He reveled in our popularity and stood by beaming as Gloria and I, dressed in our finest, faces scrubbed, heads thrown back, belted out "Over There" and "You're a Grand Old Flag." God, it was fun! I wonder if my sister's memories are as joyous as mine. We are very different, Gloria and I, and have become more so as the years pass. Gloria had a voice, too, but early on opted for marriage and children. Sadly, her marriage dissolved before mine.

A voice isn't everything and there have been times when I've wondered whether my career has been worth the sacrifices, but nothing was going to stop me from having that career. Mom always said, "Give Jackie an inch and she'll take the mile, and then some." It's true—I took that little bit of gristle and ran it around the world. I was a dynamo kid, constantly on the move, running ahead. My height had something to do with my velocity. Being short, I had to figure out angles taller people don't think about. There *were* advantages to my size, though—I was always first in line, and in group photographs I'd be right up front, full of sassiness. There are pictures of me with my tongue sticking out or grinning mischievously, chin in hand. I was always enterprising, looking for center stage, hard to control. Gloria was different; she liked to work things out upstairs before reacting. I was all action, she was contemplative —but, whatever the differences in our personalities, we were a singing team. We fought like cats and dogs and drove Mother to distraction with our sibling aggression, but when the time came to sing, hostilities ceased.

That's the reason I'm a team player now. I learned my lesson with my sister—you have to blend in order to produce the best effects. It's as true for singing "You're a Grand Old Flag" at a bond rally as it is for singing *"Mira, o Norma"* in an opera house. Even when I'm standing alone on the concert stage, Martin Katz is there at the piano and it's the combination that makes the success. I pride myself on my ability to work well with others; right now, I'm in my third generation of *Semiramide* partners: Joan Sutherland, Montserrat Caballé and June Anderson. Who knows, I may make it into a fourth generation. New singers come along every ten years or so in opera, but here I am, Old Faithful, still gushing!

Up-and-coming exponents in my repertoire are often liable to hear, "Too bad you're singing in the time of Horne." That's flattering, but there's always room at the top, and though I'll fight like an Amazon to keep my position, with my voice as my sword and training as my shield, I'll never wield them against other singers. Ideally, we're on the same side, behind the footlights. I don't think I've ever attacked a fellow artist onstage. (I'm not counting a youthful fling in *Hansel and Gretel* in which, having developed an antagonism toward a soprano, I took full advantage of a scene in which I chased her with a broom.) Those magnificent *bel canto* duets go so well because they're a combined effort. The concentrated energies of two protagonists working together to carry themselves and the listeners into a *bel canto* euphoria is heady stuff indeed. In my entire career, there has been only one singer with whom I found it difficult to mesh. Even though I admire and respect many aspects of this woman's artistry and personality, our appearance together was marked by strife. Later, I'll tell you who she is and the saga of our "collaboration," an episode which, in another era, would have resulted in a full-scale operatic feud.

For now, though, let's get back to Bradford. From the very beginning, I aimed high, which meant the Metropolitan Opera, but though the Met was my goal very early, it wasn't until I was about eleven that I became interested in the Saturday-afternoon Texaco broadcasts. Gloria listened avidly, while I was out having fun. In winter, it was movies—I'd take Tyrone Power over Jan Peerce any day!—and as spring approached, I had to play baseball. Baseball is my sports love; I just watch it now, but in my childhood I played. After an unhappy stint as a catcher—they stuck me behind the plate because of my build—I moved over to first base, where I pivoted happily throughout my adolescence. Lucky girls today can join Little Leagues, which was unheard of in my day.

In 1939, my education began at the Fifth Ward School, the same institution my dad had attended. There, Lorina Peterson, a favorite teacher, taught me two important things: good penmanship and the love of learning. Miss Peterson loved music, too, and in her honor I'm putting a lovely carol she taught me, "Bethlehem Babe," on my Christmas album with the Mormon Tabernacle Choir.

At school, I was eager to use my singing skills, but, unfortunately, they were either too refined or too unrefined. I didn't make the grade-school glee club because, according to the teacher, Sigrid Johnson, I sang too loudly. I did appear in musical skits and plays, though, and treasure the memory of my role as Jolly Molly in the fifth-grade Christmas play. I sang "Up in Santa Land" and my Dad had me put a high C at the end. When I cracked on it, the audience laughed, but that didn't deter me—I just went for it again and hit it right on.

Instead of acquiring a reputation as a singer, I began to gather renown as a "cut-up." From the vantage point of hindsight, the word "brat" comes to mind, but if I was a brat, I was a special kind, more of a Peck's Bad Girl. I didn't fool around to hurt other people. I also gradually discovered that "cut-ups" weren't taken seriously. No matter how hard I worked, all I had to do was make a joke and people would flap their hands and say, "Oh, that child, she's such a scamp!" or words to that effect. Growing up for me involved learning how to superimpose restraint on my natural delight, like putting a stopper on a bottle of seltzer to preserve the fizz. The only thing was, because self-control and discipline ruled my musical life, I naturally liked to pull out the stopper in my everyday world. I've always had zest and enthusiasm for the everyday. As the years pass, it takes more energy to get the juices flowing, but flow they must. Before he died, the grand old man of the Boston Pops, Arthur Fiedler, was asked why he refused to give up his breakneck schedule, even at the very end.

"I can't stop," Fiedler replied. "To rest is to rot." I couldn't have said it better.

The sole discordant note in the musical Horne household was the lack of funds. Though neither of my parents cared about money for themselves, they were worried about us children. How could we fully realize our potential if we didn't receive the proper musical education? The problem grew as we did. Bradford, after all, had just so much to offer. Finally, as I was approaching my teens, Mother and Dad decided to take action. We would have to move. We would have to live someplace where Dick, Gloria and I could get the best in general education and musical training for the least amount of money. The options were clear—California and New York had the best state-supported educational systems—and the choice was even clearer. Dad and Mom would never survive the rigors of big-city life, so in 1945, in true pioneer fashion, we stuffed a trailer with our belongings—including a refrigerator, more precious than gold in those early post-war years—attached it to our 1939 Plymouth and set off for California, the land of sunshine and free colleges.

Studies on the effects of moving tell us the accompanying sense of upheaval often creates permanent damage to the psyches of children. My psyche was not permanently damaged, though at first it was hard for all of us. My parents, solidly established in Bradford, must have felt trepidation about resettling, but they kept their ends up and never let Dick, Gloria or me see their misgivings. Later, we all flourished in the new setting, all except Dad. He never adjusted to the West Coast and in those early years yearned to return to Bradford. Eventually, he did go home again to die.

Pennsylvania provided a sensible down-to-earth Eastern environment for my early years. For good or ill, basic Bradford-engendered tenets have never left me. Something holds me back when I really want to let go; there's a sense of propriety I don't want to lose which I call the "little girl from Bradford" syndrome. It keeps me from doing things which might make me a more well-known figure, but which seem beneath my dignity. That's why, though I'm at the top of my profession, I'm perpetually "on the brink" of being a household word. You have to be a bit outrageous in order to be outstanding, particularly in the classical-music field.

There's the famous story about Enrico Caruso, for instance. He arrived in the United States hard upon the heels of the elegant Polish tenor Jean de Reszke, and many comparisons were made between the suave, courtly Pole and the bumptious, portly Neapolitan. Then Caruso was accused of pinching a woman in the Central Park Zoo monkey house and the press had a field day. The glory of his voice was what made Caruso a legend, but the little ape episode definitely gave his career a boost up the fame ladder. Opera singers don't reach that many people unless they cavort for the media. I like what my publicist, Lewis Ufland, has to say on the subject of fame.

"When you read the papers the way I read the papers," he told me, "you know who's pushing whom." The public is naïve about the selling of personalities. As the riddle goes, if a tree falls and there's no one to hear it, does it make a noise? If I give a remarkable performance of *L'Italiana in Algeri*, who will know, aside from the audience and those who read the reviews? Does anyone believe great fame is not the result of great publicity? Every time a name appears, other than in an advertisement or a review, it's been put there directly or indirectly through publicity. I know of very few artists who do not employ a publicist. That has its good and its bad aspects, of course. On the plus side, your name gets around, your "legend" is built up and so are your fees. On the minus side, you can start believing your own publicity and spend more time making your name than doing your work.

I can't resist telling the story of an American soprano of a generation ago who suffered from PRM (Public-Relations Mania). She was out to make it and had all the stuff—youth, talent, looks and a good figure. She'd been heavily publicized by a flashy agency when she went to Columbia Artists Management (the company Ronald Wilford now heads) to seek the counsel of Humphrey Doulens. Mr. Doulens agreed to accept her as a client if she did exactly as he told her. "A woman of your stature, and the artist you can be, must not do cheap tricks for the public," he cautioned. "It's beneath your dignity as an artist and mine as an artist's manager." The soprano acquiesced and a contract was signed. Doulens went to work planning a grand campaign, including a *Time* magazine cover, when one day he walked into his office and found on his desk the *Daily News* opened to the rotogravure section. There, on a two-page spread, was his client, bikini-clad, lying on the ground with a sailor standing on her chest. "Never Underestimate the Diaphragm of a Diva," read the caption. The contract was revoked, and though the soprano had a certain réclame for a short time, her over-active antic muse didn't carry her to the top.

I don't tell this story to diminish the accomplishments of artists who have become popular idols—that would be sour grapes—but they do pay a price, often vocally. I've been on enough TV shows myself, from Arthur Godfrey to Johnny Carson, to realize how beguiling acclaim and adulation can be. After a "Tonight Show" appearance, however, I'm never asked about myself; rather it's "What's Johnny Carson really like?" I'm sure no one is going to ask Johnny what I'm like, but the point is in fifty, a hundred, maybe two hundred years, I hope that someone will turn on a machine and *hear* what Marilyn Horne was like. For this, I honor and serve my muse—and keep sailors off my chest.

37

# Long Beach and the DooWah Years

IT WASN'T until we moved to California that I appreciated the topography of the United States. Geography be damned—when you lived in Bradford, Pennsylvania, America was hills, rivers and plateaus. Long Beach, California, was a revelation. Within months, I became a child of the surf. I fell in love with the climate and the ambiance; the novelty of coming home from school and jumping into the ocean never wore off. Long Beach was lush and lively. I still remember long walks home after parties or dates, along streets flowering with night-blooming jasmine and magnolia trees, and hearing the soft sounds of conversations, most of them centering around who wanted a kiss goodnight and who was going to grant it. Life was sweet and simple then, absolutely a kid's paradise. I've lived in lots of places since, but California remains the place for me and I want to retire there.

At first, it wasn't quite a Garden of Eden, largely because of the housing shortage. My parents chose Long Beach because mother's sister Violet and her husband, Loran Ferguson, lived there and we could all move in with them, a jolting comedown for the former residents of Number 9, Avenue B. We stayed there for several months, until Dad went back to Bradford to close out his affairs. Then, Mom, Gloria and I rented a room in a Mrs. Woodring's house. Dick had joined the Air Force in June of 1945 and was no longer living with us. We had kitchen privileges, but the living wasn't easy with three of us jammed into tight quarters. Mom and Gloria slept in the bed, while I was ensconced on an Army cot. Six months later, when Dad returned, we moved into Mrs. Loma Murphy's home on Fifth Avenue in Long Beach. Now we were four; Dad and Mother slept in one room, while Gloria and I had to make do on a fold-down couch in the living room. It wasn't very restful. We had to be up and out early, or Mrs. Murphy would have folded us up in the sofa. She was not a kind landlady. At Christmas, Dad bought a tree which took up most of one room; we decorated it as best we could and then stood around the tree singing carols. I remember Mrs. Murphy looking in at us with a scowl on her face. Dad said, "Well, maybe she's never seen a family enjoy Christmas before and this will change her disposition for the better." It didn't.

When Dick returned, we rented a small apartment from Mrs. Murphy, and though we had more space, conditions weren't much improved. Dick slept on a couch in the living room, I slept on a cot in my parents' bedroom and Gloria shared the back bedroom with Reva Abernethy, a young friend of mother's from Bradford who had appeared on our doorstep. The Old Woman's Shoe was Buckingham Palace compared to the Horne's early habitat, and what made it all the more frustrating was that we were suffering while realty went wild in post-war California. Dad and Mom should have bought their own place right away or at least greased someone's palm to get a decent rental, but they weren't sharp about real estate. It's too bad, because we'd have had it a lot easier.

In 1950, we moved into our own home. It was one of the happiest days of our lives, and after Jay was born, Nanny Horne moved West to join the household.

Upon our arrival, I was enrolled in the seventh grade at George Washington Junior High School, and I vividly remember wanting desperately to "belong," especially to the top echelon of students. Any kid who's been uprooted has had the same experience, but I had a special way of getting in—the sound of my voice broke the social barrier.

During the first semester, seventh-grade students took art; in the second semester, it was music. Oh, how I struggled in the first half, drawing and painting with no visible talent. It was like asking Mary Cassatt to sing! At last, the second semester began; on the first day, we were required to perform *en masse* for the teacher. The class stood up and started vocalizing. After a few minutes, the teacher, Mrs. McCartney, tapped her baton on the desk. We stopped.

"I hear a voice back there," she said. "Continue singing, class." We began again and once more were brought to a halt by the baton.

"I hear a *voice*," the teacher reiterated, scanning the chorus as though she were looking for a criminal rather than a soprano. She moved toward us like a worm-minded bird, head cocked to one side, eyes darting over the rows of students.

"Who is that voice?" she cried. With one move, the kids turned and pointed to me.

"What's your name, young lady?"

"Marilyn Horne."

"Come up here, Marilyn, and sing for me."

Three years old, in Bradford, Pennsylvania,
the Shirley Temple of the
Appalachian Plateau.

Dad: he set the standard.

Gloria, Mom, and I in 1939. Like Dad, Mom had a singing voice. Small wonder that in only a couple of years, the singing Horne sisters would be a regular feature at band concerts and bond rallies.

Grandma Ada Prunkard "Nanny" Horne: one of the mainstays of my life.

Front and center as Jolly Molly in the fifth-grade Christmas play. I'm about to hit a high C.

LEFT: Twelve years old, shortly after our move to California.

BELOW: The transplanted Hornes in Long Beach, California, 1948: Gloria, Mom, me, Dad, and Dick.

Gloria and I with two other members of the St. Luke's Episcopal Church Quartet, directed by William Ripley Dorr (center). Dorr and Roger Wagner helped usher in my Hollywood "DooWah Years."

My operetta debut—Lehar's *The Merry Widow* at Polytechnic High School.

A group from the Roger Wagner Chorale on a 1953 tour of Europe, yours truly second from the left in the back row. With the chorale, I sang at churches, concert halls, and sound stages—and played the Hawaiian guitar on my nose.

On the opera stage at last! The year was 1954 and the role was Hata in the Los Angeles Guild Opera's production of *The Bartered Bride*. (ALBERT DUVAL)

A publicity still taken at about the same time as my opera debut—notice the stars in my eyes. (JOHN E. REED)

In 1955, I was "discovered" by Arthur Godfrey's "Talent Scouts."
I sang "Un bel di" and won.

*Cinderella*, the English version of
*Cenerentola* and my first Rossini
role, made memorable by director
Carl Ebert—and a certain handsome
baritone. (ALBERT DUVAL)

In 1956, impresario Martin Taubman told me to get myself over to Europe and he'd arrange for auditions. The very first one was with Germany's Gelsenkirchen Opera Company—and they hired me, practically on the spot. Thus began my "galley years" of apprenticeship. Three of my roles were Minnie in *Girl of the Golden West,* Giulietta in *The Tales of Hoffman* and Mimi in *La Bohème.*

My Valkyrie experience at the San Carlo Opera in 1959—seven statuesque singers with blond wigs and platform shoes and me, black-haired and in sandals. It made an odd stage picture.

Gwen Koldofsky and I touring Alaska in 1959: nineteen recitals and thirty-three half-hour children's concerts in five weeks!

Taken soon after my marriage to Henry Lewis in 1960. Friends, family, and colleagues all warned me that an interracial marriage would destroy my career—but *both* our careers were about to blossom.

*Wozzeck* in San Francisco. It was a role I hadn't wanted to do in Gelsenkirchen, but it became my first international success and my ticket back to the States. (CAROLYN MASON JONES)

CARMEN

ROSINA

# FOUR DEBUTS:

My first Carmen, 1961, and Rosina, 1962, both at the San Francisco Spring Opera; my first Adalgisa, Vancouver, 1963; and Amneris, Toronto, 1964. (ROSINA: CAROLYN MASON JONES)

ADALGISA

AMNERIS

With first agent, beloved friend and surrogate mother Dorothy Huttenback, in 1964, after a performance of *L'Italiana in Algeri.* (CAROLYN MASON JONES)

*Semiramide* in Boston, 1965, with Joan Sutherland. Following nineteenth-century tradition, I was bearded for the role. Untraditionally, the general was six months pregnant!

Angela and her proud mom, 1966.

*Igor Stravinsky*
*1967*

*Vera*
*with love and admiration.*

Igor and Vera Stravinsky in 1967. Working with and knowing him was an incredible honor and privilege for a young singer. The dedication to his last work reads: "To Marilyn Horne."

The camera never blinks. Three television appearances: with Eileen Farrell and Carol Burnett on "The Carol Burnett Show," singing "Hey, Big Spender"; with dear friend Jim Nabors on his Christmas special; and playing Carmen with Felix Unger, alias Tony Randall, on "The Odd Couple." (CARMEN: LYN RIKER)

My 1969 La Scala debut as Jocasta in a purple plastic egg suit in Stravinsky's *Oedipus Rex*. (E. PICCAGLIANI)

Rossini's *L'Assedio di Corinto* with
Beverly Sills at La Scala one month
later. I was very nearly ready to use
that sword on Beverly.
(E. PICCAGLIANI)

With Angela, almost four, a "prisoner" in
my dressing room at La Scala.
(E. PICCAGLIANI)

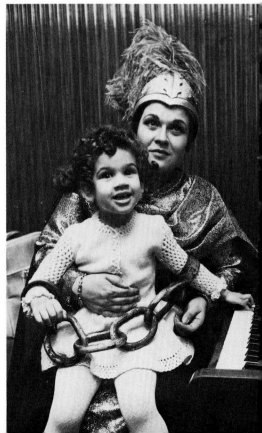

Even as I stepped forward, I knew my acceptance ticket had been issued. "Now I'm going to make it," I thought happily. Truly, it wasn't calculated. I've always known that my voice was my entree. Naturally, Dad had a comment to make on the subject: "Just remember, Peanut, they only like you for your voice." It sounds like a putdown, but Dad was trying to impress me with two things: (1) the importance of working hard to keep the voice going; and (2) the probability that others would disappoint me. Like Yeats' Anne Gregory, I've wished to be "loved for myself alone," but I'd be a fool if I didn't acknowledge my debt to that little piece of gristle in my throat.

Once word of my choir triumph spread, I became part of the scene at George Washington and began an active school life. Invitations poured in for parties, picnics and shows. I became active in school politics, a mini-FDR, and when I ran for office, I usually won. I literally sang my way into everything. Everyone said I sounded like Kirsten Flagstad, and I believed it. Imagine!

Meanwhile, Dad, who looked for opportunities in music the way Sherlock Holmes looked for clues in mysteries, discovered the Los Angeles Bureau of Music and wrote a letter extolling his singing daughters. The Bureau, a musical clearing house or melodic matchmaker, numbered among its members a choir director named Roger Wagner. An audition was arranged for Gloria and me, and we were accepted into the Concert Youth Chorus (eventually the Roger Wagner Chorale). No one could have had a better apprenticeship. At the age of twelve, I joined a group of exceptional singers, including Marni Nixon, whose career of dubbing singing voices in Hollywood films (Deborah Kerr in *The King and I*, Audrey Hepburn in *My Fair Lady*) would somewhat obscure her own talent; Harve Presnell, a big, strapping baritone, later to play opposite Debbie Reynolds in *The Unsinkable Molly Brown*; and Bruce Yarnell, another baritone, who would appear in opera as well as musicals. The last time I saw Bruce, we were appearing on separate stages in Sioux Falls, South Dakota, and were able to get together for dinner. Bruce, a happy-go-lucky guy, flew his own plane to and from engagements. Flying was an obsession with him and he carried on about it like a kid.

"For heaven's sake, Bruce," I said to him over dessert, "why don't you stop flying that plane of yours around? The next thing you know, I'll read that you slammed into the side of a mountain." Tragically, not long after, that's exactly what happened.

An exceptional organization, Roger Wagner's Chorale was equally at home in a church, the Hollywood Bowl, the Shrine Auditorium and on Hollywood sound stages. Wagner himself was an extraordinary man. Born in Le Puy, France, he came to this country at the age of seven. His father, the concertmaster at St. Brendan's Catholic Church, wanted a musical career for his son, but Roger was interested in sports as well as music, and might actually have become a professional athlete had he not broken his arm in a high-school football game. It turned out to be a lucky break for music, because the senior Wagner immediately plucked his son out of Fairfax High in Los Angeles and sent him back to France for further schooling. Roger's father, a Ph.D. in music, wanted no detours in his son's career. Roger did study at the Paris Conservatoire and received his musicology doctorate *cum laude* from the University of Montreal—he also picked up a silver medal in the 1936 Olympics as part of the French decathlon team! After his return to Los Angeles, Roger not only taught music, he coached basketball, baseball and track at Mount Carmel High and, meanwhile, formed a choral group. Alfred Wallenstein, the conductor of the Los Angeles Philharmonic, persuaded Roger to turn his chorale professional, and the rest is history. I'm proud I was part of it.

It was while singing with the Chorale that I met Eleanor Roosevelt at a Jackson Day Dinner in 1947, as I described to Sara Wilford. As part of the festivities, we sang Herbert Stothart's "The Only Thing We Have to Fear." Stothart, MGM's music director, had set FDR's famous Inaugural Address to music. I hung around after the performance and went up to that great lady as she was leaving. For once in my life, I was flustered and couldn't think of anything to say, so I asked for her place card. "Of course, my dear," she said modestly, "it's an honor to give it to you." What a gracious woman she was, and what a lesson in genuine humility.

Moments like this have stayed with me; I remember what it's like to be on the other side of the autograph book, which is why I try to accommodate everyone who asks for my signature or photograph, sometimes with unexpected results. Once, after a Boston recital, a young blind woman led by a seeing-eye German shepherd joined a line of fans in the greenroom. The woman introduced herself as Pauline and we chatted about music as the dog stood by quietly.

"Beautiful animal," I said. "May I pat him?"

"It's a she," answered Pauline. "Her name is Gloria and, sure, you can pat her."

I reached over and gently roughed the back of the shepherd's ears. She responded like a music critic and didn't even wag her tail. At Pauline's request, I took a program and wrote a message thanking her for coming, and off she went. A minute later, she returned, led by a young woman who said, "Miss Horne, would you mind signing another autograph?" For a second, I thought she was using her blind friend to get to the head of a rather long line, and was about to remonstrate, when she handed me Pauline's program. I looked down and saw what I had written: "Dear Gloria, Many thanks for being with me today. Sincerely, Marilyn Horne." It may be the only time a dog has received an autograph.

Truly, I've nothing but appreciation for fans—human or canine —who, genuinely moved by my performances, ask for autographs.

Sometimes, though, autograph hounds become a little too ardent and ask for enough signatures to fill a telephone book! People may think an artist fussy when he or she says, "That's all," yet after you're presented with nine or ten extra pieces of paper by dozens of fans in line, and asked to write to persons not at the concert, you do begin to fuss. The doyenne of opera autograph-seekers, Lois Kirsch-enbaum, lives in New York City and has become an institution because of her avocation. Very nearsighted, she has unlimited access backstage and attends nearly every major operatic event in the United States. One time, after an appearance with Renata Scotto, I went into Scott's dressing room to say goodnight. As I left the room, Lois came running down the hall waving her arms. "Renata!" she shouted, pressing a pen and paper into my hand. She peered into my face. "You're not Scotto!" she declared accusingly, snatching back the autograph material and storming away. I couldn't resist calling after her, "Wait a minute, I'm Marilyn. Remember? You were just in *my* room!"

No one was asking for my autograph back then, however, al-though in some ways my life did seem like a movie. Singing, study-ing, surfing—remember the Judy Garland/Mickey Rooney films about kids having a high old time putting on shows and getting in and out of scrapes? Well, I actually lived that life from George Washington through Polytechnic High School. I was popular, a good student and, yes, still a cut-up, specializing in verbal antics. From imitations to asides, my lips were never sealed. At one point in the eighth grade, I corrected the choir director's Latin pronuncia-tion during rehearsals. Instead of spearing me with her baton, she passed the word on to Royal Stanton, Polytechnic's music director, advising him that little Miss Horne had a very big mouth. Mr. Stanton decided to take me down a peg or two and, during freshman year, gave me low grades in choir. I got mad and quit. You can guess the rest. The *a cappella* group needed me more than I needed it, and soon Royal Stanton came around for a discussion with the "bolter." We worked out an amicable agreement, I returned to the fold and later we became great friends.

Bluntly, this only goes to show that when you have an extraordinary ability, you can throw your weight around. In general, public-school teachers of my day didn't know what to do with gifted students—by and large, they still don't—and I learned early how to get my way. Luckily, proper sanctions were established at home and I couldn't get away with the same kind of murder there. As a parent myself, I eventually discovered that the difficulty in raising children was not in setting proper standards, but in making sure they were met. I had to meet the ones established in my home.

Royal Stanton, a fine person as well as teacher, broadened my musical horizons which had been nurtured earlier in lessons with William Ripley Dorr, choir director of St. Luke's Episcopal Church. Gloria and I were in the St. Luke's girls' choir. Singing the choral works of Haydn, Beethoven and Bach, I learned to appreciate the great masters.

Because of all this choral work in and out of school, California was indeed providing the musical education and stimuli Dad and Mother had anticipated. My goal remained constant, however: I was on my way to the Met. Emelie Dodge, an English teacher at Polytechnic and later my personal secretary, remembers our first meeting, a classic teacher-pupil confrontation at which she asked what I was going to be when I grew up. "An opera singer at the Met," was the instant reply. Emelie later confided she was both amused and bemused by my statement. I was the first California student she'd ever come across who didn't want to be a movie star. Movies, however, were very much a part of my life, and they became an even greater one. Because of my work with the St. Luke's chorus and the Roger Wagner Chorale, I was about to become involved with the movies for real.

One thing Hollywood always needed for its movies was background music, and the St. Luke's and Wagner choirs were two of the groups that supplied it. So it was that I became a "chorus" schoolgirl about to begin her behind-the-scenes film career while attending classes on the MGM lot, along with such classmates as Roddy McDowall, Claude Jarman, Jr., and a pretty teen-ager named Elizabeth Taylor.

The first movie I worked on was *Joan of Arc*, a spectacular failure with Ingrid Bergman. *Joan*, Hollywood's quasi-religious epic reading of Maxwell Anderson's play, needed a background wash of liturgical music, a natural for the Wagner gang. Although a *bona fide* member of the Chorale, I was under-age and had to get special permission from the Screen Actors' Guild to participate, but when that dispensation came, my movie singing career was on its way. Surrounded by fellow choristers, I went from puberty to adolescence singing into microphones.

Whatever the music, liturgical, classical, romantic or pop, the "lyrics" were always the same. We always seemed to be singing, "DooWah, DooWah," and that's why I call this period my Doo-Wah Years. DooWahs were also incorporated into the television scene. "I Married Joan," a popular sitcom of the Fifties, was one of the first to employ the Wagner Chorale. We DooWahed in the background for season after season. In one episode, Joan Davis and her TV husband, Jim Backus, were vacationing in Hawaii. Naturally, the chorus was supposed to provide appropriate aloha-oriented DooWahs, but what's Hawaii without an electric guitar? The call went out for the instrument, with no immediate results. Production was held up—until I came to the rescue.

"I can imitate an electric guitar," I told the choir director and, to demonstrate, held my nose with my thumb and finger, pressing and releasing them against my nostrils while humming island tunes. Roger was delighted and, after a quick run-through, recorded the DooWahs with me playing solo nose. If you ever catch a rerun of the Joan Davis show and she's in Hawaii, listen closely to hear, if I do say so myself, a fabulous electric guitar. I couldn't blow my nose for a week after that, but, as Tosca sings, *"Vissi d'arte."*

At fifteen, I became a paid soloist for the California Heights Methodist Church choir. Though I didn't know it then, the conductor, Dorothy DeCoudres, actually paid my fifteen-dollar-a-month salary out of her own pocket and, not only that, bought gowns for me so I'd be properly attired for performances. She's one of two important Dorothys in my life, and there'll be more about the other Dorothy later.

During the DooWah years, my musical activities continued in school as well. Junior year, I got the lead in the school musical, Lehár's *The Merry Widow*—my first appearance in operetta and I was the star! I barely knew what a bride was, let alone a widow, which didn't stop me from reveling in the role of the *"lustige"* Hanna Glawari. Also in the cast was my friend Joanne Pagones. Joanne and I were so close that we kept our nighties at each other's houses just in case we decided to stay over on the spur of the moment. Joanne had a sparkling personality and a lovely singing voice, and we would sing around town together at Rotary Club meetings and the like. It was good practice and we'd pick up ten dollars plus reviews in the Rotary paper such as: "The little vocalists Marilyn Horne and Joanne Pagones could not only sing, but are pretty."

One time, when Joanne and I were rehearsing during an overnight stay at the Hornes', Dad walked into the living room, pointed his finger at me and said, "You, the Met," then pointed to Joanne and said, "You, Broadway." Joanne actually did appear with Carol

Channing in *Hello, Dolly!* but eventually gave up her career to devote time to her husband and *his* career. The Hornes certainly approved of her decision: she married my brother Dick.

*The Merry Widow* was a huge success and, according to the local paper, "Marilyn Horne, as the Merry Widow, was convincing. Her vocalism had a dependable security, and as it went up, it acquired considerable resonance and brilliance." So much of the joy in *The Merry Widow* production was generated by Royal Stanton. I still have a copy of the program in which he wrote, "Jackie, You have made me very proud—I anticipate the brightest future for you, since you have so much and know so well how to use it. Be assured of my continuing interest in you and all you do. Your good friend, Royal Stanton." Alas, that was his last year at Polytechnic. Recently retired, Royal headed fine arts schools at northern California colleges and there conducted very successful choruses. Whenever I'm on the West Coast, I try to catch a glimpse of Royal—he was one of the positive influences on my career.

All told, 1950 was a banner year for me. Besides *The Merry Widow* and the Rotary meetings, I was president of the Portia Society and secretary of Phi Gamma Chi sorority. In the latter capacity, I received poetic pledge cards from aspiring sisters. The poems had one subject:

> She sings in the evening
> She sings in the morn
> There's no talent lacking
> with Marilynn Horne
>
> > Pledge Marilyn Nelson

> Oh let us rejoice in Marilynn's voice
> She can make it go up or go down
> She can wiggle it, waver it

Steady, quaver it,
Holler it all over town

Pledge Ilene Durfee

Marilynn Horne
A girl whose future is assured
    In music circles she'll be heard
The "Met" perhaps her voice will ring
    And in our lives this gift she'll bring
This course she's gone since she was born
Who do I mean? Why, Marilynn Horne.

Pledge Carol Nyman

Marilynn Horne,
With voice so sweet
Makes men forlorn,
And fall at her feet

Pledge Sue Merritt

Keats was right: "The poetry of earth is never dead." It gets mangled from time to time, though. Thank heavens, that final "n" on my name would be guillotined in Germany. As a teen-ager, I thought it added a needed touch of sophistication, but it only added confusion.

In June of 1950, I was chosen as one of the outstanding music students from Long Beach's three high schools and received a season ticket to Symphonies Under the Stars at the Hollywood Bowl. The season opened with *Faust*, starring Nadine Conner, Richard Tucker and Jerome Hines. (Jerry Hines is still singing, and in 1982 published a fine book called *Great Singers on Great Singing*, in which I discourse for a chapter. If you think I talk about breath support, you're right.)

Senior year was a bit of a letdown, since Royal was gone and musicals were only given in alternate years, but, scholastically, all went well. I won a scholarship to the University of Southern California, and not just on musical ability—I had an excellent academic record. Everything seemed to be looking up for me. Was there a fly in the ointment? Well, I guess one. If I ever had a problem, it was my tendency to endomorphy.

Someone once asked me what the greatest struggle of my life was, expecting a musical answer—perhaps a particularly difficult role or a song I couldn't master—but my reply was quick and sincere: "My greatest struggle is not to weigh three hundred pounds." The late Totie Fields claimed that she wasn't fat; she was the perfect weight, just the wrong height. Me, too. I'm never going to be thin, at least not as measured by today's standards—I might have had a fighting chance in the Gay Nineties. Oh, how I wish I could keep off the twenty to thirty pounds I can drop by watching my intake. I've fought the bulge battle all my life. Psychologically, I can understand my need for food. The travel, the loneliness, the pressures—all these are insidious incentives that propel me into the cupboard. I know I'm too fat, and I'd strike a bargain with Mephistopheles for a permanent weight loss, but *The Diet Secrets of Marilyn Horne* is not a book destined for best-seller lists.

I'll tell you one thing, however. Though excess pounds drive me crazy, they haven't stopped me from enjoying life, especially the romantic life. Men are not attracted to sticks and bones, at least the men I've known. Weight and all, I've gotten what I've wanted in music—many great singers *are* great in size, after all—and I've done all right in love, too.

The latter was just as true at Polytechnic as it is now. I had plenty of men friends and, after I was graduated in 1951, had the same beau in my freshman year at USC that I'd had in high school. We exchanged cigar-band wedding rings and our names were linked in the school newspaper:

> One of the newest and steadiest of steady couples to be seen around the campus is Marilynn Horne and Terry Barkis. Marilynn and Terry were acquainted in junior high school but only as good buddies. Marilynn and Terry were at a party and with soft lights and music setting the atmosphere, Terry asked Marilynn to wear his pin. . . .

Isn't that romantic? So, you see, I had no problems with men. When I met Henry Lewis, I wasn't even looking for a boyfriend.

The wide veranda skirting the Victorian music building at USC was a favorite place for students to congregate between classes and smoke or gab. On this veranda, in 1951, I first saw Henry Lewis. Though Henry was only a year older than I, he seemed more mature and sophisticated. I was seventeen and thought he was around twenty-nine or thirty! I caught sight of him on the porch—at six-foot-one, he's easy to spot—and thought, "Wow, he's good-looking."

As it turned out, Henry was not only good-looking, he was immensely talented and already a ground-breaker. A virtuoso on the double bass, he'd been taken into the Los Angeles Philharmonic at the age of sixteen while still a student at USC—the first black ever to join a major symphony orchestra. He was the Jackie Robinson of music. There were other black musicians and conductors, but—to continue the baseball analogy—they were all in the minor leagues. Henry was always world-class. In 1955, he would become conductor of the Seventh Army Symphony in Germany, then, after his discharge in 1957, study conducting with Eduard van Beinum, music director of the Los Angeles Philharmonic. Eventually, as music director of the New Jersey Symphony, Henry would become the first major black conductor. Whatever has happened to Henry and me as a couple, nothing has changed my opinion of his musicianship; he's sensational. For a while, we made our own beau-

51

tiful music together, and though at present we don't appear together professionally that often, I consult him almost as much as I did when we were married.

All of that was in my future, however. Right then, though I admired his looks, Henry made little impact on me. After that initial glimpse, I remember little about him during the next couple of years; he was around, but so were others. Frankly, I was too busy with my music and classes to spend much time with any one man.

The exceptions to that rule were my teachers, and the way I selected them—one of them anyway—was typical Horne behavior. I went to register for classes knowing nothing about the faculty, and was pondering over the choices when a student employee in the registrar's office, noticing my hesitation, asked me my course of study. I said music and he asked with whom I planned to study singing. I hadn't given it a thought.

"Who's good?" I queried.

"Well," he replied, "I'm studying with Bill Vennard and he's terrific. Why don't you go for him?"

"Okay," I replied, "I'll put his name down." And I did.

Because of this extensive research into the matter of vocal teachers at USC, I was fortunate enough to come under the wing of Bill Vennard. Though Bill modestly referred to himself as merely a "keeper" of my voice, he was a great deal more and, among other things, taught me exercises that I still use today. I wasn't as appreciative of him at first as I should have been, though. After a little while, I decided I wanted to sound like a combination of my opera heroines, Renata Tebaldi and Ebe Stignani. Tebaldi, the glorious Italian soprano, was very popular in the United States, of course, and Stignani, the mighty Italian mezzo, was more well known in her native land, but I knew them both through their appearances with the San Francisco Opera Company and their records. Callas wasn't on my list because she had never appeared in San Francisco.

I admired them both to the point of imitation, but Bill refused to alter the course of study to turn me into a Tebaldi-Stignani clone. As a result, once again I bolted, and blithely engaged two other teachers willing to do what I wanted. Neither of those instructors did me any good; worse, one caused real damage. After four lessons, the top of my voice disappeared. I couldn't sing F above the staff, which had been duck soup before my Vennard defection. The feeling of how to go up the scale was gone. I was scared stiff and went penitently back to Bill Vennard. Within a week, he had me soaring again. I was very lucky the crisis came early. Anyone with a natural voice who doesn't understand the technical aspects of how that voice is produced will eventually get into trouble. The pressures of singing before the public, the traveling, the physical and vocal fatigue, all are important factors, and heaven help the singer who doesn't know how to open up and when to shut up. The crisis I went through at the dawn of my career made me want to learn everything about the technical aspects of my art. Today, I feel secure because I've made it my business to learn as much there is to be known about the production of the human singing voice, and this erudition is a direct result of my association with Bill Vennard.

At USC, I also studied with Gwendolyn Williams Koldofsky, head of the Song Literature and Accompanying Department, a fortuitous association in every way. In 1958, Gwen became my accompanist and, in 1967, I asked her star student, Martin Katz, to take over and we're still together! Besides acting as my social director, Gwen also interceded for me in scholastic matters. At one point, I was up to my old tricks in Harmony class, fooling around and paying little attention to the work. The professor was the composer Leon Kirchner, and I didn't think he was much of a teacher, though, in all fairness, I couldn't stand the subject. Near the end of the semester, Professor Kirchner called me into his office and delivered an ultimatum. "Miss Horne, you are capable of getting an A in this class and you are doing C work. I refuse to give you a C. You'll either get an A, which is what you can and should do, or I'll fail you."

"That's not fair," I protested. "You can't do that to me. I'll take the C!"

He was adamant, so naturally I went to Gwen. Kirchner thought he was dealing with an airhead college kid until Gwen informed him that I was one of the great hopes for singing. "Marilyn's terribly sincere about her voice," she told him, "even if she isn't so sincere about Harmony."

Kirchner relented and I got the C. This is just another indication of how unbelievably lucky I was in the people I worked with when I was young. My admiration for such friends as Gwen, Dorothy DeCoudres, Dorothy Huttenback (who will appear later), Bill Vennard, William Ripley Dorr, Roger Wagner, Jack Metz, my coach Fritz Zweig, a great musician from the old German school, and so many more, is unbounded. Thanks to them, I got through some pretty rough times, rough because I was always under financial strain. That old bugaboo, lack of funds, made it necessary for me to take odd jobs—and some of them were very odd indeed.

# I V

## *The Pirate Queen*
## *Meets Lotte Lehmann*

THE ODDEST of those jobs was a form of licensed larceny widely practiced in the recording business in the early Fifties. In those pre-long-playing-record days, popular songs came out on 78-rpm singles. The formula was to put an A and a B side on every record; the A was a possible hit and the B a filler. Sometimes, the tables were turned and the filler became the hit—Gene Autry's "Rudolph, the Red-Nosed Reindeer" is a good example. Very, very rarely, both sides scored. Singers like Sinatra, Crosby, Patti Page, Vaughn Monroe, Frankie Laine, Johnnie Ray and Rosemary Clooney recorded songs which then became anybody's property.

In the popular field today, groups and soloists are so closely identified with their product, often written by them, that they beggar imitation. In the Fifties, however, those restraints weren't there, and pirate records, pure and simple steals, became a thriving business. If a singer like Buddy Clark had a hit record with a major label, a pirate operation would hire someone to mimic Clark's voice and delivery, an orchestra to re-create the sounds of Clark's back-up and, *voilà*, it had a pirate record—for a lot less money than the original. The records were released under the Varsity label and distributed through nationwide chains, such as Sears, Roebuck.

In 1952, I swashbuckled my way into pirate recordings via my friend Charlie Scharbach. Charlie, a fellow member of the Roger Wagner Chorale, sang around town a lot, worked clubs and also performed backgrounds, the old DooWah. Charlie, Gloria and I were in the Madrigal Singers at USC, and one day Charlie came to rehearsal announcing that he'd just been hired by a record company which also needed a female voice. He'd suggested me. It not only seemed a good way to make money, it sounded like a lark. Off I went, auditioned successfully and soon was behind the mike making more DooWahs, but this time for discs. After a short run of DooWahs, I let the powers that be know that I could do more than back-up bellowing, and before long I was given solo bits, total rip-offs. Kay Starr had a big hit then, called "The Wheel of Fortune," which went something like this: "The wheel of fortune goes spinning around. While the wheel is turning, turning, turning, I'll be yearning, yearning, yearning." Miss Starr's rotary vehicle became my first hit, so to speak. Kay—she later became a friend—had a distinctive delivery in which a word like "wheel" came out "hu-wheel" and "fortune" was metamorphosed into "fah-hor-ti-yoon." It was fun re-creating and expanding her idiosyncratic style, and though I made no personal fortune from it, the recording did start me off on the right foot in my new "career."

The recordings were done in Garrison's, a studio in Long Beach where vocal teachers and groups went to make legitimate recordings of their work as well. I'd listen to the original, follow along with the sheet music and, being a trained classical musician, as well as a born mimic, I'd be ready to go. You wouldn't believe the number of singers who *can't* read music! The producers were delighted with my fast work, but not elated enough to alter my remuneration. I was paid forty dollars a night whether I sang as "Kate Smith" or did background DooWahs.

After "The Wheel of Fortune," I cut Peggy Lee's fast-paced, sexy version of the Rodgers-and-Hart waltz "Lover." Here was the future Rosina and Tancredi spilling out, "Lover, when I'm near you and I hear you speak my name, softly in my ear you breathe a flame." I did a good job of approximating Miss Lee's sibilant, insinuative style, which, by the way, is also remarkably suited to Carmen's "Habañera."

Next, they came up with a doozie. Two siblings, the Bell Sisters, had a hit called "Bermuda," after which they passed into ASCAP oblivion. The guys at Garrison's wanted me to record "Bermuda," but I needed a sister. "I've got one!" I told Hal Loman, the orchestra leader, "and she's a singer, too." Gloria came over, auditioned and was asked to stay on. Before long, both of us were DooWahing in the background and cutting solos. Gloria did her version of Ella Mae Morse's version of the "Blacksmith Blues," while I moved onto Jo Stafford's turf and recorded "Hambone." Miss Stafford's rendition included a syncopated "pop" introduced every few bars which sounded like a cork being pulled from a bottle. The Garrison studio had no bottle or cork, and in order to recreate the sound, the ersatz Jo Stafford puffed up her cheeks, stuck her finger in the side of her mouth, then pulled it forward quickly to make a "pop." Between playing my nose with Roger Wagner and popping my cheeks for Hal Loman, I was a one-woman band.

I worked at Garrison's, on and off, for about two years. Sadly, of the fifteen or twenty solo records cut, I never thought to save any. Some are still around as collector's items, and I'd love to hear one. I enjoyed my pirate career while I was doing it, but it made my frenetic schedule even more crowded and I finally had to drop it.

During my sophomore year at USC, besides flourishing as a Pirate Queen, I also marked a watershed in my classical studies. I received a grant to study with the legendary soprano Lotte Lehmann, who was teaching master classes at Cal Tech and the Music Academy of the West.

Lehmann occupies a hallowed niche in the singers' pantheon; critics and fans wax eloquent over her "human completeness," beauty of tone and technical sureness. Like other titans of the past, she has been elevated to sainthood.

Born in Perlberg, Germany, in 1888, Lotte Lehmann made her operatic debut in Hamburg in 1909 as the first or second boy (depending on which source you read) in Mozart's *Die Zauberflöte*, and in 1916 went to the Vienna Hofoper. Until 1938, she was the outstanding artist of that house, creating many roles and becoming most famous for her consummate portrayal of the Marschallin in Strauss' *Der Rosenkavalier*. Her American debut in 1930 with the Chicago Opera Company was as Sieglinde in *Die Walküre*, as was her Metropolitan debut in 1934. Lehmann sang at the Met until 1945, spent the next six years on the concert stage, and even tried a brief cinematic fling with MGM. It lasted for exactly one film—a character part in a rather saccharine movie called *The Big City* (1948). Then Lehmann retired to Santa Barbara to teach classes and occasionally sing in public. When she gave recitals on the West Coast, her accompanist was Gwen Koldofsky. It was through Gwen that I got to Lehmann.

In 1951, Lehmann arrived at USC to conduct master classes for the Adolf Koldofsky Memorial Scholarship, established by Gwen in honor of her late husband, a violinist and concertmaster of the RKO orchestra in the glory days of film-studio symphonies. Koldofsky was not only an outstanding musician, but a genuine humanist.

Among other accomplishments, he championed the music of Arnold Schoenberg when no one would listen to the German exile's work, and played Schoenberg's sonatas and concertos from memory before audiences, whether they were willing to listen or not. When Adolf died of a heart attack, Gwen established the Memorial Scholarship in his honor, and I'm very honored this year to be co-chairman of that fund with Mary Katz.

Lehmann led the Koldofsky master classes in Bovard Auditorium. To my great delight, I was chosen as a participant and, at the age of seventeen, learned my first *"Lied"* or song, *"Die junge Nonne"* ("The Young Nun") by Franz Schubert. Mme. Lehmann was satisfied with my work and invited me to join her next series of masters at Cal Tech, which of course thrilled me, but there was just one problem—how was I going to afford it?

Once again, good luck intervened. There is a woman in California named Carolyn Scott, a true patron of the arts who came by her philanthropy the hard way. Carolyn's only child, a daughter, died suddenly, and barely two months later her husband dropped dead in the street. Mr. Scott and Carolyn had been vitally interested in the arts, and with the money he left, she began to "subsidize" young people by sending a number of promising students through Cal Tech. I was not on "full scholarship" with her, but she aided me in many ways. Thanks to her, I was able to buy a car, an absolute necessity, and over the years she'd send checks or clothes, both of which were welcome and needed. She's old and enfeebled now, but I keep in touch with her and treasure our present friendship as well as her past generosity.

It was with Carolyn Scott's backing that I went to Cal Tech and the Music Academy of the West in Santa Barbara to work with Lehmann. I charged into it, chin high and eyes sparkling, certain that I was going to knock them dead. What a rude shock I was in for!

Great artist that she was, Lotte Lehmann was also one very tough lady. That's all right—talent and niceness don't have to go together —but Lehmann's vaunted "completeness" as a human being was not always in evidence to me. Indeed, my last master session with her proved to be one of the most upsetting moments of my life. To this day, I cannot figure out what motivated Lotte Lehmann's behavior.

Before the classes themselves commenced, the participants were all brought in to give a concert for students at the Lobero Theatre. I sang German *Lieder* and was warmly applauded. A few days later, the class met with Lehmann and, as is usual in master classes, a select audience of friends and musicians was on hand. The participants sat in a row near the stage, and when my turn came, I stood up and stepped forward to sing Brahms' *"Botschaft."* Before I could open my mouth, however, the great Lehmann lit into me with such venom that I believed I could actually feel the physical sting of her words.

"Your Cherman vas a disgrrrace in ze Loberrro conzert," she began. "You haf no rrright to zink a lenkvich zo poorly. A zinker must haf commant of ze lenkvich, und not learnink anozer tonk prrroperrly is ze zign of laziness. You vill neverr be grrreat becauss you cannot master ze lenkvich!"

In the midst of my anguish and fear, I couldn't help noticing that my persecutor herself sounded like something out of the Katzenjammer Kids. The realization that she hadn't mastered *my* tongue, however, didn't help my stomach, and I froze as Lehmann continued her tirade. When she didn't stop, the audience began to squirm, and I looked over to Gwen, the official accompanist, at the piano. She lowered her head in a feeble gesture of sympathy, but there was nothing Gwen could do. Ironically, I *had* worked on my German, with Gwen, until we had both considered it letter-perfect. Lehmann raved on and the audience was aghast, wondering, I'm sure, not only what had gotten into the Master, but how on earth this student was going to sing after the *Sturm und Drang*. Finally, Lehmann stopped and, throwing me a look which could have destroyed Tebaldi, Stignani and Callas combined, commanded me to "Zink!"

I did. I sang. The special ability, the something in me which I call "concentration," enabled me to block out everything that had gone before and just proceed. I gave everything I had to *"Botschaft."*

This was the first of my experiences in singing under special stress. In the years to come, there would be many more: performances after my mother's death and, even worse because it was so unexpected, when my brother Dick was killed. Then there was the performance of *L'Italiana in Algeri* at the Metropolitan with Henry conducting: I was uttering phrases like "It is he whom I adore" and that very day we had announced our formal separation. These times try your very soul.

That day, however, not only did I sing for Lehmann, I sang well, and Gwen, caught up in the drama, accompanied me, as always, superbly. At the final note, the audience broke into such cheers that Lehmann could do nothing but mumble, "Vell, dot vas much imprrroved." I returned to my seat and sat through the rest of the class, unable to hear another note that was sung. My mind was churning; I vowed I would never, ever sing for that woman again!

At the end of class, it was Lehmann's custom to rise, walk over to the participants, exchange greetings and ask what songs they'd present at the next meeting. In truth, I had a booking at the same time as the next session and I hadn't planned to attend, and when Lehmann reached me and posed the question, I answered, "I won't be here, Madame. I have another engagement." Damned if Lehmann didn't get in a final lick. "Vell," she snorted curtly, "I hope you vill be shtutyink your Cherman." The class was dismissed and soon I was surrounded by friends expressing outrage at the teacher's behavior and admiration for my performance. I never went back.

Naturally, I assumed that my relationship with Lehmann was over, but, as it turned out, I was wrong. In 1956, I was engaged for the outdoor Ojai Festival near Santa Barbara, at which Stravinsky was to conduct his *Les Noces*. I was in my trailer making up my eyes when there was a knock on the door. With one eye painted and the other bare, I stumbled over to the door and pushed it open with my elbow. I'm very nearsighted and, until contact lenses became a part of my wardrobe, had a devil of a time making up. Standing there, a warm smile on her famous lips, was Lotte Lehmann. I couldn't believe my eyes.

"Come in, Madame," I stammered. She did and, very sweetly and cordially, said she'd heard I was going to study in Germany and added that if there was anything she could do to help, just to let her know. I remember wondering as she spoke, "has she forgotten how nasty she was, or is it that she *does* remember and wants to bury the hatchet?" I was a bit torn between wanting to tell her off and letting bygones be bygones. I decided to let it rest, and we parted on good terms.

Soon after, as it happened, we were in Vienna at the same time and she invited me to join her at the Staatsoper for a performance of *Die Meistersinger von Nürnberg*. I accepted happily. It promised to be quite an evening. I already had a sense of show-biz savvy, and the chance to walk into the Vienna Opera House for the first time with the fabled Lehmann was delicious. The opera house, gutted during World War II, was the soul of Vienna and the very first building reconstructed after the war. Marching in with Lotte Lehmann was a young singer's dream.

Our entrance, however, was not only less than dramatic, it went practically unnoticed. For some reason, Lehmann arrived too early, and as we walked to our box, the standees lined up for tickets were the only ones who spotted us. Of course they burst into applause when they saw her, but by the time the rest of the audience had filed in, she'd faded into the walls. They didn't even know she was in the house! If she'd just waited and come in right before the lights went down, the entire house would have been on its feet. Why did she go in unobtrusively? Why did she pick on me at the master class? Your guess is as good as mine.

From then on, until her death, I was in touch with Lotte Lehmann, either in person or through the mail. If I was having difficulty with a song, she would help me out and, even more, suggest songs suitable for my repertoire. When, some time later, I began studying Robert Schumann's *Frauenliebe und Leben,* a cycle of eight songs in which Lehmann had excelled—there's a fabulous recording of her with Bruno Walter at the piano—I sought her advice, waiting only till I had a few performances under my belt so that my ideas would be settled before asking for hers. I wanted to get some fine points on my interpretation, not parrot Lehmann's.

*Frauenliebe und Leben* (*A Woman in Love and Life*) is a little kitschy, but I love it. A woman sings of meeting a man, falling in love, getting engaged, getting married, giving birth and, finally, of her husband's death. It's from the submissive school of female behavior, difficult to swallow in this liberated time, but it does contain great music. I went to Santa Barbara and sang it for her in her living room. She listened intently and, at the conclusion, remarked, "Zere's nozink to add. It's beeyootiful, Jackie, but vun little touch, I zink, at ze end, vould be goot. You should do somezink a bit more theatrical viz your hands, raise zem und let zem fall slowly." She demonstrated by singing the last song, *"Nun hast du mir den ersten Schmerz getan"* ("Now you have caused me the first pain"), which ends with, "The world is empty, empty. I have loved and I have lived; I do not live anymore. I silently withdraw into myself; the veil is falling. Then I have you and my lost happiness. You, my world!" She raised her hands to her breast as she sang the next-to-last line and dropped them on the final word. It looked great, and I practiced it with her. With our arms moving up and down, up and down, the scene must have looked like a mother bird teaching her fledgling how to fly. Armed with Lotte Lehmann's suggestion, I did the Schumann at my next concert in Carnegie Hall.

After the performance, Trude Rittman came to my dressing room. Trude is a German émigrée and another marvelous person in my life, a musician and composer who did orchestrations for Rodgers and Hammerstein, Lerner and Lowe and many others. We'd met when I'd sung in the chorus of the "Small House of Uncle Thomas" ballet in the movie *The King and I.* Trude had directed the musical sequences of the film, and had composed the music for that big dance number, which was based on a Siamese interpretation of Harriet Beecher Stowe's *Uncle Tom's Cabin.* Her opinion was valuable and I asked what she thought of Schumann. "It was fabulous, Jackie, just the right tone. Frankly, the only thing I didn't like was what you did with your hands at the end. It looked phony."

For all the help Lotte Lehmann gave me, however, our relationship was still not without difficulty. After all her cordiality, I didn't think she could ever upset me again, but I was wrong. We had another, more frightening encounter in 1964.

Each year, the *Los Angeles Times* gives a prestigious "Woman of the Year" award to ten or so outstanding women in fields ranging from music and science to medicine and public service. In 1960, I was voted a Woman of the Year for my appearance in Alban Berg's *Wozzeck*, and in 1964 the *Times* called and asked me, as a former recipient, to join the current presentation ceremony honoring Lotte Lehmann. Naturally, I went and, during the dinner, was approached by an old friend from the DooWah years.

"Jackie," she greeted me enthusiastically, "I hear you're pregnant. Is it true?"

I wasn't showing yet, but answered delightedly, "Yes, I am."

"Wonderful," was the reply, "and what do you want, a boy or a girl?"

"Listen," I said, "I just hope it's a healthy baby." Lehmann was standing next to me and, at my reply, turned and growled, *"Und ich hoffe es wird ein nul sein!"* ("And I hope it's a zero!")

I was stunned. What a thing to say to a woman pregnant for the first time!

"What do you mean?" I demanded.

Lehmann continued coldly, "A zinker has no buziness hafink childrren. You must conzentrate on the carreerr und only on the carreerr!"

I was shocked then and I'm still shocked. It *is* difficult to combine career and motherhood—it's difficult enough just to be a mother—but how could she say that to someone already on the way to parenthood?

Fair is fair, though. If I tell you of Lehmann's dark side, then I must also tell you that she opened the doors of singing *Lieder* for me. Her instruction is inextricably woven into my own interpretations. As exponent and teacher, she was incomparable and inspirational. My friend, Donald Gramm, the late American bass-baritone, lucky enough to see her in performance told me once of her uniqueness: "By God, when she sang something like Schubert's 'The Crow,' you really thought that bird was flying over her head! She made everything come alive!" When I started those master classes with Lehmann, I was too green to cut through some of the flak and get to the greatness. I grew into her, and am definitely of her school, as opposed to the Elisabeth Schwarzkopf school, in which every note is hugged, squeezed and throttled in order to reach a desired effect. Schwarzkopf is much more calculated in her approach to

*Lieder,* while Lehmann was innately theatrical; she used imagination to create an entire feeling or story, from the very opening of the piano chords to the final sounds and beyond. There was a residual effect in Lehmann's approach; something remained with the listener even after the music was over, and that "something" was sublime.

Schwarzkopf herself recognized the special ingredient in Lehmann's singing. One time, the younger woman went to visit Lehmann in Santa Barbara, and as they walked along the beach, Schwarzkopf said, "You know, Lotte, I get the feeling from hearing your records that you really enjoyed singing."

Lehmann stopped in her tracks. "Why, of course I enjoyed it," she replied assertively.

"I never have," answered Schwarzkopf.

"Well, it sounds it, Elisabeth," rejoined Lehmann as she resumed walking.

I never knew what Lehmann was like in an actual performance until 1961, when a friend invited Henry and me over for dinner and played a tape of the historic 1936 San Francisco Opera broadcast of Wagner's *Die Walküre.* The cast included Kirsten Flagstad, Lauritz Melchior, Friedrich Schorr and Lotte Lehmann, a singing lineup comparable to the batting order of the 1929 New York Yankees, and on the podium was Fritz Reiner. If you don't know opera, let me tell you that those names represented the finest interpreters of the German repertoire—and Lotte Lehmann completely wiped the others out. How? By singing the music and words with such incredible intensity and conviction that the result was overwhelming. I was so thrilled, I went home and wrote her a letter; hearing her in performance was a revelation, I said, like a gift from God. Her reply was poignant. She thanked me, and added, "My dear Jackie, it's just as the Marschallin says, *'Jedes Ding hat seine Zeit.'* ['Everything has its time.'] I had mine, and now, Jackie, it's yours!"

Lotte Lehmann was a true artist, susceptible at certain moments to the same petty jealousies and envious stabs ordinary people feel, but able to rise above them as a performer and, ultimately, as a person. Though I cite those momentary lapses in humanity, I really come to praise her.

# Carmen Jones

BACK TO school! Despite the master-class fiasco, and whatever gripe I had against Lehmann at the time, taking her sessions had shown the way. I decided to pursue my musical career exclusively, and so, after the fall semester of 1953, I withdrew from USC. As much as the school had given me, I just couldn't get the things there I needed as a professional singer—that is, voice lessons at least three times a week, coaching every day and extensive language study. All those things were available at the college, but they came with excess baggage—namely, a required curriculum—and I just didn't have the time for that anymore.

I didn't ask for my parents' approval; I simply announced my decision at dinner one evening, and they agreed with my plan. There was no reason for them not to. Their goal for me always had been a singing career, and I was already making between ten and twelve thousand dollars a year as a solo performer. In addition, since I lived at home, our family routine wouldn't change. Thinking back, I was right. It didn't make sense to continue my education in a general way when I knew exactly what I wanted to do. I never did receive a Bachelor's degree, but my alma mater has an honorary doctorate waiting for me as soon as I find the time to pick it up!

In the months that followed, I kept very busy, literally singing for my supper. You name it, I sang it! Besides engagements at prestigious places such as the Hollywood Bowl, I sang at weddings, funerals and parties, and only drew the line at nightclubs or bars.

Remember the movie *I Never Sang for My Father*? My life could be called "I Always Sang for My Father." Musically, Dad still called the shots. Although I was singing up a storm, for a long time he wouldn't allow me to take the big step and attempt an entire evening of opera. As professional as I was, and there were a lot of weddings and funerals to prove it, Dad cautioned me not to try to sustain an operatic performance until I was physically and vocally mature. Finally, when I was twenty, opportunity knocked.

The opera was Smetana's *The Bartered Bride* and the role was Hata, often translated into English as Agnes. How's this for a part? You're married to a rich landlord and your stammering son, the laughingstock of the village, gets engaged to a pretty young thing by virtue of your husband's wealth. Just when you think you've got this nitwit off your hands, behold, your husband's son by a previous marriage gets the girl and you wind up at the final curtain with your stuttering son who's dressed up as a bear. Is this a way to begin an operatic career? It was for me! I suppose if I could play a merry widow at sixteen, I could play the mother of a grown bear at twenty.

*The Bartered Bride* was a production of the Los Angeles Guild Opera, a professional organization founded by the city to present opera to schoolchildren. Every year, it put on a production for about twenty performances and bussed kids to the Shrine Auditorium in Los Angeles, a huge sixty-eight-hundred-seat hall. Think of it, nearly seven thousand kids at an opera!

The production was directed by Carl Ebert, another amazing personality. A Berliner trained in acting by Max Reinhardt, he was made general director of the State Theatre at Darmstadt in 1927 and then, switching gears, director general and producer of the Städtische Opera, Berlin. His productions were legendary, but he refused to collaborate with the Nazis and had to flee Germany in 1933, and subsequently began producing opera all over the world, from Firenze to Buenos Aires. With conductor Fritz Busch, he founded the Glyndebourne Festival in Great Britain, and then he organized the Turkish National Theatre and Opera. Talk about track records! Besides producing and directing for the Los Angeles Opera Guild, Ebert was also the director of USC's opera department from 1948 to 1956, and that's when I met him.

Ebert's production of *The Bartered Bride* made its bow in the fall of 1954. How did I feel at my debut? How would you feel singing in front of sixty-eight hundred kids? Truthfully, I can't remember my debut state, other than that I was tremendously excited over having learned and performed an entire operatic role, and at being able to combine dramatic and operatic skills for the first time. Hata is a contralto, and though I considered myself a soprano, my operatic debut was in the range which became my home, and that was good. And it was fabulous working with Ebert. He must have been pleased, too, because I was hired to appear again the next year in *Hansel and Gretel.*

Though no longer an operatic virgin, I still couldn't make a living as an opera singer and so continued working in other musical fields as well. At about this time, Otto Preminger decided to film *Carmen Jones,* Oscar Hammerstein's re-creation of Bizet's *Carmen* in the black idiom. Hammerstein had done a new book and lyrics for the opera in 1943, and the result had run for 503 performances on Broadway. In terms of employment, *Carmen Jones* was the "Roots" of its day, because it gave blacks an opportunity to perform in something other than occasional character roles. A show like *Carmen Jones* was a godsend to Muriel Smith and other quality performers. The barring of blacks from the cultural world has always been an American tragedy. Impossible as it seems, though the New York City Opera had presented black singers in leading roles in the late 1940's, it wasn't until 1955 that Marian Anderson broke the operatic color barrier at the Met when she sang Ulrica in Verdi's *Un Ballo in Maschera*. Even then, Miss Anderson, who Toscanini had said had "the voice that comes once in a hundred years," was past her prime, so it was more of a symbolic appearance than a musical occasion. Until then, a young black with classical singing aspirations had no place to go except the concert stage where Miss Anderson, Roland Hayes and Dorothy Maynor had found their musical homes. Even now, there's a color barrier in opera which affects men more than women. We'll accept black women as heroines, but, with a few exceptions, won't readily embrace black men as heroes. We cannot pat ourselves on the backs—there's still a long way to go.

Back to *Carmen Jones*, however. What Hammerstein had done was move the action of *Carmen* from nineteenth-century Spain to the twentieth-century American South. Don José became Joe, an Army corporal; Micaëla, the sweet young thing in love with Joe, became Cindy Lou; Escamillo, the toreador, became Husky Miller, a heavyweight boxer; and Carmen, the gypsy, remained Carmen, only now she was working in a factory that produced parachutes rather than cigarettes.

Hammerstein had also reworked the arias into songs to spectacular effect. Instead of singing the "Habañera"—"*L'amour est*

71

*un oiseau rebelle que nul ne peut apprivoiser"* ("Love's a wild bird no one can tame")—Carmen Jones oozed her way through "Dat's Love" ("Love's a baby dat grows up wild an' he don' do what you want him to. Love ain' nobody's angel child an' he won' pay any mind to you"). The "Seguidilla"— *"Près des ramparts de Séville, chez mon ami Lillas Pastia"*—became "Dere's a café on de corner," a café run by Billy Pastor instead of Lillas Pastia. Carmen's "Card Song" was flipped into "De Cards Don' Lie" ("I'm gonna keep on livin' up to de day I die"). You could start a race riot by reciting those lyrics today.

It took ten years for Hollywood to touch *Carmen Jones* and then they souped it up with Stereophonic sound and Cinema-Scope, with a result that was two dimensions short of being three-dimensional. Harry Belafonte and Dorothy Dandridge played Joe and Carmen. Dandridge, a beautiful and gifted woman, later died tragically, and I'm sure a great part of her unhappiness was due to career frustrations.

In the summer of 1954, John Noschese, a singer friend, casually mentioned over a Coke that 20th-Century-Fox was hiring singers for the recording of the chorus music in *Carmen Jones*. What's more, there was no color barrier—whites could apply. "What do you say we audition and make a little money?" John suggested. I agreed and off we went to the studio. What an incredible call it was! Hundreds of singers were waiting to "make a little money." What I hadn't realized was that the audition was for the actual soloists' soundtrack—I'd assumed it was just for one of those title backgrounds in which the chorus goes "Ahhhh, ohhhh, ahhhh, ohhhh" while the credits flash by. Instead, everything was up for grabs, even the dubbed voices of Belafonte and Dandridge. Pearl Bailey would be doing her own vocals.

When I got there, Herschel Gilbert, the musical director, was busy marshaling the troops with Ted Low, his assistant. There was a surprise for me, too—Low had brought along his friend Henry Lewis. I hadn't seen Henry very much for the past three years; he'd been around and I'd thought he was cute, but we'd never had time to date. In fact, Henry had been playing in the orchestra for *The Bartered Bride*—but it had been the production's soprano he'd been interested in, not the mezzo. At one point, after I'd sung a long, low line, Henry had turned to someone in the pit and, unable to see the stage, asked, "Who's that terrific tenor?" Tenor!

I was too busy to think about any of that just then, however. When it came my turn, I sang Micaëla's aria, *"Je dis que rien ne m'épouvante,"* in French. (Later, it would become "I'se yo' gal, I wuz always yo' gal.") Micaëla is a soprano and, of course, I sang soprano then. After my number, Mr. Gilbert said, "Very nice, very nice, thank you." I was returning to my seat when I heard someone singing the "Habañera" with the Hammerstein lyrics. I got mad at myself for being Miss Purist and doing the Bizet French, so I turned to Mr. Gilbert and announced, "You know, I can sing low, too!"

Gilbert smiled. "Can you sing the 'Habañera'?" he asked.

"Sure!" I replied, and though I'd never seen the music before— I knew the melody by ear only—the next thing I knew, I was singing words like "You go for me an' I'm taboo, But if yore hard to get I go for you, An' if I do, den you are through, boy. My baby, dat's de end of you." I'm embarrassed to say I tore into those lyrics with the most blatant imitation of "darky" dialogue this side of Catfish Row. After I'd finished, Mr. Gilbert thanked me again and said I could go. On my way out, Henry Lewis came up and spoke to me.

"Hi, Jackie," he said amiably. "You know, I think they liked you and I'm sure you'll get something nice out of this." Then he added, "You want to have dinner?" I was excited about the audition and wanted to talk about it and Henry knew music and he *was* good-looking. So, Henry Lewis walked into my life as we walked out the door.

Henry was fun to be with and the time passed pleasantly as we enjoyed a leisurely dinner and an active conversation in a little restaurant on Santa Monica Boulevard. It was late when we left and I had a long way to go to Long Beach. There was no freeway then, and I arrived home at nearly midnight. Dad was sitting in the living room reading the paper.

"Jackie," he said as I came in the door, "a man named Gilbert called and left a number where you can reach him. He said to be sure and call when you came in."

"Gilbert?" I thought for a second. "Oh, Gilbert! You mean Herschel Gilbert, Dad?"

"That's it, that's it," replied my father. Dad was casual, but I was beginning to shake.

"I can't call him now, it's almost twelve."

"Honey, he said for you to call him whenever you got in, so if I were you, I'd call him."

I did. Herschel Gilbert answered the phone and brushed aside my apologies for calling late. "We like what you did today, Miss Horne, and want you to come over tomorrow and test for Carmen."

What a stunner! I'd started out aiming for the chorus, then made a stab at Micaëla and here I was being given a chance for the leading role. I put down the phone and started jumping around the room. Caught up in the excitement, Dad dropped his paper and his reserve and hopped with me. Mother came in to see what the ruckus was and, when she found out, was so pleased, she began jumping, too. We hugged and kissed. After my parents went to bed, I called Henry Lewis.

"Guess what, Henry," I said with a new, low lilt in my voice. "I'm going to sing Carmen Jones."

I got the part.

I worked for about three weeks on the dubbing. At the same time, Henry and I began dating, a fact I didn't mention to my parents for a very obvious reason—they were products of Bradford WASP culture and Henry was black. It was Hollywood Bowl season at the time; Henry was in the orchestra and I was making singing appearances intermittently there with Roger Wagner, so we saw each other fairly frequently.

During the day, I was at the sound studio along with the other "voices." Pearl Bailey was doing her own vocals—she'd slimmed down to pencil thinness for the film and appeared every day in a different dazzling Don Loper dress. What style that lady had, and still has! Marvin Hayes sang the role of Husky Miller, which Joe Adams enacted on the screen, and LeVern Hutcherson and I did our bit for the two leads. It wasn't much of a strain—in fact, it was fun. My job entailed working with Dorothy Dandridge. I had to listen carefully to her speaking voice and try to match the timbre and the accent, so that when it came time for me to record the songs, there would be a little bit of Dandridge in my throat. She sang in a register comfortable for her, then I mimicked her voice in the proper keys. Later, she filmed her scenes with my recorded voice blasting from huge loudspeakers. The tendency in dubbing is to overdo your mouth movements. Dandridge didn't and was sensational. The sound technicians pieced music and film together and the result is a seamless performance by Dorothy Dandridge and Marilyn Horne.

The past didn't desert me entirely, though. In typical Hollywood fashion, the final chords of the opera, the bone-chilling fate theme, was augmented at the end of the movie by—you guessed it—a full chorus DooWah.

Alas, I didn't make much money out of the deal, around fifteen hundred dollars. It would have been a lot more if I hadn't sold the recording rights for a mere two hundred and fifty dollars. Damned if the record wasn't a best-seller, and recently re-released, too—with *my* picture on the cover! It makes me mad that I worked for such peanuts, but, on the other hand, it was an experience; I learned, I had fun and I had a chance to be around Harry Belafonte, one very handsome and talented man.

It wasn't until 1979 that I saw Belafonte again, when I attended a roast for Tony Randall at Radio City Music Hall. Tony's an opera buff and many people from the musical world were there, and we roasters had taken an elevator into the basement so we could re-appear on the big stage seated at a table. I stepped into the elevator, and as the doors closed, a husky voice whispered in my ear, "I love you, Marilyn Horne." I turned to face Harry Belafonte. I hadn't seen him since *Carmen Jones* and I noticed his hair was graying, but on him it looked good! I needed words fast, but could only gulp, "Likewise!" Let me tell you, I'd sing for peanuts again just to hear and see him.

*Carmen Jones* did well both in the reviews and at the box office. The *Daily News* gave it four stars and John McCarten in *The New Yorker* praised "Dorothy Dandridge, whose configurations are re-markable and whose songs, rendered by Marilyn Horne, have a highly sultry effectiveness. I had no idea," he continued, "that Miss Dandridge was not singing *in voce sua* until I was given the news by a press agent." Twenty years later, when I recorded Bizet's *Carmen* (*in voce mia*) with Leonard Bernstein conducting the Metro-politan Opera, it was an all-time operatic best-seller. In six months, it even outsold Maria Callas' classic *Tosca*. Not bad for a little girl from Bradford—with a lot of help from a certain conductor from Lawrence, Massachusetts.

After *Carmen Jones*, my work in films continued. Have you seen *The Rose Tattoo* with Anna Magnani and Burt Lancaster? Guess who's singing the song behind the opening credits. I also worked a lot for television, including such shows as the monthly "Shower

of Stars" special, which included, among other productions, a musical version of Dickens' *A Christmas Carol*, with Fredric March as
Scrooge. For that production, Maxwell Anderson did the libretto,
Bernard Herrmann did the music and Marilyn Horne did some
singing.

I worked frequently with Benny Herrmann, who's probably best
known for his brilliant score for *Citizen Kane*. Benny, a Handelian-
era nut, used to go scurrying around places like the British Museum
to unearth original material. I did many concerts with him, and
on one occasion remember singing a back-breaking program containing three Handel arias, plus *"Che farò"* from Gluck's *Orfeo*
and Arne's "Water parted from the sea," all in a single Sunday-
afternoon concert at the Los Angeles County Museum. I first sang
those arias straight, just as they were written, and then with a
famous castrato's embellishments. The embellishments on the *"Che
farò"* were so florid that they'd crucify me if I did them today.
Actually, they weren't so fond of them then!

A little digression here: *"Che farò"* is one of those glorious arias
which have been sung a certain way for so long that there's no room
for interpretation. It's usually done the same way, s-l-o-w-l-y. Henry
and I discussed the piece, however, and both agreed that since
Orfeo is telling us in the recitative that he's *"pazzo"*—Euridice has
just been whisked back to Hell—the music should be agitated.
The tempo is marked *alla breve*, two beats to the bar, but that can
mean a fast two as well as a slow two, and it makes more sense to
take it fast so that it can be slowed up in other places, as when
Orfeo says forlornly, "Euridice!" The Horne version of *"Che farò
senza Euridice"* ("I've lost my Eurydice") went quite quickly,
and every time I sang it, the critics said I was wrong. The only
person who ever said it was right was the French baritone Martial
Singher, a great male Orfeo and a consummate musician whose
opinion meant a lot more to me than most critics'. Frankly, em-

bellishments have disappeared because they went out of fashion and most singers can no longer sing them. Well, *I* can. For a while there I had to argue with a lot of conductors to sing the music as it was originally conceived.

Concerts such as that one were classical gravy, but radio, television and movies continued to be the meat of my early career. Then, in 1955, my career took a new twist when I appeared in *front* of the camera on "Arthur Godfrey's Talent Scouts."

Amateur nights and talent shows were an important aspect of American life, providing not only entertainment but the opportunity to socialize for a purpose. The big talent showcases started on radio with "The Original Amateur Hour," on which Major Edward Bowes made a small-town phenomenon into a national pastime. His show was extremely popular, and every musical-saw player, spoon slapper, accordion squeezer and coloratura in the country wanted to get on it and take his chances with the "gong," a cymbal banged if an act wasn't up to snuff. Bowes was a tough man with the gong, and the program was punctuated with ear-splitting cymbal crashes. Later, Bowes was replaced by his affable assistant, Ted Mack, who never played the cymbal with the Major's fervor. In 1949, "The Original Amateur Hour" premiered on TV and was quite successful, following close upon the heels of "Arthur Godfrey's Talent Scouts," which featured fewer amateurs—and no gong.

Whatever else these shows did, they provided a showcase for talent. We have become too sophisticated or maybe too critical for talent shows these days, which is too bad, because they were havens for would-be and almost-there performers. There's no such thing as "amateur" anymore; everyone is an immediate "professional." I see evidence all the time in opera, where young singers have made debuts long before their techniques and skills were ready. I was thirty-six years old at my Metropolitan Opera debut and may have been a bit "over-qualified," but, at thirty-six, at least I knew what I had, what I wanted and where I was going. When singers in their early and mid-twenties make debuts in blockbuster roles and in blockbuster places, it shocks and saddens me. There is no substitute for training and experience, and both take years and years.

In opera, the voice is only the starting point, then come determination, brains, acting ability, a knowledge of languages and business acumen. You must come up the hard way; shortcuts at the beginning of a career will only shorten the career's span. Unfortunately, singers today often are not guided intelligently. Teachers, coaches, managers, agents and the like take promising raw material and do little or nothing to refine it. If, by some miracle, they do try to hold the singer back, the singer bristles and insists on jumping in willy-nilly.

Bellini's *Norma* is a good illustration. The opera is so demanding that until recently it appeared only when there was a singer qualified to perform it. After performances in Philadelphia and New York in 1841 and 1843, *Norma* was given its first major production in America by Giulia Grisi at the inaugural of the Academy of Music in New York City on October 2, 1854, and made the Metropolitan Opera stage on February 27, 1890, when Walter Damrosch conducted a German-language version. Lilli Lehmann sang the title role, and avowed it was easier to sing all three Brünnhildes than one Norma. "When you sing Wagner," wrote Lilli Lehmann, "you are so carried away by the dramatic emotion, the action, and the scene that you do not have to think how to sing the words. That comes of itself. But in Bellini, you must always have a care for beauty of tone and correct emission."

After two more performances by Lehmann in the 1891–92 season, *Norma* did not appear on the Met stage until November 16, 1927, when it was revived for Rosa Ponselle, who had worked up to it gradually. Gina Cigna sang the role in 1937, Zinka Milanov in 1943, and no one else till Callas opened the Met season as Norma on October 29, 1956. Finally, Joan Sutherland brought it back to the Met on March 3, 1970. And that was it. Now it's so different. A handful of Normas in a hundred years has yielded to a plethora of Normas in the past decade. Anyone who has a hankering to sing Norma does, whether or not she's up to it or even suited for it. Some wonderful singers have come close to committing vocal suicide.

If I have any advice to give young singers on the subject, it's this: don't push, don't rush, and remember you've got resources we older singers never had. There are more opera companies in the United States than ever before. Use them!

In 1955, I used the Arthur Godfrey show. It was at the height of his TV fame and his scouts were all over the country. A fellow named Ace Goodman was his Los Angeles representative. Someone told me Goodman was auditioning for the show, and once again I was off and running. Mr. Goodman, a brusque heart-of-gold character out of Damon Runyon, had had a bellyful of "talent" by the time I got to him.

"Okay, kid, whatcha gonna do?" he queried uninterestedly when I appeared before him.

"I'm going to sing an operatic aria." He was not bowled over by my announcement. I sang *"Ritorna vincitor"* from *Aïda* and Mr. Goodman perked up.

"What else can you do, kid?" he asked enthusiastically. This was beginning to look like a scene out of *42nd Street*. I sang a popular number, at the end of which Mr. Goodman was irate.

"Are you crazy to sing junk like that with a voice like yours?" he admonished.

"Listen," I replied, "I'll sing anything."

"That's the most ridiculous thing I've ever heard. You stick to opera!" Mr. Goodman arranged for me to go to New York and appear on the show. I was excited for two reasons: (1) I would get to be with Godfrey, and (2) I wanted desperately to see the Metropolitan Opera House. Dorothy DeCoudres came along to present me, and we were off to the Big Apple.

After registering at the Taft Hotel at Seventh Avenue and 50th Street, I raced down Broadway to 39th Street and the Met. Think of my disappointment when I found that, because it was summertime, the house was officially closed! I begged a custodian to let me look inside for one minute, but, getting nowhere, had to go back to the hotel without accomplishing my goal. As it turned out, I didn't see Arthur Godfrey either. He was on vacation and Jack Paar was hosting the show. However, the scouts had done a little research, and when I stepped into the spotlight on Monday evening, Paar said that he understood my heart's desire was to get inside the Met. "Oh yes, Mr. Paar," I said emotionally. "It means so much to me just to *see* it!"

"Well, Miss Horne," said Paar avuncularly, "we've arranged for you to have a tour of the Met if you win, so maybe that'll give you an added incentive."

I sang Puccini's *"Un bel dì"* from *Madama Butterfly*, and won.

As part of the reward, the winner also got to appear on Arthur Godfrey's morning radio show for the week, so Dorothy and I settled in for the next few days. Peter Lind Hayes and Mary Healy, the popular husband-and-wife talk team of the Fifties, were the hosts in Godfrey's absence; Jerry Vale was on the show, as was Roz Russell, then appearing on Broadway in *Auntie Mame*, and they were all wonderful to me. I was in pretty rough shape, though— still on California time and unable to get a good night's sleep, I had to get up early every morning and sing an aria! It was killing. There were times when I didn't know where the voice was going to come from, but I guess it came, because when Friday arrived, Hayes asked me to stay on for another week. "Gee, Mr. Hayes, I'd love to stay," I said, "but I've got to get back to Hollywood. I'm soloing in *Carmina Burana* with Leopold Stokowski at the Hollywood Bowl." How's that for a topper?

Being on Arthur Godfrey's show was fabulous, but, alas, somehow they never did arrange for me to get into the Met, and it wasn't until several years later that I attended my first performance there. In 1966, the building was torn down. I never could understand that. Italy, France or Germany would have bought the next block in order to preserve the old house, but we tore it down. It was a hard loss for me, and not having sung there is one of my deepest regrets. Montserrat Caballé made her debut there in a third-rate production, simply because she wanted to appear on the old stage, but I wouldn't do that. I wanted to come in with style, and instead I didn't get to sing in the "Yellow Brick Brewery" at all.

# V I

## *Europe Beckons*

IN 1955, simply being *near* the Metropolitan Opera House lit a fire under me, and I returned to California more determined than ever to make it operatically. My life was a whirlwind. The *Carmina Burana* was performed on August 30, and the opportunity to work under Leopold Stokowski was indeed worth sacrificing another week of appearances on Arthur Godfrey. Earlier, I had appeared in the Los Angeles Guild Opera's *Hansel and Gretel*, first as the Sandman, soprano, then as Hansel, mezzo. I was working constantly as a soloist and in small groups.

At home, meanwhile, our ranks had thinned. By the mid-Fifties, Gloria had married and moved to Hawaii, and Dick and Joanne had married and were on their own. Jay, Grandma Horne and I were still at home, however, and Horne family life was still strong. I may have taken some solo flights, but I was still very much part of the nest.

We had evolved into Californians, except for Dad, who never made a complete adjustment. From the day we arrived, he had been a fish out of water. How difficult it must have been for my middle-aged parents to relocate, especially Dad. He loved California's climate, as any sane person would, but Bradford was ingrained in his soul. Back East, he'd been a prominent person, involved in all facets of city life, hobnobbing with the political elite as well as everyday citizens. When anything needed doing, Dad was always on the committee, or heading it up. He had a quiet charisma and was smart about so many things. Self-educated, a voracious reader and far more intellectual in his thinking than the rest of his family, he was a dreamer in many ways, but a dreamer willing to accept his role as head of a family. Above all, he was a great talker. As kids, we were always waiting around while Dad discussed politics with his cronies. The inclination to gab is another thing I inherited from him.

He took many jobs in California, including a stint as shoe sales-man in a store where he eventually became manager. He was also employed as a county assessor, a seasonal venture. By 1955, he had become a traveling salesman for the Invalid Walker and Wheel-chair Company, for which Mom was executive secretary. Dad wasn't satisfied there, either, though. In a letter dated March 6, 1955, Dad answered an ad in the paper and cited his dislike of travel as the reason for wanting to change jobs. I can't help thinking he must have been a little chagrined because Mother held a higher position in the company than he. That letter tears me apart. My father, at forty-eight years of age, unfulfilled in his work, was still trying to find his niche, and in little over a year he would be dead.

If Dad gave me the desire, incentive and discipline to succeed,

Mom gave me the strength. Berneice Horne was the rock of the family, a constant source of resourcefulness, though she tended to stay in the background. Because Mom kept quiet, her opinion counted for an awful lot when expressed. She was forty-seven years old when Dad died and left her with no support. She missed him terribly, but kept on going because we needed her. Jay was only six and I was not yet the Miss Independence I thought I was. Though she never went past the eleventh grade—Dick had been born when she was only seventeen—Mom rose from bookkeeper to executive vice president in her company, and eighteen years later, when she died, her estate was considerable: fifty thousand dollars for each of her four children and one thousand dollars for each of her grandchildren. She had earned it all herself. I like to think I inherited Mother's "spine" and Dad's spirit; I also flatter myself in thinking I look like her—Mother was a beauty. Dad— well, he was "clean-favored," with a grin that lit up his whole face, but handsome, no.

Through these years, I was a dutiful daughter, free-spirited but still obedient. True, I had been seeing a man of whom neither parent would have approved, but before it became too serious, my "romance" with Henry petered out. I can't say why; we just drifted apart as we had drifted together. My mind was on other projects and I was literally too busy for serious romance. In addition, Henry was drafted into the army in 1955. I saw him once when he came home on furlough and we corresponded briefly after he was sent to Germany, but we were no longer a twosome.

In the mid-1950's, I met Robert Craft. Bob, a fabulous musician, became my very close friend, and through him I met *the* musical genius of the twentieth century, Igor Stravinsky. When Stravinsky came on the scene, around 1910, everyone was either rehashing Wagner or, in limited numbers, doing quasi-atonal compositions. Stravinsky went back to primitive rhythms and combined them

*85*

with modified atonal music, which resulted in something completely new or "re-new." Bob Craft assisted the Maestro and eventually became his right arm.

One of Bob's pet projects was the music of Carlo Gesualdo,
c. 1560–1613, a Neapolitan gentleman whose life and work were
equally tempestuous. Gesualdo is known to have murdered his wife,
her lover and a child he would not accept as his own. The spouse
and boyfriend were stabbed by hired assassins as they lay in bed;
the child was placed in a cradle suspended from the ceiling by four
ropes and, in a scene out of Jacobean drama, was "rocked" to death.
Gesualdo's uncle was a Pope, San Carlo Borromeo, and later can-
onized, which proves that even saints have skeletons in the closet.
According to the *Larousse Encyclopedia of Music*, Gesualdo's "music displays most openly his ardent southern temperament; he
pushes to extreme lengths the most daring contrapuntal and chro-
matic harmonies." "Ardent southern temperament" is putting it
mildly!

Bob loved Gesualdo's madrigals and motets and enlisted a group
of singers to perform the ardent musician's *oeuvre*. I was one of
five singers chosen to perform the madrigals. Charlie Scharbach
was our bass, Grace-Lynne Martin, soprano, I was second soprano,
Cora Lauridsen was alto and Richard Robinson, tenor. Charlie and
Grace-Lynne have absolute pitch and had "pitched" battles about
where it was. Though Grace-Lynne disagreed, we tuned to the bass.

Among other places, we performed at the Monday Evening Concerts. These concerts, sponsored by the Southern California Chamber Music Society, took place in Los Angeles County Auditorium
and were a vital part of the musical scene. The list of artists appearing in the Monday Night series featured the cream of the young
musicians' crop, including a pianist named André Previn and a
contrabassist called Henry Lewis. I recall one evening, September

20, 1954, when we did five madrigals for five voices and Stravinsky's *In Memoriam, Dylan Thomas* premiered on the same program.

Bob arranged for us to record the madrigals, and Stravinsky was in on the sessions—in fact, he actually "composed" portions of the works which had been lost! In addition, it just so happened that Aldous Huxley was very interested in Gesualdo, and because of the fascination of Craft, Stravinsky and Huxley, Southern California was treated to an exceptional lecture-and-music series. Our contrapuntal group traveled around performing music interspersed and illuminated by Mr. Huxley's commentary on "The Court of Ferrara and Gesualdo." Huxley was brilliant and gave incredible lectures. He loved the word "extraordinary" and we singers would count the number of times it was uttered during a single lecture. The record was fifty.

Stravinsky and Huxley certainly were a strange duo, the former a gnomish, balding Russian, the latter a lanky, aquiline Englishman. Huxley was at least six-feet-three, while Stravinsky was *my* height; together they resembled a psychedelic Mutt and Jeff. Poor Mr. Huxley had terrible cataracts, and though he had got partial sight back through the Bates exercise method, his vision was minimal. Stravinsky's eyesight wasn't great either and, in fact, the Maestro always wore *three* pairs of eyeglasses, one on his head, another on his forehead and the last over his eyes. Depending upon what he wanted to see, he'd flip the required pair down and flip the other two up.

One time, while recording at Capitol Records, I was in the control room and Huxley and the Maestro were in the actual recording room. Through the window, I could see them hunched over the piano, staring intently at something which appeared to puzzle them greatly. Stravinsky's voice came over the intercom, saying, "Let's ask Jackie, she knows these things." I couldn't believe it! Igor Stravinsky wanted to check some musical point with *me*. Huxley's voice came over the mike asking, in clipped British tones, "Jackie, could you come here and tell us what this extraordinary sign means."

I went through the door, into the studio and over to the piano. There, a hand-lettered sign carried the legend, "NO COTTON-PICK- IN' DRINKS ON THIS INSTRUMENT." Igor Stravinsky and Aldous Huxley couldn't figure out what "cotton-pickin'" meant.

My brushes with greatness were, in Mr. Huxley's own word, "extraordinary," and whenever East Coast friends inform me that the Atlantic side of the States is the cultural center of the world, I love to remind them that my Southern California circle included Bob Craft, Igor Stravinsky, Aldous Huxley, Jascha Heifetz and Gregor Piatigorsky, among many others.

It was my good fortune to come into contact with people willing and able to help me in my career. I believe in a reverse domino theory of career progress: the final objective is to stand up instead of fall down. In my particular game, Dad set the blocks in motion and Gwen Koldofsky helped keep them going. Through her, I made essential professional and personal connections: Lotte Lehmann, Marty Katz—and now, around this time, Dorothy Huttenback. Dorothy was an artists' representative and manager, but oh so much more. It's one thing to represent an artist, and another to believe in, encourage and counsel that person, especially a raw recruit. How lucky I was to have Dorothy as an adviser and how lucky still to have her as a friend! It was Dorothy who managed my early West Coast career and got me local bookings, and it was she who introduced me to Martin Taubman, an impresario from Vienna and New York. Taubman offered to manage my career, but only if I would prepare in Europe and give him a couple of thousand dollars for a retainer. He could as easily have asked for a million. Dorothy got into the act and told him that *some* people had money and *some* people had talent! Mr. Taubman took the hint and waived the retainer.

"Get yourself over to Europe, and I'll arrange for auditions," Taubman said.

"Okay," I replied. "I'll be there."

All my mentors, save one, agreed with this plan, and, in fact, Dorothy DeCoudres decided I should give a self-benefit concert to raise money for a European sojourn. The only counselor opposed to Taubman's dictum was the most influential person in my life, my father. Dad, who until recently had been the total overseer of my career, teaching me, guiding me, locating the right opportunities and never allowing me to be exploited or pushed, thought I should stay in the United States.

This conflict with my father was a turning point in my professional and personal life.

From the beginning, my parents had recognized my free-spirited nature and catered to it, allowing me to believe I was a willing servant of my voice and not its slave. No matter how much Dad wanted me to work, he rarely interfered with my play and I had plenty of opportunity to fool around, after which I'd buckle down to practice. My father wisely let me feel I was doing my own dance, even though he was pulling the strings. Consequently, we had rarely been at odds concerning my professional life. Now, for the first time, I was arguing about my career with its master builder. Privately, Mother told me I should take the chance and go to Europe, but she wouldn't say that to Dad, who told me I was crazy to go overseas without even a booking, let alone a contract. What's more, he'd argue, why should I skip the country when my American career was burgeoning? Indeed, my domestic career *was* taking off. Thanks to Dorothy Huttenback's management, I was working steadily and receiving excellent notices, though there was a bit of confusion in some of my reviews. A soprano named Marilyn Hall was performing at the same time, and I cannot tell you the number of times *she* got credit for *my* singing, and vice versa. According to one critic, who apologized in his column for crediting Miss Hall with my "brilliant singing," my *Doppelgänger* finally changed her name to Maria Hall to avoid further confusion.

The controversy continued non-stop at the Horne house. Meals were spent discussing America versus Europe. Dad and I were the protagonists. Mom, Jay and Grandma just listened. One evening, after a particularly fierce donnybrook, I stood up and announced to both parents, "I'm going to bed and think this thing over for the last time. Tomorrow, I'll *tell* you what I'm going to do." With that, I retired.

The next morning when I came in for breakfast, Dad looked searchingly at me while Mother pretended to be engrossed in her coffee cup. I took my place at the table, reached for the orange juice and, looking Dad squarely in the face, said softly, "I'm going."

Once I'd made up my mind, I had to get the financing, and so Dorothy DeCoudres, Gwen and I immediately went to work on the Marilyn Horne Benefit Concert. I wrote a letter to the board of the California Heights Methodist Church and received permission to use their social hall for my personal fund-raising. Gwen and I began planning the program, while Dorothy literally forced people to buy tickets or become patrons. At one point, she unearthed a supposedly wealthy man and arranged for him to hear me sing at a concert. The mystery Mr. Bucks was impressed with my voice, but wouldn't give me any money. "He said you're too fat," Dorothy told me matter-of-factly without revealing his identity. Sometimes I wonder whether the story was true or Dorothy was just trying to get me to lose weight!

We continued to sell, advertise and promote, and then my newest ally, Bentz Horne, got into the act.

Dad was still convinced I should stay in America, but after my declaration of independence, he jumped on my bandwagon and decided there should be a second benefit—in Bradford! "After all, Peanut," he explained, "you're a hometown girl and I've got clout back there. Why, we'll have a fabulous turnout." Dad wrote to Will Davis, the church organist who'd discovered Dad's voice many years ago, and Davis asked some prominent citizens associated with the arts for support. Imagine our feelings when they told Will that, despite my Bradford ties, I was not up to the level of talent usually brought to their town.

That hurt, and hurts still. In 1979, Bradford, Pennsylvania, declared a Marilyn Horne Day, and I stood on a platform listening as some of the very citizens who'd refused me twenty years before praised me to the skies. I felt little joy. The people who might have been most touched by the tribute—Dad, Mom and Dick—were gone and, frankly, I'd have traded all those accolades for just a little support when I'd most needed it. Aside from a handful of relatives and friends, my hometown hadn't been there for me and, moreover, my father had been humiliated. His beloved Bradford let him down, and all of Bradford's medals and acclaim would not sweeten that poor memory for his daughter. Bradford may call me a hometown girl now, but the truth is, I feel a stronger loyalty to my adopted city, Long Beach, which was supportive from the beginning.

The California concert raised about a thousand dollars, and by scrimping and saving I managed to come up with an additional two thousand dollars. Meanwhile, my friends rallied round. During all that time, I had to rely on the kindness of others, and my files bulge with letters of acknowledgment to and from good people. One of them gives an idea of what I mean. Addressed to me, the letter from Burton Chace, Supervisor of the Fourth District Los Angeles County Board, reads in part:

It was most generous of you indeed to send me your check for fifty dollars ($50.00) which I gave to you on a "loan basis" for you to proceed with your musical career.

Mrs. Chace and I would like to return this money to you with our sincere best wishes for success in your musical education. We think you have a great future and we certainly know that you can find a place for this small amount.

I like this letter because it shows a double generosity on the part of the Chaces, and, I have to admit, I'm proud of myself for paying the loan back.

While all this fund-raising was going on, dear Bob Craft was making a contribution of his own by arranging for me to appear with him and Stravinsky in the International Music Festival in Venice. It was scheduled to take place in September, so I purchased a round-trip ticket to Europe for a boat sailing on July 31, with an open return date. I had no idea when I'd be back, but I wanted to make sure I *could* get back.

By the summer of 1956, with all their children settled, for the first time in their lives my parents were beginning to see a glimmer of financial security, so they decided to go East and give me a big European send-off. Dad left on a sales trip and the plan called for Mom, Jay, Nanny and me to join him in Bradford to visit with family and friends; then I would go on to Europe as they went West. The trip from Long Beach was overland and dreadful. I had a huge steamer trunk and, because I was concerned about its arriving when I did (and about the cost of the trip, of course), we traveled by train instead of plane. Sitting up for three days in a railroad car is not my idea of heaven. To top it off, there was a mix-up with the luggage anyway, and our bags went on a separate train.

We got off in Buffalo at six in the morning, where Grandpa

Hokanson and my Uncle Kenny picked us up. On the drive to Bradford, I naturally inquired about Dad, and my uncle, a shy man,
hemmed and hawed, and finally said, "Your father's sick." I asked
if he was in the hospital and was shocked when my uncle mumbled,
"I . . . ah, think he is, Jackie, but you'll have to ask your Aunt
Adelaide for details." When she heard that, Mother made them
stop the car on the spot while she called Adelaide, who confirmed
that Dad was hospitalized. Adelaide told mother to come by her
house first so we could all go to the hospital together. I think my
aunt was trying to cushion things a bit, but Mom wasn't really
listening and we went directly to the hospital.

It was early, the staff was skeletal and typically clinical, and no
one seemed to know about my father's case, so Mom called our old
family doctor, the attending physician, and asked for the straight
story. His answer was truthful: "I'm sorry, Berneice. Bentz has
acute leukemia." I screamed when mother repeated those words to
me, and nurses rushed over and told me to get hold of myself. My
anguish mixed with fury at these white-clad "machines" as I re-
torted angrily, "Get a hold of myself! What are you talking about?
This is my *father!*"

The doctor came right over to the hospital, sat Mother and me
down and related the grim facts. Dad had two days to two weeks to
live. Cortisone treatments could keep him going that long, but his
condition was hopeless. The doctor also said that the cortisone
could cause a build-up of Dad's blood cells, which would result in
an agonizing death as the patient strangled on his own blood.

"Is there any chance he might live beyond two weeks?" Mother
asked quietly.

"No," answered the doctor.

"Well," sighed Mother, "forget the cortisone. Just give him pain-
killers."

I called Dick in California and, hearing my voice, he boomed jovially, "Hey, Jackie, how are you? What's doing? Did you have a good trip?"

"Dick, Dick . . . something awful's happened. You better sit down."

There was a long silence after I finished explaining, and I wondered if the connection had broken until I realized Dick couldn't talk. He was crying. My brother, the Rock of Gibraltar to his kid sister, was weeping uncontrollably, and I wept, too.

Dad lingered for two more days, during which time the other members of the family flew out to join us. We all took turns staying in the hospital room, because we didn't want Dad to be alone. On the second evening, after Mom had gone home to rest, I sat by the bed, looking at him. His color was ashen and his breathing laborious. My thoughts were of the past: the voice lessons, the grandstands with Gloria and me standing in front of the band and Dad smiling in the background, the concerts, the recitals, Sunday mornings in church with Dad singing gloriously in the choir. I could not imagine a world without his familiar presence. I thought of all he had done for me, and was overcome with guilt. Though he had "come around," my final act had been one of rebellion against his wishes.

As though he had read my thoughts, Dad opened his eyes and looked lovingly at me. In a little while, he spoke.

"Well, Peanut," he whispered slowly, "I've been doing a lot of thinking. You know, up to now I didn't know if you really had it in you. I couldn't be sure, but I think you do. I think you were right to go to Europe and now you've got to go on. I know you'll do it, I know it." He closed his eyes and lapsed back into sleep. Those were his last words to me. The next day, he was dead.

After the funeral and burial, I told Mom I'd cancel Europe and come home with her, but she told me, "Nothing doing!" We said our farewells on a sunlit street in Bradford in front of my grand-father's house. I wore a white Lanz dress covered with tiny red rosebuds. I loved that dress because it seemed so "European." Dick was the last to enter the car that would take the family back to California and, before getting into the driver's seat, gave me a goodbye hug. Recognizing the need, Dick took over the dominant male role in the family and his words to me that day, just like my Dad's last words, will be with me forever.

"Jackie." Dick put his hands on my shoulders and looked into my eyes. "I just want you to remember, it's okay for you to fail. If things don't work out, you'll still be our daughter and sister. You can come home, we'll love you." He kissed me on the cheek, hugged me, then got into the car and drove off. I waved until the car turned the corner and then began to cry. My father was gone for good, the rest of the family was on the way home and I was headed for the other side of the world. A moment before, I had almost wavered in my resolve. I wanted to be with them, not all alone in a strange country, but then my dear brother had said what no one had ever said before—not Dad, Mom, *anyone*. Dick had told me it was okay to fail. He had assured me that I was loved whether or not I succeeded, and that assurance not only helped me leave my family, it gave me the strength to face the next four years.

# VII

# The Galley Years

"*Die kleine Dicke wird etwas sein.*"
("*That little fat one is going places.*")

MY FATHER died in Bradford on July 11, 1956. Three weeks later, I set sail on the Dutch ship *Maasdam* from Hoboken, New Jersey, to Rotterdam, Holland. I was twenty-two years old, suddenly half-orphaned, on my way to a strange continent, most of whose languages I did not speak and where, aside from my engagement in Venice, not even a *bona fide* job awaited me. What's more, I was no sailor, and the ocean filled me with apprehension, particularly at night when it loomed endless, dark and terrifying. The situation hadn't been helped any when, on the overnight sleeper from Buffalo to Newark, the conductor had greeted me at breakfast in the dining car with, "Boy, how about that ship going down, wasn't that something?" I heard about the sinking of the *Andrea Doria* on the morning I was to set sail.

96

The *Maasdam* was full of young people like myself on their way to Europe for experience or training. During the crossing, I participated in shipboard talent shows and romances. The *Maasdam* was a mini-Love Boat, and I was assiduously pursued by an ardent young painter who later appeared on my doorstep in Germany asking me to marry him!

I had arranged for an old school friend, John Meadows, to meet the boat in Rotterdam and then drive me to Salzburg to see Martin Taubman. On the way, I asked John to stop in Stuttgart, where the Seventh Army was stationed, and where there was a particular Specialist Second Class with whom I wanted to connect. Henry Lewis had pulled some strings to get into the Seventh Army Symphony, where he was the conductor and would eventually lead more than one hundred concerts in Germany, France, Holland, Luxembourg and Greece, as well as recording over fifty concerts for broadcast over the Armed Forces Network and the German radio. Our sparse correspondence had come to a standstill, but even though I hadn't heard from Henry in months, I had a yen to see him. Once again, just as she had at the *Carmen Jones* audition, in stepped Fate.

John and I drove up to the main gate of the Seventh Army compound and, at my request, an obliging sentry called Henry's barracks. Henry got on the phone and I kidded around, telling him to come on out to the gate for a big surprise. Too much time had passed for him to recognize my voice over the wire! Henry came to the gate, saw me and roared with delight. "You're not going to believe this, Jackie," he said. "I'm just leaving on a vacation. I only went back to the barracks because I forgot something. If you'd called a few minutes earlier or later, you'd have missed me." Henry, John and I went out for dinner, and poor John must have felt like a fifth wheel as Henry and I rattled on and on.

After dinner, Henry went on to Italy and John and I drove to

Salzburg, where I studied for a month. From there I went to Vienna, where I'd be living and studying. Taubman had reserved a room for me there in the Pension Schneider, a residence that made Mrs. Loma Murphy's house look like the Beverly Wilshire Hotel. I found the *pension* gloomy and depressing, but my feelings were probably colored by my situation; many other singers stayed there and found it perfectly pleasant. I do remember an overbearing maid named Fritzi who leaped around the rooms in high-top shoes, cleaning and chattering like an operetta character.

Within the month, I was taking the overnight sleeper to Venice for the International Festival of Contemporary Music. Bob Craft and Vera Stravinsky, the wife of the composer, met me at the train and ushered me into my first gondola. Bob was so excited about showing me the city, he made me promise to close my eyes while he led me to a corner of St. Mark's Square to make sure I got just the right view. The gondola let us off and with my head bowed down I scrambled onto the quay clutching Bob's hand. We walked through a narrow alley of tiny shops, past Harry's Bar and then we reached a vaulted arcade.

"Shut your eyes, Jackie." Bob took my hand again and led me through the arch.

"Okay, open them!" Bob could barely contain his enthusiasm, and no wonder—there glittering before me was the most beautiful sight in the world, the Piazza San Marco. I still thank Bob Craft for my first perfect view of that incredible scene.

The city was awesome, but the festival had fallen on hard times. A government austerity rule had cut its funds, so the administration had had to cancel all plans for costly operatic premieres, and had instead commissioned a choral piece from Stravinsky, whose opera *The Rake's Progress* had premiered at the 1951 festival. Stravinsky had composed the *Canticum Sacrum ad Honorem Sancti Marci Nominis* (*A Canticle to Honor the Name of Saint Mark*). The piece, only seventeen minutes long and featuring Richard Lewis and Gérard Souzay as soloists, comprised the second half of a program which opened with music of Monteverdi and Schütz sung by Lewis, Souzay, Magda Laszlo, Petre Munteanu and me, and conducted by Bob Craft. Because of its brevity, Stravinsky had been asked to lengthen his composition, but he wouldn't; instead, he conducted it twice!

It was eerie hearing the *Canticum* performed and then re-performed thirty minutes later in St. Mark's Cathedral. The audience had been enjoined from applauding in church, and the deathly hush which followed the music was unnerving. I still find such silence disconcerting—there's nothing better than hearing applause after you've done a good turn. I take my cue on the subject from Artur Rubinstein, who once said that if he didn't get applause after the first movement of the Tchaikovsky piano concerto, then he knew something was wrong. As a performer, I like to know that listeners are reacting, and the importance of applause should never be minimized. I don't agree with purist nonsense about not clapping, particularly in opera, when applause often interrupts an aria between *cavatina* and *cabaletta*. I think it's great to have much ado about something, and if I've sung a terrific recitative, well, let me hear it before I go into the *cavatina!*

Maybe it's better they couldn't applaud back in Venice. I thought it was a terrific piece, but the *Canticum*, a twelve-tone experiment, was not a smashing success then. Seeing Venice was enough of a thrill for me, however, and I spent long hours exploring the city with Bob Craft, soaking in everything. There are certain moments of that initial visit that I'll never forget.

Stravinsky was an indefatigable worker, always busy at something, whether composing, arranging, writing or discoursing. That September, however, the climate was not cooperative. The sirocco was up, and anyone who's ever lived through this thick, warm, damp wind knows how debilitating it is and how badly it affects people. You simply can't move in all the density and humidity.

One miserably humid afternoon, Mme. Stravinsky, Bob and I were sitting in their suite in the Bauer-Grunwald Hotel when Stravinsky appeared—he'd been composing down in the bar, which was closed during the day. He was shaking his head. The three pairs of glasses moved with each nod.

"It is impossible!" he groaned. "I cannot compose my *dry* music in this weather!"

Poor Stravinsky had already run into trouble at the festival when he had written a note for an instrument—the bass clarinet, I think —which was actually too low to play. The *cognoscenti* were agog— imagine Stravinsky making such an error!

In Venice, I also met Gérard Souzay and Dalton Baldwin, his accompanist, both of whom became lifelong friends. Dalton is one of those genuinely *good* people and Gérard is pretty special, too. I recently received a note from him which read, "I'm so proud of you that you've become so great." Both men were very solicitous of me, because they knew about my recent bereavement. I remember telling them that I had to go on because my father would have had it no other way. Still, it was hard and I often got tearful and found it difficult to work. At those times, my friends sustained me, praising me for my courage in striking out alone and sticking to my guns.

My first visit to the Dream City drew to a close, but I can't leave Venice without mentioning Nadia Boulanger, musician and teacher, gentle and wise, a darling woman. We sat in St. Mark's one evening as Stravinsky and the orchestra rehearsed and, turning to me, she said, "He's always twenty-five years ahead of everyone." When, twenty-five years later, I stood at his grave in San Michele Venice, I was flooded with memories of the Maestro. It was he who first taught me to sing in Russian, to considerable hilarity as I tried to wrap my tongue around the words. In 1968, we were in Toronto for a broadcast of *Oedipus Rex*—the last time I sang for him; he was already ill. Stravinsky, his wife, I and others were in his dressing room when someone asked if I had sung a particular work and I replied, "Oh, I've already forgotten that." Stravinsky reflected a bit and said, "Ah yes, the things we have forgotten, but I will never forget your beautiful voice, Jackie dear." He didn't. Bob Craft told me that the Maestro's last work was orchestrating two Hugo Wolf religious songs, and the dedication reads, "To Marilyn Horne."

After the festival, I returned to Vienna and began studying with Heinrich Schmidt, head of musical preparation at the Vienna State Opera. Meanwhile, Martin Taubman arranged for me to audition with a well-known German agent. I forget the man's name now, but he was one of the biggest agents in music and Taubman urged me to be on top of everything. I *was* on top of everything, including the German pastries; since the day Dad died, I'd been on an eating rampage and my weight was way up.

I arrived at the agent's office in Frankfort and was introduced to an ascetic-looking Prussian seated on the sofa in Taubman's inner office. When he saw me, the Prussian rose from his desk and said,

"*Sie sind zu dick.*" ("You're too fat.")

What's the phrase, "fight or flight"? Well, I wasn't going to run. Firmly planting my two feet on the floor, I placed one arm akimbo, raised the other straight up and pointed my finger at the Junker's nose.

"*Warten und Hören!*" ("Wait and listen!") I ordered, and then sang "*Ritorna vincitor.*" At the end, the agent turned to Taubman and said,

"*Die kleine Dicke wird etwas sein!*" ("That little fat one is going places!")

Where I was going was the Gelsenkirchen Opera Company.

The Gelsenkirchen Opera is part of a long and noble tradition. For four centuries, the German government has supported the arts by establishing theatres and patronizing artists. In West Germany today, there are one hundred and ninety-five subsidized theatres, including over fifty opera companies—small wonder Mr. Taubman wanted me over there.

The Frankfort agent arranged for me to audition for Gelsenkirchen and I was immediately hired—even though there wasn't a place for me. They wanted me badly enough to create a spot! I'd never even heard of Gelsenkirchen, but, needless to say, I was excited about my appointment and eager to begin. Soon I'd be part of my very own repertory company.

Giuseppe Verdi often spoke of his *"anni di galera,"* his "galley years," referring to the times he worked non-stop under less than ideal conditions. For the next three years, I was on a personal slave ship. My contract specified time "off" for summers at home and concerts in other European cities, but for the most part my apprenticeship was served in the Ruhr Valley town of Gelsenkirchen. Don't be misled by the lovely sound of the words "Ruhr Valley" —Gelsenkirchen was the pits, literally, since it stood in the middle of Germany's coal-and-steel area, and it boasted a climate that ranged all the way from fog to rain to snow, and don't forget the dirt.

The winters were frightfully frigid; I had colds, colds and more colds, plus bronchitis and tonsilitis; my adenoids became inflamed and were eventually removed—for the second time—and I was so lonely and homesick, it was almost unbearable. Yet I could appreciate some of the ironies I encountered. The Intendant, or Director of the Opera, was a former Nazi who'd been given a lifetime contract at the Stuttgart theatre by Hitler. After the war, he had been removed from Stuttgart and jailed as a war criminal and, upon his release, been appointed to Gelsenkirchen. He even had a son,

Adolf, named after, well, you know. I was prepared to hate this man, but I grew to love and admire him. The Intendant was a marvelous director and a fine person, a papa who ran the theatre with an iron hand but also looked after his opera family. When he left for another position, his replacement, who happened to be Jewish, proved to be a tyrannical SOB.

Post-war Germany was a complicated community and I learned a lot there about living and people, not all of it pleasant. The company did *Abstecher*, or out-of-town performances, and we were traveling by bus on one such appearance when someone picked up a newspaper filled with news about the devaluation of the British pound. A German baritone laughingly commented,

"So the English have devalued the pound, and *we're* the ones who were supposed to have lost the war."

"I'm sure there was no doubt in your minds in 1945 *who* lost the war!" I snorted.

There were also a number of Americans in Gelsenkirchen, including a guest black baritone, a sweet guy. One evening, a bunch of us were passing the time in the local café when a group of townfolk came in and drank themselves into advanced loutishness. One of the brutes detached himself, walked over to our table and stood weaving behind the baritone. He flopped his arms around the singer's chest, gave him a bear hug and announced loudly,

"You are a black man, but we don't mind you or your color. It's the Jews we don't like!"

That's all I needed to hear. I jumped up from my seat and proclaimed,

"Well, I'm Jewish, so get the hell out of here!" Without another word, the drunk returned to his companions and they left the café. I sat down and reached for a glass, and the baritone took my outstretched hand in his.

"Gee, Jackie," he said sympathetically, "I'm really sorry that happened"—adding sincerely, "I didn't know you were Jewish."

The nadir of my German years came on Christmas Eve, 1958. Christmas has to be the hardest holiday to spend alone, especially if your memories are full of family gatherings right out of Dickens. I was not slated to perform for a few days during the holiday week and had no place to go on December 25, so when a girlfriend named Karol Lorraine invited me to join her in Heidelberg, I jumped at the opportunity, took the train and arrived late on the 24th. Germany closes up tight as a drum on Christmas Eve. After dinner, we parted for the evening and I returned to the room she'd rented for me, a place with rime-rimmed windows and a cutting chill in the atmosphere. As I began to undress, I was overcome with a terrific itch in my groin. Without going into the gory details, I was hosting lice and, recognizing the infestation, let out a scream that must have reached C above high C. There was no reason for me to be infested; I've always been fastidious about personal hygiene and, besides, I'd been celibate in Gelsenkirchen! Martin Taubman's parting words to me had been "Don't sleep around, Jackie," but I hadn't needed him to tell me that was not the way I intended to get ahead.

There was no denying the miserable little mites attached to me, however. What to do? No drugstore was open, and there wasn't even a phone in my room in case I could find a doctor willing to come out on Christmas Eve. I thought of taking a hot bath, but that didn't seem right. I had to get rid of the horrid things and could only think of one way. I took out a razor and shaved the infested region, revealing skin covered with ugly red welts. I looked through my overnight case for an antiseptic and all I could find was a bottle of 4711 cologne. I splashed it on, knowing it would smart, but, God, I wasn't prepared for the intense agony of that application. It was killing! Sobbing, I put on my nightgown, crawled into bed and lay there whimpering. Stung with pain and filled with shame, I finally figured out how the damn things had probably gotten to me. My roommate in Gelsenkirchen had a boyfriend who wanted to play "Three's Company" in our flat. He was a grubby, unkempt slob, and I had never liked him hanging around and using our facilities. He looked like a walking flea circus, and now I was sure he was one.

The next day, Karol took me to her doctor and after the examination he said I'd administered the best possible treatment to myself. A hot bath would only have given the wretched creatures a warmer climate in which to fester, and by my actions I'd actually effected a one-treatment cure.

In retelling the story now, comical aspects do emerge, but there was nothing funny about it at the time. It was the worst Christmas Eve I've ever known, or, as Scrooge might put it, "Bah, humbug!"

A few things kept me going during these trying years. First, I was performing constantly, for the most part roles in the soprano repertoire: Mimi in *La Bohème*, Giulietta in *The Tales of Hoffmann*, Minnie in *The Girl of the Golden West*, Amelia in *Simon Boccanegra* and Tatiana in *Eugene Onegin*. A great deal of the soprano repertoire is still good for me, if I wanted to tackle the parts—I could sing Mimi today, though I might not be as easy on the high C as I was then. Another plus for the Gelsenkirchen years was my growing fluency in the language. German opera houses did all their operas in that tongue and I became proficient in speaking, reading and writing German. Later, I learned French and Italian as well. (My mastery of Italian many years later was thanks to Nico Zaccaria—I'm not sure Berlitz would admit this, but the best way to learn another language is in bed.) The dreariness of Gelsenkirchen was also relieved by the Monday-evening shortwave broadcasts of the "Martini and Rossi Hour," an Italian version of our Bell Telephone or Firestone Hours, which presented concerts by outstanding singers of the day. I listened entranced to artists such as Tebaldi, Callas and Simionato, and in 1959, for the very first time heard the Australian wonder, Joan Sutherland, on the West Deutsche Rundfunk.

I went home summers to touch base with my family. Jay was so blasé about my comings and goings that it drove me wild. I'd return, aching to see him, and he'd be so casual I'd want to wring his neck. That's a kid brother for you. Once when he was about sixteen, I made a transatlantic phone call and Jay answered. "Jay, Jay," I shouted, "it's Jackie!" "Wanna talk to Mom?" he said.

In 1957, Carl Ebert called me back to Los Angeles to repeat my first starring mezzo role as Cinderella, the Guild's English-language version of Rossini's *Cenerentola*. I'd first performed it for Ebert in March of 1956, and, as usual, Ebert had had a great deal to offer, not only in the staging but in his interpretation of the Rossini style. It was heady stuff indeed for a twenty-two-year-old, and made all the more bubbly by the presence of a certain handsome baritone, who will remain nameless for reasons which will become obvious.

From the very beginning of rehearsals, we felt a strong attraction, an immediate empathy brought about, perhaps, because he and I were the youngest members of the cast. Though we spoke to each other only on a professional level, I felt the tug throughout the preliminary run-throughs. Then, one day, it happened.

Ebert was standing in front of the stage directing a walk-through. I was standing, center stage, listening to Ebert's instructions and the rest of the cast was positioned around the set. Suddenly, without a word, the baritone walked over, took me in his arms and kissed me like I'd never been kissed before—right in the middle of a rehearsal in the Shrine Auditorium. My score hit the floor as I wrapped my arms around him and kissed him right back!

I'll never forget the look on Ebert's face. His blue eyes widened and he said loud and clear,

"I would like to get kissed like that, too!"

After that, the baritone and the mezzo embarked on a long, wonderful love affair. It wasn't perfect bliss, because my friend was married and, though he and his wife were unhappy, there were children whom he adored. I didn't want a backstairs relationship, so eventually I gave him the classic either/or option. He couldn't leave his family, and so the affair ended. A few years later, he did get a divorce, but by then Henry Lewis was back in the picture and it was too late.

While indentured at Gelsenkirchen, I started corresponding again with Henry and, as usual, the lion's share of the letters came from my pen. Since Vienna was phonable, Henry didn't feel the need to write, but the wires between Waltz City and Stuttgart hummed. Finally, Henry arranged to visit me in Vienna. You can bet I was eager to see him, but when he arrived on the appointed day, he was with his *mother*. Good old Henry had neglected to inform either his parent visiting from the States or his girlfriend that the other would be there. I know Mrs. Lewis was as delighted to share her son with me as I was to have her as a chaperone.

Now that Mrs. Lewis is in the picture, it's time to tell you a little bit more about Henry's background. He was born October 16, 1932, in Los Angeles, the only child of Mary Josephine Turnham Lewis, a registered nurse, and Henry Lewis, Sr., an automobile dealer. His musical genius emerged early, though neither of his parents was musical, and at five he began playing the piano. Henry was enrolled in parochial school and on the first day discovered he was the only black kid. During recess, he was taunted with cries of "Nigger, nigger," and finally ran to the Sister in charge. Tearfully, he told her the kids were calling him "nigger." The Sister turned and matter-of-factly said, "Well, you *are* one, aren't you? Go back and play."

Later, other nuns encouraged his musical gift. Henry's favorite story of those early years concerns a recital at the Holy Name School during which he had to play a Handel piece from memory—and drew a blank halfway through the selection. Quickly improvising Handel-sounding music at the keyboard, Henry finished the performance. "I'll never forget the look on the Sister's face as I walked off the stage," he recalled to me. "She knew something was wrong, but couldn't quite put her finger on it." Eventually, Henry persuaded his parents to enroll him in public schools, where he became interested in band instruments and finally wound up on the double bass. At his father's insistence, Henry went out for the football team, made it, then, on his own initiative, quit. "I wasn't interested," said Henry, "but I wanted to show him I could do it." After finishing Dorsey High School in Los Angeles, Henry got a scholarship to the University of Southern California, where, of course, we met.

The senior Lewises divorced when their son was twenty years old, and from then on Henry had to divide his loyalties, though remaining closest to his mother. Henry, Sr., remarried, and though he took pride in his son's accomplishments, it was Jo who thrilled to everything Henry did.

Almost from the first, Henry's family embraced me with open arms. I say "almost" because that Vienna visit was not exactly a bed of roses. Jo Lewis was surprised to find me with her son, and though Henry and I felt very close, our affections had to be filtered through her formidable presence. She barely let us out of her sight. Henry had asked me to do some singing with the Seventh Army Symphony and we were scheduled to do a recording of *Cavalleria Rusticana* together in Stuttgart after the Vienna interlude. I learned the part of *Cavalleria*'s Santuzza in two days. Considering the constant, hovering presence of his mother, this has to rank as one of my great operatic accomplishments.

In spite of Jo's initial coolness, Henry was consolation and inspiration indeed, and by the time he was discharged in 1957, we were involved again, sort of.

Meanwhile, I continued to shuttle back and forth between Europe and the United States. For four years, Dorothy Huttenback got me summer bookings in America, which barely paid my fare but gave me the opportunity to go home, while Martin Taubman arranged engagements on the Continent. One memorable appearance was in Naples, where I was engaged to sing in *Die Walküre* at the San Carlo Opera.

There are eight Valkyries in Wagner's opera besides Brünnhilde —four sopranos and four mezzos and contraltos—and they all appear in Act III. I sang Gerhilde, a high soprano. In Naples, the Valkyries looked like a Las Vegas chorus line; each was a statuesque five-feet-seven or more, and all had been issued long blond wigs and platform shoes which raised them another three inches off the ground. All, that is, but Gerhilde. I was presented with a long *black* wig and a pair of flat sandals. Standing on the stage with my siblings, I looked like a thumb on an eight-digit hand. What's more, since we were warriors, we all wore coats of mail. My sisters' mail hung neatly to just below their rears, while mine dangled somewhere around mid-calf. And that's not all. In *Die Walküre*, one of the Valkyries is "the runner," required to dash back and forth with messages. With seven leggy sprinters and one runt to choose from, guess who played Mercury. I took off weight chasing around that stage. The stagehands were very sweet; they called me *"La Valkirietta"* and, as I raced in and out of the wings, would hold my spear and shield while I straightened my ebony tresses, which threatened to fly off every time I ran. As ridiculous as the situation was, however, I was so happy to be in sunny Italy after somber Gelsenkirchen that I didn't care how stupid I looked. It was a joy just not to have black coal dust in my nose.

While at the San Carlo Opera, I lived in a hotel overlooking

Naples Bay and, during my stay, struck up an acquaintance with a well-mannered, swarthy-complexioned man who would stop me in the lobby to ask how things were going and offer to help in any way he could. I usually talked to strangers and was very friendly to him until the concierge called me over and gave me the scoop on my newfound friend. He was Lucky Luciano, the Mafia kingpin who had been deported to Italy by the U.S. government and was living in exile. Luciano had taken a liking to me. He was in the habit of taking what he wanted, said the concierge, and suggested I steer clear of Luciano, lest I'd be made an offer I'd find difficult to refuse. Thereafter, the *Valkirietta* ran from the lobby whenever a certain expatriate was around.

Also in Naples, a filling in my front tooth started acting up and, though in pain, I was not keen on seeking professional aid. Naples' many natural splendors did not include medical excellence—every opera singer knows Caruso died there! Alas, the tooth would not wait until I returned to clinical Germany and became so bad I had to call the hotel doctor. He gave me a shot of codeine and told me to find a dentist as quick as I could. I did—and entered the most modern, well-equipped office this side of Central Park South. The dentist, a double for Rossano Brazzi, had studied in the United States and had imported every new dental device there was, including the jet-stream drill. The nerve on my tooth had to come out, he said, and warned me that the tooth would probably turn black in six months because of exposure to the air. Thereupon, he whipped that nerve out and plugged my tooth so fast that air barely had a chance to get into the shell. It took five *years* for that tooth to blacken. You can say what you want about the practice of dentistry in Naples, but you'll never hear a disparaging word from me.

After his discharge, Henry returned to his position as bass player in the Los Angeles Philharmonic, and though he was still not a zealous pen pal, our correspondence was steady and full of allusions to mutual affection and musical happenings. I guess you could call them love letters with a downbeat.

In one letter I wrote from Vienna, where I was appearing in the Vienna Festival, I told him about some taping sessions I was lucky enough to attend with Martin Taubman. *Don Giovanni* was being recorded under Erich Leinsdorf's direction, with Leontyne Price, Birgit Nilsson, Cesare Valletti and Cesare Siepi in the cast. I advised Henry that the real star of the recording would be Leontyne Price as Donna Elvira. "Hen," I wrote, "this is *great, great* singing of the first rank." All my life, great singing has knocked me out; I don't care if the artist is my biggest rival, I *adore* great singing. For one singer to be moved to tears by another is very rare, and Leontyne has touched me that deeply. In Vienna, after Price had finished singing in the "balcony trio," I turned to Martin and said, "I quit." She was so fabulous I didn't feel qualified even to squeak in her presence.

Leontyne has always been a favorite of the general public—she could make a charm bracelet out of her Grammy awards! No matter what she records, she seems to win. I was asked to sing at the Grammy presentations once and told them, "Why bother with me? Why don't you just ask Leontyne to sing, so she can be there to pick up her Grammy?"

I've been privileged to appear with Leontyne on several occasions, and each time her greatness as a person as well as an artist has been revealed. In February of 1976, we barged down the Nile together as Aïda and Amneris, and I received a lovely note from my co-star saying:

Dear "Jackie,"
   I haven't words to express my deepest thanks for your thoughtfulness to me on opening night of our Aïda. What

an exquisite moment for recalling that special night.

You're not only the greatest singer alive but the greatest female colleague I've ever worked with. Please, no idle promises, we must sit down and really "gab" about "pros" and "cons" one of these days soon.

Your idea about our concert is fabulous. Meanwhile, deep affection and gratitude. Bravissima!!

Much love,
Leontyne

In February 1982, at a rehearsal for a special performance of the Verdi *Requiem* at the Metropolitan Opera, Leontyne spun out a high B flat at the end of the *"Libera me"* that could have melted steel—and, mind you, the lady was fifty-five years old! I told her afterward that she'd done me in with her singing.

"How do you do it? How do you get those high notes?" I asked.

"How?" answered La Price, tucking a wisp of hair under her turban. "Why, I've been listening to *your* records, honey, that's how." (Not for high pianissimos, I assure you!)

I was supposed to be performing in the *Requiem*, too, but, as it turned out, I became ill and had to cancel—the only Met performance I've ever missed and a painful action since it was a broadcast memorial tribute to Francis Robinson, Assistant General Manager of the Metropolitan and a dear, dear friend. I desperately wanted to be there, but had major throat problems due to a cold, and was told by my doctor to keep my mouth shut. The minute my cancellation was announced, Leontyne called to see how I was doing and wouldn't listen to my apologies for defecting.

"Don't you worry about the *Requiem*," she said firmly. "*You* just take care of *you*, honey!"

What a thrill when we finally *did* do a joint concert, in March of 1982 at Lincoln Center. For me, the shining moment came in rehearsal as we sang the *"Mira, o Norma"* duet. After we had finished the opening slow *cavatina*, we were holding each other, and I could feel "Norma" trembling. Leontyne Price was in tears and, for the moment, unable to continue. Tears are a luxury singers rarely allow themselves in actual performance, but there are times when the glory of the music simply overwhelms you. Leontyne had never sung Norma, that most challenging and glorious of operatic roles. Perhaps it was the realization that she never would be performing it that had gotten to her; perhaps it was simply the beauty of the moment, or a personal sadness or happiness. Only she knows.

"Oh, rats," she muttered, dabbing at her eyes with the back of her hand. "Forgive me, I'm so silly." Silly? No, splendid is more like it.

My professional relationship with Leontyne Price has grown into a warm friendship, and after the joint concert she paid me one of my highest compliments. "Working with you, Jackie, has been beautiful," she said. "You give so much. I just never expected to get these things back from another singer."

Ditto, dear Leontyne, and I'm so happy I was able to pay witness to your greatness twenty-five years ago in Vienna.

My letter to Henry in praise of Price also contained insights into my own status. "I definitely am staying lyric for at least five years, this is where I belong! Natch, I'm no light lyric and lean towards spinto but I'm going to stick to it with a vehemence." I got vengeance and vehemence mixed up, but I *was* sure about my voice. And I was right, too. It would be years before I turned mezzo.

To this day, I look back on the German experience with mixed emotions. While they were often painful to get through, those years made my future achievements possible; I literally paid my dues. I don't believe singers *have* to go to Europe anymore—careers certainly can be made in the U.S.—but performers can never get the flavor of languages as they're used in opera or song unless they experience it over there.

When I came to Europe in 1956, most of the other singers in the group were older. Then, I was usually the youngest; now, I'm often the oldest—that's what happens when you sing long enough. The same was true in Gelsenkirchen, where I was the "baby." Though they were more mature than I, many of my compatriots couldn't take it, and quit. The loneliness, hard work, lack of success and sheer boredom drove them out. I suffered, too, but my suffering had to do with my incredible drive to succeed. I was Bentz Horne's daughter and had to stay on track; emotional problems had to be set aside. Like Scarlett O'Hara, I was going to think about other things "tomorrow." The career didn't suffer, but I did. The trauma of leaving at twenty-two, losing my father and going alone to a foreign country should have been dealt with on its own terms. I shelved it, and put all my energies into my singing, determined to make the best of the situation and *get* the best out of it.

# VIII

## Triumphs and Disasters

MAKING THE best of the situation was not always easy, however. It was often an uphill battle, not only emotionally but physically.

My Gelsenkirchen days were filled with upper respiratory disease. Then, in 1959, I developed a breathiness that made it difficult for me to make the passage of air smooth and supportive. I'd already experienced minor troubles in Vienna and seen a Dr. Kriso, a well-known throat specialist with a fine reputation for helping singers. An excellent diagnostician, he was married to Emmy Loose, a soprano of the Vienna State Opera, and knew vocal problems first-hand. When my problem wouldn't go away, I revisited the good doctor to find out why I was taking two or three breaths instead of one.

Dr. Kriso examined me and was loath to say what was wrong,

later confessing he felt singers were not models of stability about voice-related problems and he'd feared I'd be too rattled by the truth. Having been raised with facts, not illusions, I wanted to know the facts, however, and, perceiving my no-nonsense attitude, Dr. Kriso told me the story. It wasn't pretty.

The vocal cords constitute the lower of two pairs of folds in the larynx that vibrate when pulled together and, when air is passed up from the lungs, produce vocal sound. Dr. Kriso drew a picture of my folds, with an added illustration: a swollen spot on one of my cords. When the vocal cords shut, that lump was hit first, and so more air was required in order to stretch out and shut the cord. Kriso, who had been assistant to a famous throat doctor in Vienna, told me that, years ago, nodes had been discovered on Lotte Lehmann's cords. The surgeons had wanted to remove them, but Lehmann said no; she was convinced the tiny calluses gave her voice a special quality which she didn't want to lose. Lehmann made her entire career with nodes on her vocal cords. When he said this, a bell went off in my head: no wonder she took two or three breaths to others' one. Lehmann was always short of breath. She made it effective—God, she made it effective!—but it was unmistakable. Unlike my erstwhile teacher, however, I had no intention of going through life with anything less than perfect vocal cords.

"What do I have to do?" I asked calmly.

Dr. Kriso immediately began a treatment program which ran concurrently with my rehearsals for the Vienna Festival. In the morning, I went to the theatre and rehearsed, then walked over to the doctor's office, where he applied deep heat or ultra-sound waves on the outside of my throat for a few minutes. After that, I wouldn't speak for the rest of the day, only opening up the next morning at rehearsal. In a remarkably short time, only two days, the red spot went away. We even determined the cause. Dr. Kriso said that within the last six months I must have sung a performance on a dreadful cold, and I pinpointed it exactly to a *Girl of the Golden West* in Frankfurt that I had indeed sung over one of the most blooming colds imaginable. The doctor said that if I was careful for a year and did not overtire myself singing, the cord would strengthen itself and everything would be fine. He also added, "You should have your adenoids removed."

"What?" I squeaked. "I've already *had* them out."

My adenoids, excised in childhood, had made a return visit, and a few weeks later I did have them taken out. I sat in a chair in Kriso's office as the tissue was cut away. A friend of mine, waiting in the outer office, later said she'd overheard the doctor and me mumbling and conversing in German for about half an hour as we prepared for the minor surgery, then, after a short silence, the German gave way to English. *"Ow! That hurts!"* cried the patient. Forty-five minutes later, I drove myself home. No nonsense, that's me.

Dr. Kriso reconfirmed what my father had said many years ago about proper training and care of the vocal equipment. Along with the retina of the eye, the vocal cords are the only tissues in the human body which, when damaged, do *not* come back with full elasticity. The muscular membrane, originally yellow in color, turns almost black after such damage. That's what probably happened to Callas and to a former patient of Kriso's, another dynamic soprano named Ljuba Welitsch. (The doctor, with admirable discretion, only discussed his singer patients who were no longer performing.) Welitsch was a red-headed sensation in Richard Strauss' *Salome*, a lurid one-act opera based on Oscar Wilde's play, and she sang the part often and everywhere. It's a wickedly demanding role and Kriso warned her not to do it more than six or seven times a year. Kriso, a modest, unassuming little man, only *advised*, however, and Mme. Welitsch didn't listen. Tragically, by her mid-thirties Welitsch's career was over. *Salome* wasn't her only problem. Kriso said Welitsch also lived a life of tension—*"gespannt,"* he called it.

"Remember," he cautioned me, "a singer must try to create an atmosphere of calm in order to continue singing." Truer words were never spoken and harder advice to follow was never given! Prima donnas can become highly strung just *trying* to be calm.

Dr. Kriso's medical skill and personal attention greatly impressed me. He didn't have to counsel me; I was just another young singer with an undetermined future, but this man really *cared* about the "instrument," and I'm so thankul I listened to him. His advice has stood me in good stead all these years. I don't abuse my voice and I frantically try to remain calm.

Vocal troubles weren't all that was bedeviling me at that time. That winter, I had a hair-raising experience that I hope never to repeat. I'd bought a car, a little Renault Dauphine, and, after a trip to Vienna, was returning to Gelsenkirchen via Salzburg, accompanied by my friend Uta Wagner. It was a miserable journey in every way. I had just gotten my period, had awful cramps and was doubled over the steering wheel. It was January of a very severe winter and there had been record-breaking snows. We were traveling on the Autobahn at a very reasonable pace through thick forest regions—the Autobahn has no speed limit, and big Mercedes usually whiz by at Mach 1—when suddenly we found ourselves on a sheet of ice: "*Glatteis*," the Germans call it. I felt the car skidding and took my foot off the accelerator—not smart, I now know!—and the car went into a long slide, spun around for three complete revolutions and then flipped over onto the snow piled in the center of the highway.

If it hadn't been for the snow, I think someone else would be pushing Rossini today; the car roof surely would have caved in, had the impact not been cushioned. Uta and I were wedged in upside down, and remained so till some truck drivers stopped and pulled us out. They turned the Renault right side up and told us to sit in the car while they went for a tow truck. Uta and I got back in and sat there freezing and waiting on the shoulder of the road. As we huddled in the tiny front seat, I looked in the rearview mirror at the approaching cars and then it dawned on me we were sitting ducks, practically on top of the *Glatteis*. Sure enough, a car came up behind us, hit the ice and crashed right into the back of the Renault. By now, we were practically embedded in the snowbank. The car backed off, the tow truck arrived, then hooked up and towed us to a garage in nearby Munich. I had to call Martin Taubman and ask him to wire money for repairs and return fare to Gelsenkirchen. Martin came through, and Uta and I took the first train back. All this time, I'd been a model of decorum, talking, arranging, discussing what had to be done without a hint of panic, but the minute we reached Gelsenkirchen, I went into shock; I climbed into bed and slept for one solid week, rising only to eat and use the bathroom.

When I returned to the opera house, my makeup lady was *"gespannt"* herself. Rumors had been flying. According to all reports, my face had been severely gashed, and it had sent my dear dresser into a tizzy. *"Ach, ach,"* she moaned. "When I thought that beautiful face was ruined, *ach, ach."* As it happened, my face wasn't ruined, but my figure was. During my recuperation, I had done a lot of eating and returned to the stage as big as an opera house. Of course, that meant a major diet, but it wasn't until March that I was back in shape. Dorothy and Martin wrote letters of encouragement telling me to keep slimming. I don't think I mentioned the weight gain to Henry.

In April, I wrote a sad letter to Taubman. The loneliness was getting to me and I wanted to take a quick visit home. He advised me to stay put, adding that travel would be bad for my health, so I stayed put and got the grippe and bronchitis. Gelsenkirchen was one big Petri dish where germ after germ was cultivated for my benefit. The coldness and dampness were excruciating and my bones were permanently chilled. Why, oh why hadn't some Caribbean government thought to subsidize the arts?

Meanwhile, back in the States, Gwen Koldofsky had been working on a tour idea for my next visit home, a month-long series of concerts which would feature me as soloist and Gwen as accompanist. Where do you think Miss Horne and Mrs. Koldofsky were scheduled to appear—London? Paris? Rome? Montego Bay? Not quite. Alaska and Canada. Here I was miserable from the cold in Germany and Gwen wanted me to tour Alaska. She thought it would be an excellent training ground for me to prepare recital programs, and of course she was right, and, as it happened, I was so used to being frozen that Alaska actually seemed *warmer* than Gelsenkirchen.

Kitimat, Ketchikan, Wrangell, Petersburg, Sitka, Juneau, Cordova, Kodiak, Anchorage, Seward, Fairbanks and Grande Prairie —from October 31 to December 2, 1959, I played them all to appreciative and hospitable audiences. Television had not yet replaced live concert-going and the houses were packed. The *Petticoat Gazette*, published by the Women's Club of Seward, had this to say about our recital:

> Miss Marilyn Horne came to sing for us and Mrs. Gwendolyn Koldofsky play piano. All of us enjoying your song, what you sing for us and Mrs. Gwendolyn.

It's one of my favorite reviews, and don't be misled by the ingenuousness of the *Petticoat Gazette*'s reporter—the Alaskan critics knew their stuff. One of them wrote then what could be written about me now:

Miss Horne does not seek to overpower an audience with her voice as some vocalists do, but has excellent dynamic control. She has the best diction many of us have heard in a vocalist.

One erudite reviewer wrote that I sang okay, but that my German diction was poor. I called up the newspaper and, without identifying myself, asked to speak to the critic. When he got on the phone, I began to chatter non-stop in German.

"Excuse me, excuse . . ." my critic interrupted. "I don't speak German."

"Oh," I replied sweetly. "Well, this is Marilyn Horne, and I do!"

We packed nineteen full recitals and thirty-three half-hour children's concerts into those five weeks. The only way we didn't travel was by dog sled! Poor Gwen sprained her ankle almost immediately. A doctor taped the ankle and then we climbed aboard a single-engine prop plane to Kodiak. I sat in the cockpit gabbing with the pilot while Gwen practically passed out in the back from the bouncy ride and vertigo. She had to make the whole trip with her pedal foot strapped tight.

During this "have lungs, will travel" tour, we performed in any available arena, mostly high-school auditoriums. In one, the only room available between numbers was the girls' lavatory. Off I'd trot after each section to get myself a drink of water or wipe my brow. At the end of the performance, Gwen overheard a kid say to her mother, "I like that lady's singing, but why does she always go to the bathroom?"

The Sitka appearance was special. As a performer, I was used to looking out and seeing a variety of people; in Sitka, for the first time in my life, I looked out at a school audience composed entirely of people with black hair—Eskimos!

During the tour, my correspondence with Henry boomed. I wrote almost daily, about everything that was happening to us, including one moment that has always remained special. On the walls of my apartment right now are many works of art by contemporary masters, not to mention original portraits of me in favorite roles, but buying or commissioning them has never equaled the pleasure of a picture I bought in Alaska. Until then, I'd never indulged in extras, but when the painting, a lovely watercolor by Claire Fejes, caught my eye, I had to have it. In the letter, I cautioned Henry not to tell my mother or anyone else in my family, because, unlike him, they wouldn't understand. I could just hear their admonition, "You spent your money on a *what!!*" It was the first time I'd ever spent my money on a "what"; the first time I'd ever *indulged* myself in something other than the mundane and the practical, and I've never regretted it.

Henry wrote back, too. In fact, on Thanksgiving Day, Henry mailed a three-page typewritten letter, a record length for him and a wonderful bonus for me. In it, he told of visiting my mother in Long Beach to discuss our plans for the future. That future included marriage.

Before I had left Europe, Henry and I had finally decided it was time to do something permanent about our relationship, and had even set the time for the summer of 1960. Understandably, Mother was not happy. She liked Henry very much as a person, admired his intelligence and his character, but he was a Negro, an insurmountable barrier in those pre-Selma days. According to Henry, Mother's stand on our marriage was based on a purely social perspective. He wrote:

> She is mainly interested, she says, in our mutual welfare. That is, she feels we are both so much artists, and our careers have been our main thoughts, our lives with such intensity that she doubts that we could be happy as individuals (indi-

visibles) should our careers suffer or not materialize because of bigoted people in high places or not so high places, placing (perhaps quite unknown to ourselves) obstacles in the way, or perhaps not removing obstacles when they might have otherwise. She felt you had not even admitted to yourself the possibility of this situation, and was, I think, quite relieved when she saw that at least I had thought of them.

What nonsense—of course I'd thought about what my marriage might mean in terms of my career, long, hard and in excruciating detail. However, I was used to thinking for myself, and Mother didn't appreciate my independent status. I wrote Henry back, "Independence is something we never acquire if we live with or near our parents. I've seen this over and over in the years I've been in Europe where I could do just as I damned pleased. On visits home, I've had to answer (even if unknowingly) to Mother." She really thought I wasn't capable of decision-making and, until the last minute, tried to forestall our wedding day.

"What do you have to marry him for?" Mother said shortly. "Why can't you just live with him? Be his mistress, for God's sake, not his wife!"

I couldn't believe my ears—my mother from Bradford was telling me to "sin"! That was in 1960, long before live-in relationships became commonplace. Mother's *avant-garde* suggestion was not the solution for me, however. Even at the risk of a family rift, I was going to marry Henry Lewis!

I returned to Gelsenkirchen for my final season and for the next six months was sent subtle messages from well-meaning friends, cautioning me against marriage. They came every way but Pony Express. One came before I left for Germany on Christmas Eve, 1959. Roger Wagner telephoned and warned, "If you marry Henry, you're finished in America. You can carry it off in Europe, but you'll never have a career in your own country. Americans won't tolerate it!"

My brother Dick wrote endeavoring to "enlighten" me on the subject of race problems and wondering if I really knew what I was doing. After answering him, I wrote to a friend, "I am certainly 'thought out' on the subject of marriage and race problems, having had to write a small thesis to my brother yesterday."

That was just a sample. It was hard to find myself so much in conflict with my family, but I stood my ground. It was tough to take these dire predictions, but I took them. I don't know how many of my "friends" were put up to their actions by Berneice Horne, but she pulled out all the stops. It didn't work, though. I was engaged to Henry Lewis. There were different kinds of dissuasion, too. One nineteen-year-old German boy I knew casually and who was crazy about me—at twenty-six, I was an "older" woman —was so heartbroken over losing me, he actually threatened to kill himself. It sounds like a bad movie script, but when I was appearing in Hamburg in 1980, this same man called and said he'd been waiting twenty years to see me again!

From January to July, I was in such a state, I picked up every malady under the sun, including, for a brief scary time in June, a pulse rate of 110. My agitation was over my impending marriage, of course, and the running battle I was having with my family and some of my friends, but that wasn't all. Although I didn't know it yet, I was about to make my return to the American operatic stage in one of the most difficult roles of the soprano repertoire.

Oddly enough, it was a role I'd almost turned down when it was first presented to me in Gelsenkirchen, and it turned out to be my first international success. Mimi, Giulietta, Minnie, Amelia, Tatiana—most of the roles I sang in Gelsenkirchen were pretty standard, until this one came along. I was preparing Mimi in *La Bohème* when the Intendant announced that my next assignment would be Marie in Alban Berg's *Wozzeck*. Mimi and Marie are polar opposites as roles. *Wozzeck*, a twentieth-century masterpiece based on Georg Büchner's play about a poor, simple-minded soldier who murders his prostitute mistress, Marie, is full of lung-busting twelve-tone music, and, frankly, the idea of learning the part was not appealing. Though I had sung plenty of modern music, it requires a great deal of energy and stretching, and is often concentrated in the most difficult areas of the tessitura. Berg's music lay halfway between speech and song, murderous for the voice, and with so many leaps, jumps and skips you had to be a vocal acrobat to get through a measure. What concerned me about taking on the role was that I'd be too busy thinking about the notes and rhythm to even think about my voice, and when Martin Taubman just about forbade me to attempt Marie, I seriously considered refusing. The Intendant needed me, however, and singers who showed loyalty and didn't fuss about assignments received greater consideration when they wanted favors from the director. I said I'd learn the first scene and see how it felt. I asked Henry to mail me a copy of the Mitropoulos recording of *Wozzeck*.

Usually I don't listen to other interpretations, because I'm too good a mimic and it would only interfere with my musical freedom. Under the circumstances, however, I felt I needed all the help I could get. I played the Mitropoulos recording for guidance, and there were so many errors in the first scene alone, I realized I could never use it. In those days, nobody knew *Wozzeck* well, so errors went practically unnoticed unless, like me, you followed it with the score. Now I really was set to throw in the towel. Already miffed that I'd been cast as Marie and not as Maddalena in *Andrea Chénier*, a part I wanted, I tried to wriggle out of *Wozzeck* by saying it would hinder my vocal progress.

The Intendant was adamant. "You *will* sing Marie," he said emphatically, and then mentioned a few items to convince me. Marie was a formidable role to *act* as well as sing, he pointed out; you could really sink your teeth into it. Maybe five other women in the *world* knew the role—Eleanor Steber was the Metropolitan's Marie in 1959—so I would be in exclusive company. What's more, if the critics liked me in the part, my career could be greatly enhanced, and since *Wozzeck* was scheduled for the inaugural of Gelsenkirchen's new opera house, critics would come from all over. I had to do it.

I sank into Marie gradually and made myself comfortable in the role. Those years with Bob Craft and Stravinsky proved to be excellent preparation for the modern musical idiom and in a few months I was up on Marie and ready to roll. It was grueling, though, and not only vocally. Performing Marie is like going through an emotional wringer, especially in the haunting scene where Wozzeck goes mad and slits Marie's throat. You can't help being overcome by the sadness and, I suppose, nihilism which pervade the work.

*Wozzeck* opened on May 22, 1960, to complete acclaim. Because of the new house, even the United States sent press representatives and Irving Kolodin gave me a rave in the *Saturday Review of Literature.* According to the renowned Berlin critic H. H. Stuckenschmidt, I was the greatest Marie he'd ever seen, and he'd seen them all.

Then, once again, Fate stepped in.

I sent my reviews to Henry and he showed them to Dorothy Huttenback. Grass never did grow under Dorothy's feet and she passed the reviews on to Kurt Herbert Adler, Director of the San Francisco Opera, where *Wozzeck* was scheduled for a fall premiere and where Brenda Lewis, engaged to sing Marie, had just taken ill and dropped out. That left about four other women in the world who knew the role. The next thing I knew, I had an audition with Mr. Adler for Monday, the 4th of July!

If my pulse had been a mere 110 before, it must have raced up to 210 that July 4 weekend. On Friday evening, I flew from Düsseldorf to Los Angeles, arriving at two a.m. At two p.m., in the presence of Henry's mother, father and stepmother; my sister, Gloria, and her husband, Jack Palacios; Gwen, Dorothy Huttenback, Bill Vennard and his wife; and our witnesses, Poldi and Susie Engleman, Henry Lewis and I were married by Dr. Stephen Fritchman, a Unitarian minister. That evening, we flew to San Francisco, and on Monday I auditioned for Kurt Adler. I was so pumped up I could have floated off the stage. He later said it was one of the greatest auditions he'd ever witnessed in all his years at the San Francisco Opera.

And so, my galley years in Gelsenkirchen came to a close. Besides giving me an opportunity to learn and perform in a professional company, they provided me with many lessons in humanity. Postwar Germany hardly loomed as Xanadu for a liberal Democrat from California, but I found good and bad among the people there, just as anywhere else in the world. I could not have survived without the help of such individuals as the Molwitz family, who always had a place for me at the table or around the hearth; and the members of the Gelsenkirchen company, from artists to stagehands, were true cohorts. Generous with praise, they could criticize, too, and their standards were fairly high. Once, I was appearing as Amelia in Verdi's *Simon Boccanegra* and had just finished singing in a gorgeous trio which ended with two treacherous high C's. I got the first, doggedly scrambled up for the second and then walked off into the wings, where a stagehand said curtly.

*"Das war kein 'hohes C.' "* ("That wasn't a high C.")

I said, *"Scheisse!"* and kept on moving. His words got to me, though, and when the recording of *Simon Boccanegra* with Victoria de los Angeles singing Amelia was released, I bought it to hear how the high C's should sound. They'd cut the second one!

At my last performance in the opera house that summer, I sang Marie in *Wozzeck* and, to my complete surprise, was brought back onstage for a farewell. For once, the normally garrulous stagehands had kept their mouths shut. Flowers piled up all around me, and gifts, and the audience rose, cheering. The stagehands gave me a huge picture of myself as Marie and I stood next to my cardboard counterfeit and bawled.

Ruth, my makeup lady, told me it was the first such demonstration ever held for *anyone* in the history of the Gelsenkirchen Opera.

I've never returned there, but that *Kohlenpot* (coalpot), a place a California kid could only loathe, will always be in my heart.

# I X

## *Ritorna Vincitor*

RETURNING TO the United States also meant that for the first time Henry and I would be living together as man and wife. We were delighted, of course, but also a little nervous after all we'd already been through. Our wedding ceremony was just an example.

You'll notice that in my brief description a few pages back, the only member of my immediate family to attend was Gloria. Everybody else had stayed away out of respect for Mother. On the morning of my wedding day, I had telephoned Mother from Dorothy Huttenback's house and asked her to please come, but she had refused. Her absence had weighed heavily upon me, and it took a lot of courage for me to marry without her being present. Years later, Dick confided that he'd felt terrible boycotting my wedding. He knew he was letting me down. At the time, though, he felt that Mother needed him more than I did.

Two weeks after the wedding, Mother called and declared a truce. She'd made her point by doing what she as a parent had felt was right, but now that the marriage had taken place, she had the grace to accept the change. It takes a big person to concede, and Berneice Hokanson Horne was a very big person. There are times when I miss her so terribly it hurts, but the memory of her courage and her love helps to ease the pain. I remember her with adoration, and she was never more wonderful than when she finally embraced Henry as one of her "children." Dick, Gloria and Jay rallied around, too, and forever after provided the necessary family supports for me, Henry and later Angela, even after Henry and I went our separate ways.

In October of 1982, my sister-in-law Joanne Horne went with me to hear Henry conduct *Dialogues of the Carmelites* at the San Francisco Opera. Henry was staying with friends, and when he told them Joanne and I were not only going to the opera but celebrating Henry's birthday afterward, their comment was, "Didn't you divorce that family?" The truth is, though Henry and I are no longer together, he is still as much a part of my family as ever.

Meanwhile, the new Mrs. Henry Lewis was working just as hard as the old Jackie Horne. Rehearsals for *Wozzeck* were due to begin in September, and there were other engagements to fulfill. Henry, too, was caught up in his work with the Los Angeles Philharmonic, as well as a number of splinter organizations he'd formed, including chamber-music and opera groups. We were both terribly busy, the only difference being we were together—a big difference indeed.

*Wozzeck* proved to be a perfect choice for my re-entry into the American operatic orbit. The West Coast premiere on October 4, 1960, was a smash, the critics and the public hailed me as a new star, and to think that this was the role I hadn't wanted! Thank goodness the Gelsenkirchen Intendant had prevailed.

One of the most enthusiastic members of the audience at the *Wozzeck* premiere was Dorothy Huttenback. Never one to rest on her laurels, Dorothy continued to promote my career by bringing me to the attention of Colbert Artists Management. Anne Colbert and her husband, Henry, ran a successful agency out of New York City, and Dorothy handled some of their West Coast business. Now that I'd returned as a "discovery," the Colberts were willing to take me on as a client.

Henry Lewis wasn't sitting by idly, either. Newspapers all over the country carried the story on February 10, 1961, and though it was the race issue that the headlines stressed, the news was thrilling anyway. "NEGRO CONDUCTS COAST SYMPHONY," *The New York Times* wrote; "Henry Lewis, First of Race to Lead Major Orchestra in Regular Concert." I can't count the number of times since that day that papers have announced a black man was conducting a symphony for the first time, but I was there and it was Henry Lewis. The key words in the headline are "major" and "regular." Henry had led the Los Angeles Philharmonic before, but outside Los Angeles, and there had been other black conductors, but not with major orchestras. Dean Dixon did lead the NBC Symphony back in 1941, but as a substitute in a radio concert. Of course, race really had nothing to do with it. The L.A. Philharmonic was Henry's home base, he'd studied with its onetime director Eduard van Beinum and was a member of the bass section. He'd been given the chance to take the podium because of his own talent and the strong support of George Kuyper, the Philharmonic's manager, not because he was black. Whatever the reason, Henry scored an enormous hit that night and received a rousing ovation from an audience of strangers and assorted Hornes. Oh, *The New York*

*Times* did point out another interesting fact, too: the soloist for the performance was Marilyn Horne, Mrs. Henry Lewis.

Mr. and Mrs. Henry Lewis were living in a modest aerie overlooking the Golden Gate Freeway. I loved "playing house," but even then had little time for steady domesticity. Concerts, appearances with Henry and his Los Angeles Philharmonic Chamber Orchestra and with other orchestras were piling up almost faster than I could cope with them—and then, early in 1961, my next big break came. Another artist's indisposition paved my way to Joan Sutherland, about to make her first appearance in New York City, and to my debut as a *bel canto* singer.

*Bel canto* literally means beautiful singing. Thirty years ago, Maria Callas was responsible for the return of this eighteenth-century Italian vocal style and technique which emphasizes beauty of sound as well as ease, flexibility and brilliance of performance. To this, Callas added dramatic and emotional expression previously thought incompatible, and the combination was electric.

Until then, except for surefire hits such as *Lucia di Lammermoor* and *Il Barbiere di Siviglia*, the operas of Rossini, Donizetti and Bellini had been put aside. Only sporadically was a particular antique work dusted off, usually because a superstar, such as Lily Pons in *La Fille du Régiment*, wanted to do it and had enough clout at the box office to make it worthwhile for the management. Callas became interested in the repertoire, and, one by one, presented masterworks such as *Anna Bolena, Medea, La Sonnambula* and *I Puritani*. Alas, I never saw Callas perform, but I became very familiar with her recordings. Instinctively, Callas plumbed the depths of music, infusing understanding, passion and meaning into her interpretations, most notably in the recitatives. Recitative is the declamatory portion of opera in which the plot is generally advanced, as opposed to the more static or reflective lyrical settings. It's one thing to sing a beautiful aria and quite another to present a beautifully conceived recitative. Listening to Callas on records and working with Henry taught me how it was done.

When Callas tragically lost her agility and ability, Sutherland was there to carry on the tradition. Her husband, musician Richard Bonynge, recognized his wife's singular gifts for the *bel canto*— she'd been thinking of becoming a Wagnerite—and together they were largely responsible for the re-emergence of *bel canto* operas in the United States and elsewhere. It was in one of them, Bellini's *Beatrice di Tenda*, that we sang together for the first time. It was Callas who started the renewal of interest in *bel canto*, Sutherland who furthered it, and then I came along. Like an Olympic torch of song, the light was passed. Through Joan's generosity, I became part of the great chain of *bel canto* singing.

*Beatrice di Tenda* is the story of the wife of Filippo Maria Visconti, Duke of Milan. The Duke is in love with Agnese del Maino, who is secretly in love with Orombello, Lord of Ventimiglia, who really loves Beatrice, the Duke's wife. In the course of two acts, Filippo tries to rid himself of his wife, while Agnese helps matters by turning over some of Beatrice's letters to her accuser. At the opera's end, poor Beatrice, scheduled for an appearance on the executioner's block, takes time out on her last voyage to forgive Agnese. Agnese faints dead away as Beatrice is led away. All this happens to some of the loveliest music Bellini ever wrote.

Joan, in the title role, was making her heralded New York City debut in a Town Hall concert version of the opera presented by the American Opera Society. Giulietta Simionato, they said, was scheduled to sing Agnese, but had to withdraw and suddenly the opera was minus a mezzo. Anne Colbert, who was Sutherland's agent as well, called to ask if I could do it. Could I do it? Nothing on earth could stop me. I learned the part in three weeks while sing-

ing concerts with Henry and the Los Angeles Chamber Orchestra
—and those concerts, back to back, were no pieces of cake.

Three weeks after Anne Colbert called, I arrived in New York
and was greeted by a major snowstorm. Getting to the first rehearsal was a nightmare. I hadn't been so bundled up since Gelsenkirchen. When I got there, however, Joan couldn't have been more
lovely and gracious—and tall!—nor could the other principals,
Richard Cassilly and Enzo Sordello. It was wonderful, because, in
truth, I was the unknown quantity of the company and, in a sense,
had to prove myself.

The opportunity to sing with Sutherland was enough to constrict
any tyro's vocal cords. To say her New York debut was eagerly
awaited doesn't quite capture the attendant frenzy. Joan had made
her Covent Garden debut in 1952, as the First Lady in *Die Zauberflöte*, then, eleven days later, appeared as the handmaiden Clotilde
in Bellini's *Norma*. The High Priestess was portrayed by Maria
Callas herself, with the great Ebe Stignani as Adalgisa—an awesome moment, this symbolic crossing of Callas and Sutherland.
Since then, she had been dubbed Callas' successor, and the New
York music world had screwed itself to fever pitch at the prospect
of hearing her in the flesh. This was the musical comet to which I,
an unknown *"nova,"* was attaching myself.

At the first rehearsal, Ricky Bonynge went to a telephone in
Town Hall and called Terry McEwen, then director of London
Records, now General Director of the San Francisco Opera.

"Get over here, quick," insisted Ricky. "We've got a girl who
sounds like Rosa Ponselle!"

Like Ponselle? Me? But maybe he wasn't wrong. Years later,
when I met Ponselle herself, Rosa commented on our similarity.
Giving me a picture of herself as Carmen, she wrote, "To Jackie,
Does the face look familiar? Sisters under the Skin, Love, Rosa."

According to her, our faces were constructed along the same lines (wide!) and that's why we sounded alike. Such comparisons were very flattering, since her own face had been compared to Caruso's by the great tenor himself. Skull cavities constitute an important part of the singer's equipment. Air is something we learn to control, but bones are bones—if you've got 'em, you're lucky.

Terry McEwen did come over, heard me for the first time and became not only an eager champion of my voice but later a true and beloved friend.

*Beatrice di Tenda* had all the ingredients of a smash, but I knew I needed to do a lot of preparation for my maiden voyage into the *bel canto* style. Though I had done Rossini's *Cenerentola* in Los Angeles, it had been in English, which was very different from *"vero" bel canto*. I considered *Beatrice di Tenda* my premiere excursion into the *bel canto* repertoire and worked assiduously on the score with my husband as coach. Henry provided a lot of insights and counsel, but he was a bit skeptical of what I was doing with my voice. I'd become increasingly comfortable in the mezzo range and occasionally mentioned the possibility of concentrating there.

"Mezzo-soprano means half a soprano," warned Henry, who thought the switch a bad idea, and he had a point. Operas have been composed since 1597, and in almost every one of them the leading female role has been written for the soprano voice. Except for a handful of parts, mezzos stand around and watch the soprano get the hero and the big arias. As a result, sopranos are content to stay put, while mezzos are always on the lookout for ways to move up. Even Amneris, a top "low" role, got a raw deal from Verdi: he was going to name his opera after her, but at the last minute gave the title to the soprano, Aïda.

I put the decision aside for the moment, and alternated between soprano and mezzo right through to the late sixties. It wasn't until

about 1968 that I came out of the musical closet and declared myself a true coloratura mezzo.

Henry and I worked with a vengeance. The *bel canto* requires
intense concentration, particularly to get the *rubati* and shape of
the recitatives. In Italian, *"rubato"* literally means "stolen," from
*"rubare,"* "to rob," and in music the term denotes liberty or freedom
in tempo. You rob from one note to give to another note. Jazz musicians take liberties, too, but opera is stricter; we have to stick to
the printed music and the most we can do is embellish and ornament
around it. I went crazy trying to learn Agnese, and at one point,
after a harrowing session in which Henry kept interrupting and
correcting, threw the music across the room at him and screamed,
"I cannot sing this shit!!" I was wrong, but it took years and years
of study to reach the "perfection" attributed to me now. The key
to success was *concentration.* By marshaling all my forces to get the
technique down pat so I could work on "beauty of tone and correct
emission," I was able to move freely and this, as Lilli Lehmann
wrote, is the signature of *bel canto.*

*Beatrice di Tenda* was performed on February 21, 1961, and
Sutherland conquered completely. I can't recall anyone giving her
less than a rave. Playing Eve Harrington to Joan's Margo Channing,
I picked up a few raves myself, but as second banana—in fact Harold Schonberg's *New York Times* review didn't mention me at all.
*Beatrice di Tenda* was definitely Miss Sutherland's evening and how
lucky I was to be part of it! Both personally and professionally, we
proved to be completely compatible. Terry McEwen remarked on
the incredible blending of our voices. It's partly because I'm such a
good mimic. Not that I imitate the "sound"; rather I pick up the
phrasing and the breathing which works so well with Joan. Terry
says many mezzos want to do this but can't, and I'm so happy I can!
The desire to form a united singing front has its roots way back in

In 1970, my dream came true—I sang at the Met at last and in one of the world's greatest operas. I'd turned down all Rudolf Bing's previous offers, because they hadn't been first-rate, but who could resist *Norma* with Joan Sutherland?
(HENRY GROSSMAN)

Joan and I in *Semiramide* in Chicago in 1971, our last performance together for several years. For the record, she's on a high D and I'm on a high B. (CHICAGO DAILY NEWS PHOTO BY M. LEON LOPEZ)

My first Met prima donna starring role and one that remains special for me: Rosina in *Il Barbiere di Siviglia*, 1972. (LOUIS MELANÇON, METROPOLITAN OPERA)

*Orfeo ed Euridice* at the Met: not one of the high points of my career in that house. (LOUIS MELANÇON, METROPOLITAN OPERA)

Marilyn Horne singing, Henry Lewis conducting the New Jersey Symphony at a United Nations Day concert, 1972. By this time, our marriage was pretty rocky.

With Angela after *L'Italiana* at the Met— a production as wonderful as *Orfeo* had been awful. (HENRY GROSSMAN)

*Mignon* at the Dallas Opera. I was so depressed by my recent separation that it took a lot of persuasion to get me there—but was I glad I went! I fell head over heels for the gentleman in the picture, Nicola Zaccaria. (ANDY HANSON)

On tour with the Met in Japan, 1975, along with a certain tenor.

*L'Italiana,* La Scala, 1975, being applauded from the box by General Manager
Dr. Paolo Grassi. (E. PICCAGLIANI)

Fides in *Le Prophète.* A bad case of bronchitis led to rumors that I was in vocal difficulty. A long-time dream became a nightmare. (METROPOLITAN OPERA)

Recording *Mignon* in London with Frederica von Stade, 1978. (CLIVE BARDA)

Dick, Gloria, me, and Jay—our last picture together, 1978.

*Orlando Furioso*, Verona, 1978. A mad scene played to the hilt. (DANIEL CANDE)

Amneris in *Aïda*, Salzburg, 1979. The face behind the mask is seething at conductor Herbert von Karajan. (ELLINGER)

Princess Eboli in Verdi's *Don Carlo* at the
Met, 1979. It was a great role, but for some
critics I committed the unpardonable sin:
transposition! (METROPOLITAN OPERA)

With Nico at a rehearsal for *Tancredi*
at the San Francisco Opera, 1979. (ROBERT MESSICK)

*Semiramide*, Aix-en-Provence, 1980.
(AGENCE DE PRESSE BERNAND)

A glorious moment: Joan, Luciano, and I live in concert from Lincoln Center,
March 1981. (LOUIS PERES)

*Tancredi* at Aix-en-Provence, 1981, with Katia Ricciarelli.
(AGENCE DE PRESSE BERNAND)

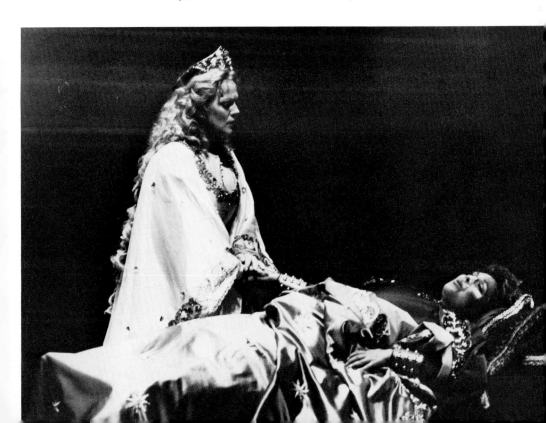

Twenty-five years after my debut in Venice, I "came home" to perform *Tancredi* in the opera house in which it had had its premiere one hundred and sixty-five years before. (GIACOMELLI)

With Angela in Venice—grand opera *and* soap opera. (JANE SCOVELL)

One more time: Sutherland and Horne in *Norma*, September 1982. Be prepared. We may yet bring in the millennium with "Mira, o Norma." (DAVID POWERS)

*Cenerentola* at the San Francisco Opera, 1982—a lot had happened since that first *Cenerentola* in 1956. (ROBERT CAHEN)

My friend and accompanist, Martin Katz, taking a well-deserved bow at the first-ever televised recital at La Scala.

Angela and I at an autographing in San Francisco, October 1982.

With Francisco Araiza, Montserrat Caballé, and Samuel Ramey after a concert performance of *Semiramide* in Hamburg. I love working with Montserrat, not only because she's a great singer—but because I can crack her up on stage. (JANE SCOVELL)

With James Levine and Leontyne Price at our 1982 Lincoln Center concert. I first heard Leontyne in 1957 in Vienna and immediately wrote Henry, "This is *great, great* singing of the first rank."

General Horne strikes again. In the summer of 1982, I performed Handel's *Rinaldo* in Ottawa, and in January 1984, I'll bring it to the Met—the first Handel opera ever performed there. The Met will be one hundred and I will be fifty—but we both plan to be around for a whole lot longer. (FERNAND R. LECLAIR)

Bradford, in those days on the bandstand with Gloria, and in the principles my father taught us. If you're determined to outsing, outshine or outdo everyone else, you don't belong on an opera stage. The greater the cast, the greater the result.

The conductor for *Beatrice di Tenda* was Nicola Rescigno, which may come as a surprise to some Sutherland/Bonynge fans who think Ricky always conducted her performances. The truth is, for a long time Ricky was more a musicologist, teacher and pianist. Furthermore, I can tell you exactly when and how Ricky got into the podium business. It was at my house in Los Angeles.

The Bonynges were out there for a Hollywood Bowl appearance and Ricky was scheduled to lead an orchestra for the second time in his life. He'd done one concert in Rome, I believe. Terry McEwen was around, too, and got the Lewises and the Bonynges together. One afternoon, the five of us were gathered around our pool, swimming, cavorting and taking pictures, acting goofy as most friends do when they get together around water. Joan took a terrific snapshot of Terry jumping into the pool holding his nose which I'd love to have printed in this book, but Terry's planning to write his own memoirs, so we'll have to wait. (There's also one of Norma and Adalgisa as mermaids!) Sometime during the course of the day, Ricky started questioning Henry about conducting and Henry began giving him tips, or, as Terry put it, "your basic fifteen-minute conducting course." Terry is convinced Henry could be the greatest teacher of conducting in the world if he wanted to be. The lesson my husband gave Ricky that day at poolside was so fabulous that Terry and I are certain Ricky began to take himself seriously as a conductor from then on. Today, he always conducts for Joan's performances and makes guest appearances with orchestras all over the world.

That afternoon was significant for music in another way as well.

After the session at poolside, Ricky took me into the living room and, sitting down at the piano, asked me to sing some selections from *Cenerentola* and other works of the *bel canto* repertoire. At dinner that night, he told Henry and me flat out I was a *bel canto* singer, and should chuck *Wozzeck*, *Fanciulla*, *Pagliacci* and the rest to concentrate on the repertoire that suited me. Unknowingly, Ricky Bonynge was putting me on the road to the Rossini medal.

The successful combination of *Beatrice di Tenda*, Joan Sutherland and Jackie Horne had a good deal to do with the unbelievable generosity of Joan and Ricky in allowing me to share not only their limelight but their musical knowledge.

Although Henry knew a lot about the style, it was Ricky who taught me how *bel canto* worked. With a dramatic composer like Verdi, you need support to carry the full weight of the sound all the way up; it's like a column of sound moving from the basement to the penthouse of the voice. In Donizetti, Rossini and Bellini roles, however, the orchestration is usually light and the middle voice is lightened. Because you don't have to sing an incredibly big middle register, you can open up on the top and let the coloratura fly. I actually "move the center of my voice"—Ricky's term—when I do certain roles: up for Adalgisa, down for Arsace. Since that "center" is positioned differently, however, I have to alternate my roles carefully in order to preserve my voice. I space my appearances in vehicles that call for a lightening or darkening of the voice. In 1982, over a well-spaced four-month span, I sang Handel's *Rinaldo*, returned to *Carmen* for the first time in seven years, performed *Norma* after a twelve-year layoff and then went waltzing into *Cenerentola* after twenty-five years away—and things didn't fall apart. The center of my voice held for each. It would be easier to sing roles that lie in the same range, but a lot less fun and fulfilling, and the fact that I'm still learning and adding operas to my repertoire is a tribute to careful planning as well as training. I've learned quite a bit about *bel canto* since those early days. I learned how to ornament from Ricky, but I must also mention Fritz Zweig, my coach in Los Angeles, who taught me style and ornamented for me, and, of course, my in-house coach, Henry Lewis, who was my *real* teacher.

Joan's execution of the *bel canto* material was as phenomenal as Ricky's erudition and I wasn't the only beneficiary of her generosity. Another colleague whom Joan pulled right into the spotlight was an up-and-coming tenor of hearty proportions whom Joan dubbed "The Big P." You know him as Luciano Pavarotti. Luciano sang with Joan on records and in performances way before the public fell in love with him. Then he took off like a rocket.

Pavarotti is very bright, with a positive genius for salesmanship as well as music. He came to this country, saw it was good for him and learned English immediately. Foreign singers don't always master the language—they usually just get by—but somewhere in that big, wide, wonderful Pavarotti a little voice said, "You've got to make contact, and in order to do that, you've got to speak the language." Luciano is only *one* of a number of fine tenors of intelligence and wit performing today, but he's got a special ingredient which has made him *the* one—a quality of sound that produces goosebumps on listeners, especially women.

In October 1979, Joan and I gave a televised joint concert at Lincoln Center. It was a smashing success, and after the performance we went to a fancy Chinese restaurant on the upper East Side. I know it was fancy because the waiter had never heard of duck sauce. I was very happy that evening, not only at being reunited with Joan and singing well, but because I'd lost a great deal of weight and really looked and felt good. Not long after we sat down to moo shoo pork without duck sauce, Joan was called to the telephone.

In a few minutes, she returned and said, "Jackie, it's Luciano and he wants to talk to you, too." Pavarotti was appearing with the Chicago Opera. I went to the phone and said hello.

"Jackeee," boomed the big boy. "Jackeee, I saw on the television, Joan an' you. Oh, Jackee, you were so wonderful, you sang so beeyootiful, you look so beeyootiful, you look so . . . so fuckable!"

Yes, Luciano Pavarotti has definitely mastered the language.

Our mutual history probably accounts for the special alchemy when Joan appears with him, or me, or, most magical of all, when the three of us are onstage together. Now we're *all* stars, but in the Sixties, Joan Sutherland was our fairy godmother—a wave of her wand, and we were performing. She was the sun and we reflected her glory.

After the *Beatrice di Tenda*, Joan, Ricky and I knew we had a fabulous combination and it only remained for us to find other operas calling for a *bel canto* one-two punch. Not long after, in 1963, we found one, again from Bellini's pen—his masterpiece, *Norma.* The Vancouver Opera wanted Joan and Ricky to do the opera and they said yes, but told them to hire me for the mezzo role of Adalgisa. Vancouver readily agreed. Thus did Sutherland and Horne begin their partnership as the Druid Duo, in the vehicle which would eventually bring me to the Metropolitan.

# X

## Henry, Judy and Angela

FROM THE day of our marriage, Henry and I had been embarrassingly happy together. Those first years were heaven. We worked, played, fought and loved together. In direct contrast to what had been predicted, both our careers were advancing, in many instances side by side, as in my appearances with Henry's Los Angeles Chamber Orchestra. In the fall of 1963, the Chamber Orchestra went on a tour of Western Europe sponsored by the State Department's Cultural Presentations Program, and Henry asked to take me along as soloist. The trip was memorable for me as my first success in Italy. When we appeared in Milan, I sang a show-stopper, *"Superbo di me stesso,"* and the headline in the *Corriere della Sera* said, "Three thousand were on their feet yelling Bis Bis [Again Again] at the end!" You can imagine what a thrill that gave me.

Before we left for Europe, we celebrated our anniversary, and among my souvenirs is a card which gives a good idea of my state of mind and heart:

We've made it three years,
　Not without tears.
Breakfasts not many,
　Tantrums aplenty.
And come a long way,
　While it's still just beginning,
Both you & I know,
　We're not yet to our inning.
The trying of patience,
　Has unfortunately been your part.
You've had it all along
　From your sweet & loving heart.
But, darling, you must know,
　Whate'er may come & go,
We won't have the peace of a dove,
　But year in & year out,
A very Great love.

I couldn't love you more
　& wouldn't change a thing,
Not even all the mess that
　happens when I sing.
Just last a little longer,
　It really is much stronger.
I owe it all to you, and will
　for all my life.
But what I still love most

Is being your old wife.
        H. & M.
            per sempre
        1963

Scansion aside, life was, as they used to say on the old radio soap opera, *beautiful.*

In the Sixties, Henry and I became part of the Los Angeles social scene and, not surprisingly, found ourselves in the Hollywood set. From those giddy years came everlasting friendships. I was working with a vocal coach named Jack Metz, for instance, and kept seeing a tall, shy Alabama boy at the studio. I thought the fellow was studying to be an opera singer, until I saw him on his own television series playing a sweet non-commissioned nincompoop in the U.S. Marines. In person, he was a far cry from the dolt he acted on the screen, and he possessed a marvelous, rich baritone voice! Jim Nabors has come a long way since Gomer Pyle, but he's the same wonderful person today as he was then. After Gomer, Jim starred in variety shows which gave him an opportunity to display his singing talents and people were amazed to hear his deep, warm voice. I appeared on a television special with Jim, and the two of us had a wonderful time singing duets and doing skits. Today, Jim's a resident of Hawaii and lives in a beautiful oceanside home in Honolulu. In 1981, while in Australia filming a "Love Boat" episode, Jim generously turned his home over to me, and in that incredibly lovely setting I began work on this book.

Through Jim, I met another superstar, Carol Burnett, on whose television variety show I also appeared. With Eileen Farrell rounding out the trio, we dressed up like three Mae Wests, the three little pigs, the Andrews Sisters, and Cinderella and her two stepsisters, and performed skits and songs. There's a pirate record of the three of us still around. Like Jim, Carol transcended her great gift for comedy and became a powerful dramatic actress.

Henry and I were also friendly with a hunk by the name of Roy Fitzgerald, Jr., whom you'd recognize better as Rock Hudson. I'm reminded quarterly of this friendship because of one Christmas when Rock gave each of his friends a gift of stock—one share in a company which had something to do with that particular friend's life-style. Henry and I got stock in an airline company because we traveled so much, and little Angela became a one-share holder in a baby-food company. To this day, we receive twenty-five-cent dividend checks.

In addition, I displayed my histrionic abilities on an episode of "The Odd Couple" with Tony Randall and Jack Klugman. I came on the set with one aria to sing and one line to say, and by the time we finished filming, I'd worked myself into a featured part! Just recently, a young man came to the stage door and told me he had never even heard of opera until seeing me on that "Odd Couple" program and then he had gotten hooked. Never underestimate the power of television.

Though I was seriously and studiously at work on my music at the time, the Hollywood scene was captivating and a trickle of hedonism seeped into the mainstream of my life. For a while, the little girl from Bradford, the one who bottled her ebullience, pulled out a few stoppers, going to parties, eating and, worse, drinking a bit. Don't misunderstand—I won't be able to boost the sales of my autobiography by claiming I was a serious drinker who had to battle her way back to the straight and narrow. First and foremost, I'm a serious *singer*, and every singer knows alcohol is bad for the voice. Going to social events meant social drinking, however, and, without realizing it, in a low-key manner I was becoming a bit of a party girl. It remained for a very special star to set me straight.

Though she never knew it, Judy Garland was responsible for my reformation. I learned my booze lesson at a party Rock Hudson gave for Princess Grace and Prince Rainier of Monaco.

Rock's gathering was a typical intimate Hollywood soiree of around four hundred people, consisting of a galaxy of stars and a number of assorted meteors, celebrities who shoot by fast and burn themselves up. At these extravagances, tongues are sabers, and the weapons certainly flashed that night. Surprisingly, no one had much to say against Grace and Rainier. She was utterly beautiful, though I was amazed to find her shorter than I'd expected, and the Prince, a soft-spoken, serious man, discussed the Monte Carlo Opera with me and impressed me with his astute and informed commentary on operas and artists.

Meanwhile, Henry was completely captivated by the goulash sisters, the Gabors. He was lost in a sea of peroxide and I was thoroughly involved in star-gazing, mentally oohing and ahhing non-stop. What an experience to stand next to Henry Fonda—I couldn't resist telling him he was one of my favorites and he, perfect gentleman, responded graciously to my gaucherie. Jim Garner had grown a beard and was running around telling everybody who he was, as if they didn't know, and Elizabeth Ashley stood outside the bathroom waiting for George Peppard to come out.

Of all the people there, however, I was most thrilled at seeing Judy Garland, as anyone from my generation of movie-goers would understand. She was one of the main reasons I had spent those Bradford Saturday afternoons at the movies! It grieves me when people equate the Judy of those drink-and-drug-ridden last years with that lovely, lively girl and woman I saw on the screen. Judy Garland was a *great* entertainer, as unique in the popular field as Lotte Lehmann was in the classical. Like Lehmann, Judy sang words with such meaning and coloring that you had to be moved, and on top of that, she was a damn good actress. Judy could really touch you, and before it got out of hand, her vulnerability endeared her to audiences. I adored her.

Judy looked fantastic in a red velvet dress which had mink trim on a curving décolletage and at the end of her sleeves. She'd had so many ups and downs in weight, mood and career that you never knew how she was going to appear—but that night she was radiant.

As a rule, no matter how convivial they may seem to be, Hollywood parties always contain an undercurrent of misery. Someone is suffering. When life is so high, someone's bound to be feeling mighty low. Rock's gala was no exception. One of the saber tongues that night announced that Judy Garland had told our host that Inger Stevens was taking pills from the medicine cabinet. Everyone was a bit skeptical and assumed instead that Judy herself was taking the pills—she had a reputation for reaming out the contents of medicine cabinets. This time, Judy may not have been crying wolf, though, because a few years later Inger Stevens, a disturbed, unhappy woman, did kill herself.

I wanted to talk to Garland, but in the crush never got to her. On that particular evening, Henry and I were in the throes of our first *real* marital squabble and I had left home ready to drink, even though I didn't like alcohol. I whirled around the celebrity maze like a top and, every time I stopped, found a drink in my hand until, finally, I found myself alone, sitting on the floor in the middle of Rock's red-walled guest bedroom enveloped in the fuzzy miasma bred by the bottle. I was swaying back and forth, humming to myself and feeling no pain, when the door opened and in walked Judy Garland. Her red dress seemed to blend into the walls, so all I could see clearly was her face. She came over and sat down next to me.

"Hi," she said, continuing in words which may have been as blurred by my hearing as by her speaking. "You're the opera singer, aren't you?"

"Yes," I answered.

"Well, I'm a singer, too," she said. "Why don't we sing?"

We did. Putting our arms around each other, Judy Garland and Marilyn Horne belted out medley after medley of popular songs for no audience but ourselves. Gershwin, Porter, Kern, Youmans—we sang them all, and Judy wasn't surprised in the slightest that I knew all the lyrics. Every so often, she'd put her finger to her lips and shush me as she sang a song that went, "Louis A. Louis B. Louis C. Louis D. Louis E. Louis F.," and at the end of the refrain she'd switch the words and growl, "F. you, Louis!"

I assumed she was singing about Louis B. Mayer, the head of MGM, who'd made her a star, but at a tremendous cost to her personal life. Though she'd been groomed as another Deanna Durbin, the pretty teen-age singing queen of Universal Pictures, Mayer had thought Judy was homely and poured thousands into re-creating her. After all the remodeling, Mayer would point Judy out to others as an example of his ability to create stars, saying, "What do you think of my little hunchback? Look where she is, thanks to me." Judy had a weight problem and MGM gave her pills to reduce. She also took pills to stay awake and then to go to sleep. All those drugs along with alcohol finally did her in, but still she was fabulous, an irreplaceable artist.

Garland and I crooned together for a long, long time, and, amazingly, in the *bass* clef. Eventually, Henry sailed away from the Gabors and found me, and what a sight I was! My mascara had dribbled down my cheeks and somewhere in Rock's house was a false eyelash belonging to me. After Judy and I had sworn eternal friendship, Henry took me home.

The next morning, I had a classic hangover and, worse, a raw throat. When I thought of what had happened the previous evening, how I'd overindulged and was suffering the consequences now, and, even more frightening, what had happened to someone as gifted and charming as Judy Garland, I felt even sicker. A performing artist has to be in control of herself, and my controls, on automatic pilot since childhood, needed a permanent resetting. I vowed then and there to stay away from liquor, a vow I've kept. You may see me with a single glass of wine at dinner, but that's it. That party in Hollywood was my one and only "lost weekend."

On Tuesday, February 18, 1964, Joan, Ricky and I returned to New York in a *bel canto* concert performance. This time, it was Carnegie Hall and the opera was a practically unknown *opera seria* by Gioacchino Rossini called *Semiramide*. While Rossini's comic operas were fixed in everybody's repertory, the many serious operas he had produced had only begun to be resurrected A.C. (After Callas). Premiered in 1823, *Semiramide* proved to be an immensely popular work all over the Continent for a while, but after a brief run at the Metropolitan Opera in the 1893–94 season, it virtually disappeared in the United States, its only performances an occasional revival in Europe.

The story concerns Semiramide, the Queen of Babylon, who murders her husband, aided by Prince Assur, who has his eye on the throne. Semiramide is attracted to the young commander of her armies, Arsace, who is in turn in love with the Princess Azema, and thank goodness for that, because he is in reality Semiramide's very own son! In the middle of the opera, the ghost of the King appears and tells an assembled crowd that Arsace will be his successor. Assur tries to prevent that eventuality, and when Arsace moves to stab Assur, Semiramide, who has slipped in unbeknownst in the dark, receives the fatal thrust. Arsace is proclaimed King, and whoever is left lives happily ever after.

Joan sang Semiramide, I donned my trousers for Arsace and, with Ricky on the podium, the "Trylon and Perisphere" of *bel canto* triumphed onstage.

Though my success that evening was fantastic, and though my association with Sutherland brought me worldwide recognition, it would be another six years before I realized my operatic goal, the Met. Not that Mr. Bing didn't send out feelers and offer possibilities, but none of them was acceptable to me. I didn't want to debut with a ragbag production or an unsuitable part just to get onto the Metropolitan stage. I wanted something special, and for that I had to wait.

At the moment, I didn't mind that much, though, because I was awaiting something else, something more wonderful than my Metropolitan debut. I was expecting a child.

At the end of a television interview I once saw, Alexandra Danilova, former prima ballerina of the Ballet Russe de Monte Carlo, was told by her interviewer, Mike Wallace, after she had recounted the story of her life, "Mme. Danilova, you've been a very successful woman."

Danilova shook her head. "No, no," she replied. "I am not a successful *woman*. A woman's success is in marriage and children. I wasn't successful in marriage and I have no children. I am a successful 'creature,' not a successful woman. I have never known of a dancer who combined motherhood and career. You can't have both."

Lotte Lehmann said the same to me about singers and I've had almost two decades to find out whether or not it's true. My marriage ended as a failure, but it wasn't a mistake. We had some fabulously productive years together, and we had Angela.

Angela's birth was the most important moment of my life, and she's the most important thing in my life. Singing *is* my life, however, and that sometimes made motherhood very difficult. I was thirty-one years old when Angela came and had been singing all my life. She's eighteen years old now and I'm very proud of her, but it hasn't been easy for either of us. Being the child of career-oriented parents is notoriously difficult—the stuff of sensational biographies, in fact—but one thing is certain: I did my best. Combining mezzohood and motherhood was one hard business; guilt is one of my vital signs. I've learned to live with it, though, as I'm sure all caring parents do. Berneice and Bentz did what they thought was right and so did Henry and I.

I learned I was pregnant while in London. My Covent Garden debut came in October 1964, as Marie in *Wozzeck*, at the very time London was stricken with a major pea-souper of a fog, the kind Jack the Ripper used to pick his way through. The difficult role was aggravated by my condition, which was further aggravated by the weather, and by the time my throat was slit onstage, it was a relief! I had morning sickness *all* day and after every scene in *Wozzeck* went into the wings to throw up. There are fifteen scenes in *Wozzeck*. Between my personal nausea and the heavy weight of *Wozzeck*'s message, I was a wreck! The doctor prescribed some pills which he assured me would clear up the nausea, but though the pills were on my dresser, I never took one. I didn't like the idea of taking medicine while I was carrying a child. That pill bottle was marked Thalidomide.

In the spring of 1965, I performed Arsace in *Semiramide* in Boston with Joan, and waddled around the sets looking more like a Sherman tank than a conquering hero. I wore a funny little beard, and at the curtain call Joan looked over, started giggling and tugged at my Assyrian Vandyke. Singing to a pregnant bearded lady was too much even for Joan. I may have been the first pregnant general since the Amazons. Then I sang *Italiana* in Vancouver, and though I expected to stop and wait at least two months for the birth, I felt great and sang several concerts, my last at USC three weeks before Angela was born. My dressmaker had made two dresses with big darts to let out along the way—and I was out to the outermost dart when I stopped.

I could not, however, appear in Donizetti's *Lucrezia Borgia* for the American Opera Society in New York City. It was just too much. To replace me, the Society plucked a Spanish girl from the Bremen Opera House and put her on the big stage. Her name was Montserrat Caballé, and whenever she sees my Angela now, she gives her a very *special* hello.

It wasn't until 1976 that Montserrat and I finally met, but since then we have appeared together on many grand occasions. I love working with her, not only because she's a great singer but because I can make her laugh onstage. It's bliss to have a colleague of the highest artistry, but absolute heaven to know you've got a stooge, and Montserrat has a built-in comic vehicle. She's from Madrid and speaks Castilian Spanish, so her "v" is pronounced "b." In the course of an opera, Montserrat sometimes gets lazy with her Italian "v's," and, I must confess, I sometimes take advantage of it. We were doing *Semiramide* in San Francisco, she in the title role and I as Arsace. The production was visually stunning, and we wore elaborate baroque costumes with huge white powdered wigs, and probably looked like two snow-capped peaks. A grand duet occurs in the court scene, after which Semiramide sings *"I vostri voti omai."* We finished the duet and, according to the stage directions, embraced as hero and heroine, and held on to each other, arms enfolded, heads buried in each other's necks. The applause held up the show, which was fortunate, because Montserrat became confused and lost her place.

"What are my first words?" she hissed in my ear.

*"I bostri boti omai,"* I answered.

If anyone present at that performance wondered why Arsace and Semiramide were locked in embrace for an eternity, the answer is that they were hysterical with laughter and could not move apart until Semiramide got enough control to sing out her first words.

Angela was born on June 14, 1965, in the Cedars of Lebanon

Hospital, just as my career was going into orbit. For a while, though, it looked as though my career would be shot down. I was given a caudal block for the delivery, but, according to an anesthetist, the contours of my spine weren't "right," and consequently I went into paralysis. The pain was excruciating. I couldn't move. I couldn't even give my baby her bottle—I wasn't nursing her since I was scheduled to travel soon after and didn't want to start something I couldn't finish. Henry went into a panic and raised hell with the obstetrician. I was put on saline solutions and almost immediately developed a bladder infection. Meanwhile, the doctors, concerned with my inability to move, put me in traction and began a physical-therapy program. My mother-in-law came to the hospital to look after me, thank God, and one week after the delivery I was back to normal. It was as though a scrim had been lifted, and by the time we took the baby home, everything was wonderful.

Eight weeks later, Henry and I had to leave for Europe, where we had recording sessions. Leaving Angela then caused more pain than I'd ever experienced in the hospital. Torn between wanting to be with her and the legitimate demands of my profession, I knew I *had* to fulfill my career commitments. At such times, I've never been sure where the impetus comes from—is it all from me or is there somewhere deep inside me a residual fear of disappointing my father? I've never known.

We left our baby with Henry's mother and flew to Switzerland. I cried almost the entire flight, but should have saved some tears. The next crisis nearly finished me.

Just after our arrival, we received news that Henry's mother had been hospitalized with a heart attack—and for a while we had no idea where Angela was! We finally located her, through a torrent of transcontinental calls, at the home of Bill and Barbara Kraft, friends who'd taken Angela to Hollywood, very near by. We got through to my mother and she went to get Angela and, though she had a full-time job, put Angela in her bedroom, got a baby-sitter and came home every day for lunch to see how her new boarder was doing. She was ecstatic, but I was frantic with worry and guilt.

Jo Lewis recovered, though she had a heart condition for the rest of her life, and Angela stayed with Mother for a month. Later, my mother said it was a wonderful time for her. I'm glad someone enjoyed it!

My "afterbirth" experiences were vocally scary, too. My throat muscles didn't come back until about six weeks after the delivery, and with professional commitments rushing in on me, I still didn't feel I was ready to support my voice. I wish I'd known that nursing helps to tighten the muscles, because it would have saved me weeks of worry. Where are the doctors when you need to know things like that? I was recording an album called *Souvenir of a Golden Era*, which was full of *bel canto* excursions, and I kept cracking on the high notes. "This is it," I thought—"curtains!" Fortunately, the muscles did come back and I was able to continue. But that wasn't all.

We were in Geneva and staying in a lovely, chic hostelry with charming decor. Charm? I'd have traded it all for a good night's sleep. Henry and I were shown into a comfortable room on the top floor and moved in, but the mansard roof over us was also home for an army of squealing rats. Good old Henry went out like a light the minute he hit the pillow, while I lay there listening to the rodents running in the roof. The next morning, we moved down three floors. I was so tired I spent the whole afternoon in bed, dozing and going over music scores. I ordered a steak from room service accompanied by a side dish of spaghetti bolognese. The waiter, nattily dressed in his hotel uniform, brought in the meal and went out with bows and smiles.

I took a bite of the pasta and it tasted strange. That impulse to make sure what you've tasted *is* what you tasted made me take another mouthful, and this time I put the dish aside, figuring the Swiss didn't know what to do with Italian food. That evening, I developed the worst case of ptomaine poisoning you can imagine, and all from two bites. If I'd eaten the whole thing, I swear I'd have died. I threw up everything, and all night long, acid bile passed over my vocal cords. The next morning, Sunday, I had no voice. A doctor came over and gave me a prescription; I couldn't keep anything down, so was treated to suppositories. Mind you, all this happened in one of Geneva's most celebrated hotels.

If I had thought my voice was in trouble before, now I was certain of it, convinced those high notes were gone for good. B is the money note in Rossini arias and Henry had to rearrange cadenzas like crazy. All the great arias I sing are in the key of E, and so all high notes are B and they were out of my repertoire for six months following Angela's birth and my food poisoning. Even today I can't listen to some of the records made during those sessions without a sense of horror.

The American Medical Association hasn't asked my opinion, but it's my belief a woman does not feel normal until a year after she's given birth.

When we returned to Los Angeles, I'd made up my mind how I'd greet my daughter. I knew she was too little to actually remember us—after all, we'd been away for months and she'd been tiny when we'd departed—so I determined to approach her calmly and not to push. Sure enough, when we arrived home, Angela didn't know me. I'd go to pick her up and she'd start to bawl. Henry said, "Just grab her and hug her, Jackie," but I played Mother Courage and remained "casual." Though I wanted to scoop her up and smother her with hugs and kisses, I smiled and cooed to my own flesh and blood as though she were an adorable stranger. I didn't want to overpower her with my love any more than I wanted to overpower audiences with my voice. Finally, Nature triumphed;

something clicked and Angela stretched out her arms to me. I cried with relief and happiness and must have held her in my arms the rest of the day.

Looking back, I have very few complaints about the Sixties. Besides Angela, my career moved forward steadily. I was appearing with major symphonies as well as opera companies from coast to coast. In 1967, for example, to commemorate the hundredth anniversary of Toscanini's birth, I sang Verdi's *Requiem* with Leonard Bernstein and the New York Philharmonic. There was no question but that I was arriving.

Home life was good, too. Angela was young and mobile, and we took her everywhere. The troubles with her wouldn't start until later, when she began school and her flexibility ended. When Angela begins her litany of how many times she was left in the care of others, I wish I had those early years on videotape so I could slip in a cassette and show her how much her dad and I were around. It might have been easier if she'd had brothers and sisters, but it wasn't to be. Not that I didn't want more. Angela was no vanity child, conceived and produced to prove her mother's total womanhood. I really believe we're here to procreate. It just never happened again.

Meanwhile, Henry's career was steadily advancing, too. After his Los Angeles Philharmonic conducting debut, he took over all the orchestra's youth concerts, then, in 1967, was offered the position of assistant conductor to Zubin Mehta, the music director of the orchestra. Henry didn't really want the job and asked for what he thought was an impossible salary, certain they'd reject the figure and leave him alone, but they agreed, and Henry spent the next year as Mehta's assistant.

At the end of the year, Henry's agent, Ronald Wilford, called and said the position of conductor of the New Jersey Symphony was open. Henry told him he was nuts. The New Jersey Symphony was strictly bush-league, a community ensemble which gave about fifteen concerts a year—hardly an organization Henry wanted to wave his arms in front of! There were some selling points, though, primarily the fact that Henry would be in the driver's seat and could fashion his own orchestra. We talked an awful lot about it, with friends, agents and just the two of us. In the end, the idea of making a silk purse out of the New Jersey Symphony intrigued him, and in February of 1968 he accepted the appointment.

New Jersey is not a commute from Los Angeles, however, and when Henry took the assignment, I had to return East with him. I was happy in Los Angeles and had no yen to return East, but I did, and we bought a home in Orange, New Jersey, a large brick Tudor manse on two woody acres, where I reigned as chanteuse chatelaine for the next nine years.

Angela's odyssey, from West to East, was the reverse of her mother's two decades before, but she was a lot younger and accustomed to travel, and her adjustment went smoothly. She, as well as her parents, made friends quickly and lastingly. We enrolled her in nursery school and I'll never forget her first day at the Temple Israel Nursery School in South Orange, the best school around. That it was affiliated with the Jewish temple was no problem for me, but even though she hadn't been baptized, Angela had been raised in a Christmas-and-Easter way. Could she cope with Rosh Hashonah and Hanukah? I was silly to worry, of course. She was so adorable, eager and loving that she adjusted to school without a hitch, and in fact she never asked why she was in a Jewish temple. I guess she just assumed that was the way you started school. Before you could say the Four Questions, Angela had a best friend named Elissa Cohen. She and Lissy grew up in each other's homes, and, indeed, all the Lewises were taken into the fold and made to feel welcome.

Every Friday, one little nursery student was appointed Shabbos girl or boy and whoever was chosen invited his or her parent to be Shabbos mother. I had that honor and it was one of my greatest roles. As Shabbos mother, I baked challah and went with Angela to school, where the Sabbath was celebrated with candle-lighting and prayers. I sang many a *B'rucha* in Temple Israel.

I'd spent my DooWah Years in Hollywood, my Galley Years in Gelsenkirchen, and now began my Balabosta Years in Orange, New Jersey. It was the best of times and we were in the best of places: 273 Elmwynd Drive was a sylvan paradise, with incredible azaleas, seventeen dogwood trees, twenty pines and an apple orchard. Angela was settled at school, my husband would soon pull the New Jersey Symphony up to a Class A rating, and my debuts at La Scala and the Met would take place within the next two years. Most important, I was in love with Henry Lewis, and was so happy . . . for a time.

# X I

# *La Scala*

MILAN'S TEATRO alla Scala ("Theatre of the Stairs") is some-times called "The House that Verdi Built," for all the successes he had there. Designed and erected in 1778 by the architect Pier-marini, the theatre replaced the burnt-down Royal Ducal Theatre, and was named in honor of Duke Barnabo Visconti's wife, Regina della Scala, who had founded a church on the same site in the four-teenth century. The first performance, on August 3, was Salieri's *Europa Riconosciuta*, and thereafter La Scala was opening-night headquarters for scores of new works, many of which are still per-formed today. All the great Italian composers wrote operas for this venerable house, among them Rossini, Bellini, Donizetti, Verdi, Puccini, and the operas, *La Gazza Ladra*, *Lucrezia Borgia*, *Norma*, *Otello*, *Falstaff*, *Madama Butterfly* and *Turandot*. Arturo Toscanini reigned as director for two glorious eras, from 1898 to 1908 (except for 1904–1905) and 1921 to 1929, at the end leaving only because of his opposition to the Fascist government. Among other things, Toscanini refused to play the Fascist anthem before performances. In the Thirties, Mussolini attempted to turn the Rome Opera into the premiere company of Italy, but, as in other instances, the Italian people ignored Il Duce's mandate and La Scala held sway. Alas, the theatre was heavily damaged by bombs in 1943, but by 1946 was completely restored and today looks much as it did in the past. Toscanini returned to conduct a reopening concert on May 11, 1946, and one of the soloists on that memorable occasion was a rookie soprano named Renata Tebaldi.

Though the Metropolitan Opera was *my* goal, La Scala beckoned first, and I made my debut in that musical mecca, not, as many think, in the widely publicized revival of Rossini's *L'Assedio di Corinto* (*The Siege of Corinth*) in April 1969 but, one month earlier, in Stravinsky's *Oedipus Rex.*

The success of the Rossini opus somewhat obscured the Stravinsky evening—and thereby hangs a tale.

I had signed my contract with La Scala to appear in *L'Assedio* and was working in Canada when I received a phone call from La Scala asking me to make my debut as Jocasta in Stravinsky's *Oedipus Rex* rather than in the Rossini. *Oedipus*, to be conducted by Claudio Abbado, was scheduled to be performed a month before *L'Assedio*, and because of my great feeling for Stravinsky, I agreed. It seemed fitting that my La Scala debut should come in a part written by a man who'd meant so much in my musical life.

I was studying both *L'Assedio* and *Oedipus* and singing the *Barber* at the Vancouver Opera when I received another phone call from La Scala. They were having casting difficulties with the Rossini. Originally, Montserrat Caballé had been mentioned for the soprano heroine, Pamira, and I had been put into the trouser role of Neocle. Then Renata Scotto had replaced Caballé—which was fine with me, Scotto was a first-rate artist—but now Mme. Scotto was expecting a baby and had to step out. La Scala called and suggested that, since I was still singing soprano and mezzo, I should take over the role of Pamira and they'd get a tenor to step into my pants as Neocle. Rossini had written two versions, one for tenor and one for mezzo. Oh, no, not for me! I'd been learning the part of Neocle and was very comfortable in the range. I refused to go up to Pamira.

"Who can we get?" asked La Scala. They mused a bit. "Do you know a soprano named Teresa Zylis-Gara?"

"I know her name," I answered, "and I understand she's a fine singer, but I've never heard her sing."

We batted around a few names for a while until I had a brainstorm.

"What about Beverly Sills?" I asked.

"Who?" answered La Scala.

"Beverly Sills. She's a fabulous American singer who's had a great success with Handel's *Julius Caesar* at the New York City Opera. I think she could sing it, but why don't you ask Tommy Schippers?" Tommy, the fine young American conductor (who later tragically succumbed to cancer just a few years after his attractive young wife, Nonie Phipps, died of the same disease), was scheduled to conduct the *Siege*. La Scala thanked me and hung up. Afterward, I called Bev, whom I knew professionally, and told her to alert her agents that La Scala might be calling. I'll never forget her excitement at the news. *"La Scala!"* she cried. *"La Scala!"*

The next time we spoke was over lunch at the Beverly Hills Hotel. Beverly was practically airborne with excitement and kept saying, "I'm going to La Scala, I'm going to La Scala!" I, too, was looking forward to appearing there and eagerly anticipated working with Bev, a fellow American and a woman of intelligence and humor.

I arrived in Milan along with Angela and her governess, Schicki Hansen, and we settled in for a three-month stay. I began rehearsing for *Oedipus Rex* with time out to explore the city and my daughter. Angela was nearly four and utterly delightful, and it was great fun to be together. Onstage, I was busy giving my son an Oedipus complex, but offstage I was enjoying the company of my little girl.

*Oedipus Rex*, a fifty-two-minute opera-oratorio with Latin text based on Sophocles' *Oedipus Tyrannus*, had its world premiere in Paris on May 30, 1927, in oratorio form and in Vienna on February 23, 1928, as an opera. Stravinsky all along envisioned it as a staged piece, but he wanted it to be static, noting there should be as little movement as possible. The chief characters were to remain like figures in a frieze, moving only arms and heads. "They should give the impression of living statues," said the Maestro. Stravinsky got his wish on the occasion of my La Scala debut. Giorgio de Lullo was the director of the Pier Luigi Pizzi production. "Pigi" Pizzi was known as being *avant-garde,* and *avant-garde* was certainly the term for this production.

We voyaged deep into Freud territory. The motif of the entire production was eggs. Jocasta was literally encased in a purple plastic egg. The first time I tried on the costume, I made Humpty Dumpty look like Twiggy. When I thought of the lovely classic Grecian costumes Jocasta usually wore, and how I was got up like a hard-boiled lavender balloon, my blood curdled. Surrounded by this plastic case, with only my head visible, I had no choice but to be static. I could barely move my arms and legs, and, what's more, I couldn't hear. When conductor Claudio Abbado stopped me in the middle of one solo and said, "Can't you hear what your music is?" I rolled down to the front of the stage and answered, "*My music? I can't hear what this* opera *is!*"

It was true: my ears were covered with plastic and everything sounded as though it were coming through glass. I made them alter the costume by cutting away the headgear to expose my ears, so at least I could hear my cues. The rest of the outfit consisted of little plastic eggs attached in strategic spots around my plastic shell —fortunately, not *that* strategic, or I'd have resembled a High-Tech Gypsy Rose Lee.

In the center of the stage stood a huge prop egg which was home base for Jocasta. Antaeus-like, I had to clutch this gigantic ovian replica at all times. I'm sure you get the symbolism. Oedipus, played by the Hungarian tenor Lajos Kozma, had a terrific bit of costumery after the eye-gouging. A golden blindfold was wrapped around his head and two huge red beads dangled from both eyes. Again, I'm sure you get the symbolism.

The production was further enhanced by the use of conveyer belts and elevators. Oedipus and I were conveyed by an elevator at our entrance. One critic called the production *"Oedipus in Ascensore"* ("Oedipus in the Elevator").

Mom couldn't make it to Italy. She had been operated on for cancer shortly before my departure, and though she had come through the surgery okay, recovery was rough and made her far too weak for travel. I still have the telegram she sent on opening night, though:

> SOCK IT TO THEM BABY, WITH YOU ALL THE WAY
> MOM & JAY

We opened on March 13, 1969, and the production was fairly well received. I came through with flying colors, though my purple egg suit turned out to be a veritable incubator. Things got so hot, I almost hatched! I received fine notices; however, my actual debut was overshadowed by the upcoming revival of *L'Assedio di Corinto*. With Beverly Sills, Justino Diaz and me in the leads and Tommy Schippers on the podium, there would be an All-American line-up at La Scala, and that was news indeed, more newsworthy than *Oedipus*.

After the premiere of *Oedipus Rex*, Wally Toscanini, the Countess Castelbarco, daughter of the late conductor, and reigning queen of La Scala social life, threw a gala fete for Italian opera society. She neglected, however, to invite the stage queen, Jocasta, or, indeed, King Oedipus himself; even though we were the stars of the opera, Mr. Kozma and I weren't "well known" enough to warrant inclusion in the celebration. The slight didn't bother me, since I don't like big parties, but even if I was in the slightest miffed at being left out, I certainly got my revenge four weeks later—thanks to Gioacchino Rossini!

*L'Assedio di Corinto* tells the complicated story of Pamira, daughter of Cleomene, governor of Corinth, who wants her to marry Neocle, a young Greek officer. Pamira, like all operatic daughters, is in love with someone else, a certain Almanzor whom she'd met in Athens. Shortly thereafter, Cleomene goes off to battle the Turks; the Turks, led by Maometto, are victorious and Cleomene is brought in as a prisoner. Pamira arrives on the scene —and discovers that Maometto is Almanzor! He offers to marry Pamira and make peace with the Greeks, but Cleomene says Pamira must marry Neocle and, when she refuses, stalks out, leaving her to Maometto. Poor Pamira is torn between love of her father and her fatherland and love of Maometto. Maometto tries to comfort her, but they are interrupted by the arrival of Neocle, who has come to take her back. Maometto is not pleased to see him, and Pamira saves Neocle only by claiming he is her brother.

Meanwhile, the Greeks are preparing to fight again, and Pamira goes back to her people with Neocle. Maometto vows that all

Greeks will be dead by sunrise; the men rush off to battle, and Pamira and the women say their prayers. Alas, the prayers aren't answered. The Turks win and Maometto comes to get Pamira, only to find that she and the rest of the sisterhood have killed themselves.

Justino Diaz would sing Maometto, Beverly would be Pamira and I was scheduled to perform Neocle.

Early in March, the cast members began arriving, including the Kid from Brooklyn, Beverly Sills. Right away, I had a sense that something wasn't quite right.

Looking out for number one is essential for any performer, and, as I've noted, it's necessary to hire others to do the looking-out for you. I had wanted press coverage for my La Scala debut and there's a lengthy correspondence between my then publicity agent and me, in which he told me there was little or no interest back home in the *Oedipus*. *Newsweek* was considering a cover on Sills and *L'Assedio*, which about wrapped up the space they'd give to opera, and the other periodicals and newspapers felt the same way. With its Yankee Doodle cast, *L'Assedio* was more newsworthy. All the same, I was disappointed. Beverly commiserated and said that our press for *L'Assedio* would make up for it.

On opening night, April 11, 1969, I was in my dressing room putting on my costume—standard army issue, complete with sword and shield—and listening to my dressers chatter. I wasn't paying much attention to their actual words until I picked up a recurring theme, the gist of which was that a gentleman had arrived from America and that he was busily going over the pictures and publicity releases to be forwarded to the United States, and that, in fact, they were in Miss Sills' dressing room at that very moment. The dresser smiled shyly and said, "We like you so much, Signora, and you've been so kind. We wanted you to know because it seems this man is pulling out all the pictures with you in them."

*Our* press, eh? Granted, this night was Beverly's debut and she was entitled to special recognition, but not to an exclusive! When a La Scala press officer dropped into the dressing room and confirmed the reports, I was out the door and marching into Sills' adjoining quarters. Though appropriately garbed in armor, I had fortunately forgotten my sword, because I was angry enough to run it through a certain redhead.

I knocked on the door, walked in, found the two of them in conference, then strode right over, pushed my chin into the publicity agent's chest and said, loud and clear,

"Look, I don't know what you're doing, but I'll tell you one thing: if *The New York Times* runs a picture and I'm *not* in it, I'll find you when I get back to the States and smack you right in the face, you son-of-a-bitch!"

He winced. A soft-spoken European of taste and refinement, he was taken aback by this double-barreled dose of straightforward American push. Frankly, what could he expect? Was I supposed to stand by and let them rob me of my notices? I *was* rather bellicose, but don't forget that I was dressed and ready for battle! What a sight it must have been, a sawed-off armadillo taking on a courtly gentleman, not to mention a certain strawberry blonde who stood by innocently fluttering her eyelids. Both of them protested—too much, as far as I was concerned—and couldn't understand where I had gotten such an idea. I didn't hang around to hear the demurrers. Reiterating my opening statement, I clanked out of the room.

To think, I fumed, that I had been the one who had suggested Beverly in the first place. That should have been a great night for us *all*—for Rossini, for opera and for America, not just for Sills. With hindsight, that was what prevented me from truly meshing with Beverly vocally during that production. I never got the feeling that she was interested in the whole, but just in her part, at least when I was singing with her. I know that nobody's perfect—I'm no June Allyson myself—but still that whole episode left a bitter taste in my mouth. For years, I felt that I had extended my hand in friendship and Beverly had bitten it.

With more hindsight, I began to wonder why I had to fight my own press battles. If you think about it, Beverly's press agent was simply doing his job; he was there working for his client for *her* opening night at La Scala, but, aside from my four-year-old daughter and Schicki, I was alone. I brooded about that for a while, too.

Nevertheless, the show must go on, and it did. We had a great success. Beverly made the cover of *Newsweek* and became the darling of the land. Despite the friction, I wanted our appearance together to end on a positive note, so I decided to let the whole business slide. In addition, after our return to America, we were scheduled to appear together with the New Jersey Symphony at Carnegie Hall and I wanted that to go well. I spoke to Bev about the concert while we were in Milan and was uneasy about her unenthusiastic response. Again, I suspected that something was going on. Henry, as conductor of the New Jersey Symphony, called Bev's New York manager and was told, "After Miss Sills' great success at La Scala, she is no longer available." In truth, Beverly backed out of Carnegie Hall to return to La Scala for *Lucia di Lammermoor.*

Beverly Sills and I have long since made a practical peace, but I regret that we never had a chance to get along when we were both singing.

*L'Assedio's* success stunned Milan and a certain Countess Castelbarco *née* Toscanini. I had been successful in *Oedipus* and word had gotten around before *L'Assedio* that the other American singers weren't bad either, so the Countess quickly sent the cast invitations to her *Siege* soiree. Beverly went, but I couldn't, because Jim Nabors had come over for the opening and arranged a bash at Biffi

Scala, the restaurant adjoining the theatre where parties were traditionally given on opening nights. When I told her I was unable to come because too many friends were with me, the Countess said, "Bring them all." I told her we were going to Biffi Scala to a prearranged party, and finally she gave up. I didn't bear any grudge against her, though, and ordered a magnificent spray of flowers to be sent to her, along with a note explaining how sorry I was I couldn't join her. I guess she was overwhelmed that a "star" should send her flowers; maybe it was the first time that anyone had bothered to thank her. In any case, the next thing I knew, Wally was on the phone with me every day, inviting me over to lunch. I did go many times, along with Angela, and grew very fond of La Scala's doyenne. I also discovered an incidental piece of intelligence: we had been born on the same day and her great father had died on that very day, too!

Jim's party was terrific, just the kind I like, brimming with people I know and love and vice versa. Angela was in her element. She had a great ear and memory for music and knew entire scores. She loved *L'Assedio*—she used to go to sleep listening to tapes of the opera—and sang all the parts herself. Like her mother, she's a mimic. Sills never sounded more like Sills than when she came out of my daughter's mouth, and Jim was flabbergasted when Angela hummed *Oedipus* to him!

Despite my altercation with Beverly, I had a happy time in Milan. Obviously, I enjoyed my successes, and it was here in the foyer of Scala that I was introduced to a distinguished member of the company on his way to Africa for an appearance. I'd heard this man on records and in Vienna and Salzburg and admired his artistry, which I quickly told him. He smiled, kissed my hand and was off to the Dark Continent.

And that's how I met Nicola Zaccaria, though it'd be years before I'd realize how significant that meeting would be.

# America's Opera House

IF ANYTHING marred my stay at La Scala, it was the news of Ada Horne's death. Before leaving for Italy, I'd called to say good-bye and Nanny had sounded so weak over the phone, I'd had a sudden premonition that this might really be goodbye. At four a.m. after the opening night, Gloria called to tell me Nanny had died on April 10, peacefully, in her sleep. After all the tension, the tears flowed for a worthy reason.

Ada May Horne was right out of Central Casting under the heading "Grandmother." She never asked anything for herself and was only interested in giving. Her life was long, ninety-plus years, and full of love generously distributed to her family. I'm only happy I was able to give some pleasure back to her. Intensely proud of my achievements, she often mentioned how pleased Dad would have been at what I'd done. He certainly would have appreciated the next landmark.

"At the heart of the cities stand the great opera houses," wrote Franz Werfel, and the Metropolitan was *America's* opera house. Certainly the Texaco Saturday-afternoon broadcasts had brought its music into cities and hamlets all over the country. The Met is one hundred years old today—not such a long time for opera houses when you consider those ancient temples of music in Milan, Naples, Venice, Paris and Vienna, some of which were standing a century *before* the Metropolitan opened its doors. The story of the Met's founding is typically American. Unable to buy their way into the boxes at the Academy of Music, a group of wealthy New York businessmen got together, put up $800,000 and financed their own new house. They were all in their boxes on opening night October 22, 1883, to see Gounod's *Faust*.

For an American girl intent upon a classical-music career, where else was there to go! The Met was the pinnacle, and to appear on its stage was the realization of childhood dreams. Then progress reared its ugly head. The old house had many problems because of inadequate backstage space—sets even had to be propped up on the sidewalk in back of the building on Seventh Avenue. As I've said, another country would have bought the next block and annexed it to the old house, but we tore it down and, with scarcely a backward glance, moved over to Lincoln Center.

The new Met opened in September 1966 with the premiere of Samuel Barber's *Antony and Cleopatra*. That I never appeared on the old Met's stage still hurts, but I wanted something worthy and paid the price.

For a few years, the Met had been making feeble overtures to my manager, suggestions ranging from silly to insulting. As I recall, they proposed a number of supporting leads, including Teresa in Bellini's *La Sonnambula*. Teresa is the mother of Amina, the lead soprano. I didn't mind playing Mom on stage—I'd done Hata at twenty—but there wasn't enough in the mother part for me. I had a certain feeling about myself. I wanted the Met debut more than anything in the world, but I wouldn't go in with a second-class production or in a secondary part. Of course, now that I'd declared myself a mezzo, there was a built-in dilemma—finding the proper vehicle.

Mezzos are *always* looking for interesting roles, because there are so few in the standard repertoire. Later, I solved that problem by specializing in the *bel canto* and baroque, which, luckily, I could handle—you don't have to delve too deeply into Rossini, Handel and Vivaldi to come up with fabulous mezzo roles. True, many are *travesti* parts, but the opportunity to sing those works hand-tailored for a particular artist by the composer himself makes what you wear unimportant. Whether you're in knickers or a fancy ballgown, it's heaven to sing beautiful music of the kind Rossini wrote for his favorite artists. The truth is, I helped unearth so many of them that there are now more current mezzo roles—and more mezzos —than ever before.

During the Metropolitan's pursuit of my services, the only Rossini opera in the Met's repertoire was *Il Barbiere di Siviglia,* and it wasn't even mentioned as a possibility. What I did best was unavailable.

To some extent, the Met-Horne situation reminded me of the old Borscht Circuit joke about the resort-hotel mixer. A gentleman approaches a lady and the following dialogue ensues:

MAN:   You dancing?
GIRL:   You asking?
MAN:   I'm asking.
GIRL:   I'm dancing.

The Met couldn't just *ask* me and expect me to leap to my feet. Even though it was risky to play such games with a musical monolith like the Metropolitan Opera, I was determined to go in by the front door. Still, it looked for a while as if I might not achieve my goal—until the redhead from Australia got on my case.

Originally, Joan Sutherland was to have opened the 1964–65 Met season as Norma, but decided, according to Rudolf Bing, "rather late in the game that she was not quite ready for the part" at the Met. Mr. Bing didn't mention that Miss Sutherland had wanted to do Norma, but had also made it clear she wanted me along as Adalgisa. "Miss Sutherland is not in charge of casting," said Mr. Bing.

After a while, however, not even Rudolf Bing could say "no" to Joan. I signed a contract in 1968 to appear with the Met during the 1970 season and was pleased with the chosen vehicle.

Joan and I had had a smashing success with *Norma* in Vancouver and at Covent Garden. The opera was perfectly suited to us, a noble and beautiful study of love and sacrifice with roots in classical tragedy. Even Richard Wagner liked *Norma* and he hated just about everything he didn't write, particularly Italian melodramas.

The music itself was simply beautiful. Bellini was a supreme melodist. There's a wonderful story about a soiree at which the hostess handed manuscript paper to two of her guests, Rossini and Donizetti, and asked each to write a beautiful melody. Later, when compared, it turned out they'd both written the same thing.

"You see?" said the hostess. "Two creative talents can arrive independently at the same result."

"Oh no," protested Donizetti. "We both stole it from Bellini."

Bellini's masterpiece takes place in ancient Gaul, during the Roman occupation. Norma is the daughter of the chief Druid and herself the High Priestess. Adalgisa is a virgin of the temple. Pollione is the Roman Proconsul and, unbeknownst to the Druids, he and Norma have been lovers and produced two children, who are hidden away.

The plot concerns Pollione's new infatuation with Adalgisa, who of course does not know of his liaison with her own High Priestess. When Adalgisa comes to Norma as her mother confessor and reveals her own love for Pollione, the women are thunderstruck. Norma is so enraged she actually contemplates killing the children of her union with Pollione, but as she stands over their sleeping bodies with a dagger in her hand, she realizes she cannot do it.

She decides that Adalgisa must marry Pollione and take the children with her. Adalgisa refuses and tells Pollione that *he* must stand by Norma, but Pollione refuses in turn and swears that he will abduct Adalgisa from the temple. This so enrages Norma that she declares war on the Romans. Pollione is captured and, face to face with her former lover and knowing that the penalty for his deed is death, Norma undergoes a change of heart and offers herself as victim by telling her congregation that there is a priestess among them unfaithful to her vows.

"Who, who?" cry the people, and Norma straightforwardly answers, *"Son io"* ("It is I"). After her stunning declaration, she asks her father to look after her children and prepares to go to her death on the funeral pyre. She reaches the top, and there standing on the kindling is none other than Pollione, who has been so moved by Norma's majestic dignity that he has fallen in love again and will join her in death. The opera ends.

Perhaps you wonder what Adalgisa is doing during the last scene. I can tell you from experience: she's in her dressing room getting her makeup off and preparing to beat the traffic back to her home.

Ricky Bonynge himself has said that "the singer who can be a complete Norma probably has never existed—maybe never *will* exist. The opera requires almost too much of one soprano—the greatest dramatic ability, superhuman emotional response, the greatest *bel canto* technique, a voice of quality and size. . . ." Giuditta Pasta created the role of Norma at La Scala on December 26, 1831, and sang it very little thereafter. The first Adalgisa, Giulia Grisi, eventually took on the title role and probably fared better than Pasta, who had great difficulty with the part. According to contemporary accounts, Pasta had pitch problems, with intonation so wavering the violins had to play out of tune to accompany her. Though she is famous as the first Norma, the dominant roles in Pasta's career were Rosina and Cenerentola, both Rossini, and one truly has to wonder how she sang Norma. Although I've been asked several times, I know *I* would never attempt it.

Apocrypha clings to *Norma* like a barnacle. One story concerns a performance in which Mme. Barili-Patti sang the lead while her little daughter Adelina portrayed one of the children. During the great *"Mira, o Norma"* duet, little Adelina got carried away and began singing along, until her mother stopped the show and administered a sound spanking. Of course, Adelina Patti became a great prima donna, so perhaps it's one instance where discipline paid off.

W. C. Fields hated working with children in the movies, and kids can get in the way of opera, too. On another occasion, Mme. Teresa Parodi and Amalia Patti were singing *"Mira, o Norma,"* and the two wee ones, taxed by sitting still so long, answered the call of nature. Patti fainted and Parodi had to be carried off as the curtain was dropped.

Once the offer of Adalgisa had been made by the Metropolitan, Henry and I got together and discussed whether it was the right role for my debut. We decided it was. Though Adalgisa plays a secondary part, she has some glorious and powerful music to sing and, besides, I liked the woman. Adalgisa represents pure lyric innocence. She's a *real* believer and, in the end, her purity of thought triumphs as she sides with Norma and takes her stand against Pollione. I can sympathize with her conflicts and her feelings, as well as revel in her melodies. Besides, as Henry pointed out, Adalgisa makes an ideal debut role because, though she is in every sense a star, the burden of the evening really falls on the High Priestess. If for any reason Adalgisa should fade—or faint from Met debut nerves—Norma can always pick up the evening with her immolation. And Norma, of course, was my beloved Joan. I couldn't lose.

I'd been living the suburban-housewife role in New Jersey, but when the time came for the first *Norma* rehearsal, Henry stopped in and, with typical Lewis largesse, pulled me out of the kitchen in style.

"Jackie, today is a very special day in your life," he said on the morning of the initial *Norma* run-through. "You're making your first appearance at the Metropolitan Opera, so I'm ordering a limousine to take you!" Henry called and ordered the limousine, then went off to the New Jersey Symphony.

I waited and waited, but the limousine never showed up. Finally, I got into our station wagon and drove into New York in pouring rain. I couldn't help thinking of the *Beatrice* rehearsal which had taken place in a snowstorm. It seems I'm always dealing with the elements on big occasions.

God, I was nervous! I tried to keep cool, but the overwhelming reality of stepping onstage at the Met kept coming into my head. Remember Mr. Dick in Dickens' *David Copperfield*? He's gone a little soft in the head because of family difficulties and, though capable of talking sense, can't get rid of a vision of King Charles' severed head, which keeps cropping up in his correspondence and conversation. Well, the Met debut had become my King Charles' head and popped up in everything I saw, said or did. Though doubts had crept in here and there, I'd always been confident the day would come. Now here it was, and the fact of it made me dizzy.

What a beautiful reception I got from the artists rehearsing at the time, though. Birgit Nilsson, Thomas Stewart and Placido Domingo all came over to wish me the best. Mr. Bing was right there, too, to shake my hand and welcome me into the Met family, a tradition of courtesy which seems to have gone the way of all amenities now. Bing knew the importance of the personal touch, and though he was subject to much criticism in his time, I never joined in. I believe in dictatorship in the opera house, because only a benign despot can handle singers. Though he may have been a dictator, Rudolf Bing was also a gentleman. I can and have worked with people I don't like, but cannot work for those I don't respect. I both liked and respected Rudolf Bing—even if he hadn't brought me into his house as early as he might have.

Rehearsals began, and the Lincoln Tunnel was the beneficiary as I commuted back and forth. There were surprisingly few points of contention. Joan, Ricky and I had been down the path before, and Carlo Bergonzi as Pollione and Cesare Siepi as Oroveso, the chief Druid, were the very best singers and colleagues. Naturally, there had to be trouble concerning my outfit. I realize I'm not the easiest person in the world to costume, but I was no longer a Valkyrie chorus girl and I wasn't going to let anyone put me into a costume that was less than right! They tried. My costume was brought in and, lo and behold, there was the long blond wig which had been denied Gerhilde back in Naples, but which had little to do with the Adalgisa I played. As for clothing, someone had determined I would shine in a gold dress. I got into it, took one look in the mirror and blew up.

"What the hell is this all about? I look like Sophie Tucker. I'm not the last of the red-hot mammas, goddammit, I'm a vestal virgin in a temple!"

Off went the wig, off went the dress and off went the mezzo.

The next day, the same garb reappeared, and the next, and the next, until one day they came back with another dress in brown. It wasn't a warm, attractive shade of brown, either. I'd gone from gold to mud, and at this juncture, the day before dress rehearsal, I called my manager, Ronald Wilford.

"Listen, Ronald, you're on!" I said firmly into the mouthpiece. "This is going to be your shining moment. If my costumes don't come in here perfect tomorrow, I'm walking!"

I meant it, and Ronald knew it.

The next day, two suitable garments appeared in my dressing room, along with my appropriately virginal wig of lustrous brown tresses.

I wasn't just having a temper tantrum. As with my Tancredi cloak, I *had* to put my foot down. My entire energies would be spent on the creation of Adalgisa, and the mechanics and accouterments had to be perfect. All I needed my first night out was a silly-looking wig or a ludicrous dress.

Thanks to Ronald, that was one crisis easily resolved, but the next one involved a lot more attention and angst. This time, only I was responsible for it, and it was a gamble that could make or break my debut.

Adalgisa's Act I entrance comes after Norma finishes the *"Casta Diva,"* her hymn to the moon goddess, and, after a powerful ensemble, leaves with all the Druids.

The stage is bare until, accompanied by a stately, poignant melody, Adalgisa enters and sings her recitative and aria, *"Sgombra è la sacra selva"* ("The sacred grove is cleared"). The words translate thusly:

> The sacred grove is cleared:
> the rites are fulfilled.
> At last I can sigh unseen here,

where for the first time
I met that fatal Roman
who has made me rebel
to the temple and to the god.
Let it be the last time, at least!
Vain hope!
An irresistible force draws me hither,
and on that dear face
my heart feasts,
and the very breeze that blows
repeats for me the sound of his dear voice.

Protect me, O god, for pity's sake!
Protect me!
I am lost, lost.
Great god, have mercy,
I am lost.

As you can see, Adalgisa no longer qualifies for temple duty. My problem was how to present this girl to her audience for the first time, and I had an idea.

A long time ago, Bentz Horne had told me, "Peanut, if you want to get people's attention and hold it, sing softly." Like a piece in a jigsaw puzzle, Dad's advice fit perfectly. I decided to take a calculated risk on opening night.

Most Adalgisas enter on the crest of a wave of sound; "The sacred grove is cleared," they sing forcefully, but that wasn't the way I would do it. To me, Adalgisa's entrance called for quiet, reflective singing, and not just to grab people's attention: it was in keeping with Adalgisa's character. I would begin the recitative pianissimo, very softly, from all the way backstage, and walk downstage holding it to front and center. I would sing softly because I felt *she* would sing softly. It was a calculated risk on two counts—

177

first, that it would be effective and, second, that I'd be heard! Even though the orchestra is silent, pianissimo from the back of the stage simply might not carry over the footlights.

My then-press agent sat in on one rehearsal and spoke to me afterward.

"You know, Jackie, those are the first notes you're ever going to sing at the Metropolitan. Don't you think you should sing them a little louder?"

"Go to hell," I answered. "Just get out of here."

Though he was speaking as my press agent and friend, I was mad at him for throwing a monkey wrench into my plans. I wanted reassurance, not criticism, but it wasn't forthcoming. I was all alone; this was "my baby." "Oh, my God," I thought, "he said it wasn't right; maybe I'd better sing it louder." I was worried, because my plan called for incredible breath support. It was like a control pitcher threading the ball *past* the batter rather than mowing him down with a fastball. By going pianissimo, I was tossing a vocal change-up. My press agent had correctly pointed out that, since it was my debut, I'd be on pins and needles anyway and my breath might be a little shaky right at the beginning. Why put my technique to such a rigorous test on the very first notes? I vacillated for a brief time, but finally shook off his warning. I'd made up my mind that this was the way I would do it, and that was that. I knew one thing, though: no Adalgisa had entered that way before, and, unless it worked, no Adalgisa ever would again!

Dress rehearsal came and, as usual, could have been called Dress Bedlam. Jim Nabors was there and later told me he was going back to television where everything was calm. He'd never seen such confusion backstage.

The rehearsal went well, however, and after my final exit, knowing that it would be my last opportunity to hear Joan in full regalia, I slipped out into the audience in costume to watch the final act. I was standing at the side of the orchestra in the darkened hall when someone came and stood behind me. I was too involved with listening to acknowledge anyone, but at the end of Norma's plea to her father, *"Deh! non volerli vittime,"* I was so moved I said aloud, "My God, I forget sometimes how fantastic she is!"

"You are not so bad yourself, Miss Horne," said the person behind me. I turned and found myself face to face with Rudolf Bing.

All systems were go for the big night, with one rather glaring exception. Mother was coming East for the event, and Auntie Maybelle would be there, along with cousin Jeanne Hokanson Hadley and her husband, Jack. One very important person would not be at my Met debut, however: my husband, Henry Lewis.

The truth is that Henry and I had been experiencing difficulties for the past four years. Angela's birth had brought us together in the special way a child unites parents, but our careers *were* getting in the way, or, I should say, *my* career was getting in the way. As my star rose, our troubles deepened.

I certainly would have had a career without Henry, but it was he who really led me into the paths of *bel canto*. Ricky Bonynge, among others, pointed the way, but it was Henry who actually hacked through the underbrush. He labored and sweated and did everything he could to teach me the style. He wrote cadenzas, arpeggios and two-octave drops which were both true to the period and showcased my voice. All this he did, often under immense time pressure.

Once, in 1962, I was asked to sing Donizetti's *La Fille du Régiment* for a student performance in San Francisco. Marie, the daughter, is usually sung by a coloratura soprano such as Pons or Sills, but none of the Donizetti parts are that high, because they were written for *bel canto* singers. I learned the part quickly and Henry was writing cadenzas up to the last minute. A cadenza is an elaborate flourish ornamenting a final cadence at any point in an aria.

In *da capo* arias, there are three opportunities for cadenzas and the last is reserved for the "best shot," to show off the singer's vocal virtuosity. Because of many production snags, *La Fille* was not really polished for its opening—actually, it was a mess and Kurt Adler knew it. He came to me after the performance and apologized. "Even *we* don't do things this badly," he moaned.

We just weren't ready to go on, and I had to keep changing my cadenzas, which meant the conductor, Oliviero de Fabritiis, had to figure out how to accompany me. Cadenzas are free-wheeling, but they're also supposed to adhere to the main body of the work. Unfortunately, the trunk wasn't supporting its branches, and at the opening performance I reached the final cadenza, crossed my fingers and launched into my vocal pyrotechnics, hoping the conductor would come along for the ride. De Fabritiis did yeoman service in the pit and kept the orchestra going in the face of many surprises from Marie. At the curtain call, he came onstage and, as we stood hand in hand, smiling and bowing, he leaned over, kissed my hand and said,

"Signora, you don't need a conductor, you need a prophet."

Well, Henry Lewis was my prophet and my teacher and my right hand. I depended upon him for advice and support, but, because my fame had eclipsed his, he was known in some circles as "Mr. Horne." We both knew it wasn't true, but sometimes when people brought up the subject, I'd get furious and start to fight, and then Henry would get angry at *me*. One time, we had a slam-bang argument after I'd lit into an acquaintance who'd made a dumb remark.

"Don't *defend* me," Henry said sternly. "Don't you *dare* defend me, because there's nothing to defend! Listen, I was the main breadwinner of this family all those years. I knew if you became successful you'd make more money than I could ever make in my career, because you're a diva! But I've got my *own* career, so *don't* defend me!! If you want to make me feel good, then try to reconcile your role as Mrs. Henry Lewis with being Marilyn Horne!"

Ricky Bonynge had never tried to make a career away from Joan; he was primarily his wife's conductor. Henry was, first and foremost, a conductor with his own orchestra, but at the beginning his career had been tied to mine, and for many years the New Jersey Symphony had sold a great many tickets because of a certain featured soloist. Eventually, the situation became too much for Henry to take, and though I understood how he felt, I still didn't think there was much that could be done about it.

"Your career comes first," he complained. "Next is Angela, and if there's anything left over, I come a poor third." As a husband, he wanted me to be the "little woman" waiting at home to attend him, while at the same time reigning supreme as prima donna. The fact was, I was pouring so much energy into my career that there wasn't a lot left over for my home life. In addition, I guess I did put Henry in the position of being "Mr. Horne," because I *wanted* him to conduct for me and coach me and guide me. I'm only amazed we lasted as long as we did. How we managed to tread water for so many years is a tribute to both of us and our love, and before we got into wholesale fighting, we did have great moments together.

Apparently, my Met debut was not to be one of these moments.

Because of recording sessions with the Royal Philharmonic Orchestra in London, Henry was going to be out of the country at *Norma*'s opening. It was a perfect example of conflict in careers. As teacher, friend and coach, as well as husband, Henry should have been with me. He'd contributed so much to my success, he should have been there to enjoy it. He had a commitment, however, and though somewhere in my heart of hearts I felt the most important career moment of my life should have taken precedence over what was a relatively non-essential engagement, I accepted the fact he wouldn't be with me. Henry actually said to me he hadn't wanted to "interfere" with my big night. Perhaps his taking the London recording assignment had been a way of saying, "I don't want to be around you that night, so I'll arrange to be out of the country." Unable to face the possible hidden meanings in Henry's action, I buried the hurt and went about my business.

The Italians have an expression, *"in bocca al lupo"*—"in the mouth of the wolf"—which they use to wish someone luck. I was put in the mouths of many wolves the night of March 3, 1970. I accepted it gratefully, though, unlike some performers, I don't drag along any lucky talismans or go through any pre-performance rituals, other than vocalizing. I used to have a bunch of stuffed animals which had been given me over the years; I'd throw them into a plastic bag, lug them to the performance and set them up on my dressing table. One day, though, I took a look at my inanimate zoo and realized that those little creatures weren't doing anything; *I* was the one who had to sing—let them put *me* on *their* dressing table. No longer slave to superstitious nonsense, I swept out my menagerie with no dire effects.

I arrived at the Metropolitan on the big day with my regular bundles containing makeup, score and a thermos of hot tea. I went into the dressing room assigned me and began to prepare. There's usually a piano in my room—if there isn't, the management is respectfully requested to get one—and I vocalize. It takes up to thirty minutes to do my exercises, but before a concert or an opera I can do the whole shebang in twenty minutes. Those exercises are hard and some singers don't vocalize at all, but I think it's absolutely necessary. Most singers who don't vocalize take two acts to warm up, and I don't think it's fair to the audience to have singers warm up at its expense.

I did my vocalizing that night and then colleagues dropped by to chat and give good wishes. Again, Mr. Bing appeared, kissed my hand and wished me well. (If I dwell upon these gestures of a bygone era, it's in hopes that present administrators in certain opera houses will take the hint.) Joan, dressed and ready to go, stopped by, hugged and kissed me, and went off to the stage. The house lights were dimmed, the overture began and my Met debut was on its way.

In a short while, I found myself standing in the wings waiting to make my entrance. I wasn't nervous anymore—eager and excited, yes, but not afraid. I immediately put myself into the character and mood, which is easy in opera. I find I don't have to psych myself up, because the composer has already done a good deal of the preparation for the singer; the music paints a clear picture and you just follow your own sounds.

At the opening strains of Adalgisa's music, I became that young girl and moved onto the rear of the stage where a huge rock stood. I walked around the boulder and ran in quickly. I don't remember hearing any applause, though there may have been some—I'm sure Mom and Auntie Maybelle and the Hadleys must have slapped their hands together. The speedy entrance was my idea: I felt Adalgisa had "forgotten" the Druid meeting because she was agonizing over Pollione. She's like someone coming in late for church services. When she rushes into the sacred grove, she expects to find everyone there, but they're not; she's missed the sermon.

The house was absolutely still. Not a cough punctuated the brief moment of silence between the opening passage and my first words. I pushed against my diaphragm, just as Mrs. Luce had taught me, and opened my mouth to let loose a taut thread of pianissimo, and as I moved into the *messa di voce*, I felt the audience's presence and knew I was home!

As originally written, *Norma* is a four-scene, two-act opera, but the Met version was divided into four acts, and thus Adalgisa was finished after Act III, which ends with the magnificent *"Mira, o*

*Norma."* One of the most glorious weavings of melody in all music, in which the younger woman begs the High Priestess not to kill herself and to return to her lover for the sake of their children, the duet was sung by Joan and me with every ounce of available skill, finishing with the bright, brilliant cabaletta *"Sì, fino all'ore,"* in which the two women pledge their devotion to each other. By the time we finished, everyone in the opera house was sky-high.

The curtain fell on Act III and my debut was over. Joan and I stood in the center of the stage, hugging each other until it was time to step before the gold curtain to take our bows. I followed Joan through the parted gilt cloth and was met by a solid wall of applause that took my breath away. Joan stood stage right, bowing and smiling and gesturing toward me; I gazed back at her, smiling and calling, "Thank you, thank you." The next thing I knew, Joan was gone. She had left me alone on the stage, a beautiful and generous gesture from one artist to another, one friend to another, which I'll never forget. Joan Sutherland was not only willing to share the spotlight, she turned the lights on *me* full force.

I saw her standing in the wings applauding. Next to her stood Rudolf Bing and next to him, his hands flashing back and forth with enthusiastic claps, was my husband, Henry Lewis.

I thought I was hallucinating, but I could only stare at him for a moment. The house still reverberated with cheers and I stepped forward to the edge of the stage. In the first row sat the legendary Maria Jeritza, and suddenly she was on her feet. Following her lead, the entire audience rose *en masse.* I looked all around that golden house from the topmost tier to the very pit and drank in every sight and every sound. Somewhere in the audience, Mother and Auntie Maybelle stood applauding till their hands were sore, tears rolling down their cheeks. I saw everything through my own tears.

This was the fulfillment of my dreams, the goal I'd pursued for so many, many years, and I knew, somehow, some way, my father was with me. I stepped off the stage and walked into the embrace of my husband.

# XIII

## *The Met and I*

High among the list of satisfactions
is the arrival of Marilyn Horne upon this
stage, years overdue but anyway here at
last, in the full prime of her voice and
dramatic assurance. Hers is a sound that
fills the house, a luscious and plangent
tone across the full tonal range of the
female voice—all the way from deep
contralto to somewhere high up in soprano
territory. Miss Horne can act too, and
what is even more rare, she can *give*—to
her colleagues on stage and to the total
artistic result. As Adalgisa she passed
up many opportunities for personal
glorification in favor of close and
supportive teamwork. The very best
moments of the evening, in fact, were the
Sutherland/Horne ensembles; and "Mira, O
Norma" was an unforgettable blend of two
distinctive but totally compatible voices
and personalities.

George Movshon,
*High Fidelity/Musical America*

Horne's entrance in the first act was
not a big voice cut down; it was a big
voice far away, an eerie effect and a
triumph of technique.

Francis Robinson in
*Celebration*

As we threaded our way backstage, Henry explained how he'd come to be there. The London recordings had gone quicker than expected and he'd made special arrangements to have cars waiting in London and New York to speed him directly from the final recording session to the performance in New York. The plane between the cars, alas, had had to be rerouted to pick up passengers, so Henry had lost a few hours, but he had arrived a little before ten p.m. and raced to the Metropolitan, arriving in time to witness the ovation.

I returned to a dressing room blockaded with eighty, ninety, maybe a hundred floral tributes overflowing into the hall. I plowed my way through the tulips, anemones, orchids, roses, asters and balloons and flopped down on a couch to collect my thoughts. Onstage, *Norma* was going into the final phase, but for me the night was over. My goal had been achieved.

The day after *Norma*, Rudolf Bing offered me the top mezzo coloratura role at the Met, Rosina in *Il Barbiere di Siviglia*. He called my manager, Ronald Wilford, told him the fee for *Norma* —seventeen hundred and fifty dollars per Adalgisa—was ridiculous, actually *tore* up my contract and put me on top salary. In the future, like any superstar, I'd be paid the highest amount, four thousand dollars. Usually, this procedure is reversed—personal managers call opera directors to get higher fees—but by initiating the upgrade Rudolf Bing was, I think, endeavoring to make amends for the unnecessary delay in my debut. He was also a shrewd businessman and his move was smart public relations. Since my triumph was overwhelming, Ronald would have negotiated my salary into the stratosphere at the next juncture anyway. Bing wisely took the opportunity to be magnanimous. He was a long time opening the door, but once I was on the threshold, he swept me up and carried me over.

Bing always was the gentleman in negotiations with me, though not always above trying to pull off cozy deals here and there. Later that year, I was to sing at Covent Garden, outside of which was the central produce market for London made famous by Eliza Doolittle and *My Fair Lady*. Before I left for England, I was called at home by Mr. Bing.

"Hello, Miss Horne. I've called to offer you a wonderful opportunity," said the General Director, oozing cordiality. A strange, hollow sound surrounded his voice.

"Hello, Mr. Bing. You sound as though you're down a well." The minute the words were out of my mouth, I realized Bing was using a conference phone. There were probably a bunch of people sitting around listening to our remarks—I could hear tittering in the background.

Mr. Bing proceeded with the conversation as though it were strictly *entre nous*. "Well, Miss Horne, I called to tell you we're putting together a June festival and I'm prepared to offer you Rosina in the *Barber*."

Obviously, Bing had thrown my name before the lions in his office. He was calling me and not Ronald because he had to go directly to the source, probably to impress the gentlemen gathered around the amplifier. Anyway, I was sure he'd checked my schedule and knew damn well I was busy. Maybe he thought a direct plea from him would get me to drop my commitment.

"When was that?" I asked innocently.

"This June," repeated Bing.

"I'm so sorry, I'm not available, Mr. Bing. I'll be at Covent Garden."

"My dear Miss Horne," answered the General Director, readying his putdown of any other opera house, "what do you do at Covent Garden?"

"Why, I sell fruits and vegetables, Mr. Bing!"

My phone audience howled with laughter!

I liked dealing with Rudolf Bing, but by the time I finally made it to the Met, he was near retirement, and left at the end of the 1971–72 season. My future at Lincoln Center would be linked with a bright, warm, witty man from Sweden named Goeran Gentele.

The ways of the Metropolitan were continuing strange. You'd think that, as a result of *Norma's* incredible success, Joan and I would be invited to appear together again, but we never were. "Can you believe," I asked in one newspaper interview, "that the Metropolitan Opera has the most winning combination they have had since Flagstad and Melchior, and they have not planned another opera for us?" It was true, however, and thereafter Joan and I went our separate ways at the Met.

By this time, we had become grist for the gossip mill. At one interview, I was asked by an inquiring idiot if there was any truth to the rumor that we were lesbians! To this brilliant query, I replied,

"Of course. We're just like Semiramide and Arsace—only *she's* the boy because she's taller."

I learned a long time ago to pay no attention to backstage blather. In the world of calumny, people repeat gossip they don't even believe themselves just to feel important. I'm skeptical when told anything secondhand, and give credence only to what I see or hear myself or learn from a few reliable sources. Then I shut up if it's destructive, or let fly if it's a good juicy story.

Such rumors still pop up now and again, but I don't think anybody believes them. In our case, the evidence against it is too overwhelming!

Joan and I made a fabulous team, and the pity is, after a Chicago *Semiramide* in 1971, we did not appear together again for nearly a decade. I'm not sure why—maybe I had become so big I began to be viewed more as a competitor than a complement—but, whatever the reason, Joan and I finally did get back together in September 1982 for *Norma* in San Francisco. I went to the West Coast feeling sad as well as excited. Joan was fifty-six years old, perhaps the oldest woman ever to sing Norma, and I was forty-eight. I couldn't help thinking this might be our last set of *Norma*'s.

Ha! We dazzled both the critics and the public. We may even have sung better than we ever had, even in *Norma* together twelve years before. Those San Francisco performances weren't the end. Be prepared. Sutherland and Horne may yet ring in the millennium with *"Mira, o Norma."*

In the next few years, I had long stretches of work at the Metropolitan and, because of those engagements, was able to curtail my European career. That enabled me to stay home with Angela and take part in her growing-up years. When she was around seven, I began to travel again, but still endeavored to be available for special occasions. Once, Angela was in the Met's *Hansel and Gretel* while I was scheduled for a concert in Syracuse, New York. I watched Angela play a gingerbread girl in the dress rehearsal before a full audience, and then a private chartered plane flew me up to Syracuse to perform. Angela may not remember all the hours I logged and the things I went through, but, given the perimeters of our artistic nest, she got all there was to give.

Another major problem was household help. Marty Katz remembers me calling home from the Tampa, Florida, airport one time and, upon receiving the news that the couple working for us had quit, burst out crying on the spot.

For all that, however, the Lewis family became staples of Sunday magazines, and because we were good copy, journalist after journalist extolled our life together, making much of our "salt and pepper" marriage and its product, Angela. On the surface, we were a neat, tidy package of artistic personalities getting along as marrieds and professionals. I was Mrs. Bubbly Loudmouth, Henry was Mr. Reserved Intelligence and Angela was Baby Snooks. Interviewed by a magazine for a series on children of famous parents, Angela, age seven, had this to say about us:

> She sings and Daddy conducts.
> Mom uses her voice. I think that's harder than conducting because you're using up your voice when you sing. My Mom sure sings loud. I can sing higher than she can and I like rock 'n' roll because I like to jazz around.

We weren't trying to pull the wool over anyone's eyes—we *were* a happy family in many respects. Henry and I were still good friends and colleagues who were willing to share our thoughts. When I look over some of the rosy reports of our domestic life in the early Seventies, though, I see, under the tip of compatibility, the iceberg of frozen discontent. Henry's resentments were building up, and he offered clues to his feelings with such quotes as "When she's been on tour, or like now, when she's in the middle of a heavy rehearsal schedule at the Met, she comes home and all she wants to do is sit down and put her feet up. . . . Yet I feel okay, now my wife's home and I can relax. I mean I can understand that she's tired and all that, but I've been working hard here at home on all the millions of things I have to do with my orchestra."

"And all that . . ." Henry had a picture of a wife and mother in his head that I wasn't fitting properly. Even if I could have read all the danger signals clearly, however, there was nothing I could have done. Henry and I were drifting apart, and our marriage had only a few more years to run.

In December of 1970, the Board of Directors of the Metropolitan Opera had announced that Goeran Gentele, Director of the Royal Opera House in Stockholm, Sweden, would succeed Rudolf Bing as General Manager in July 1972. As far as musical managerial arrangements went, this was practically a love match. The Swede, an outgoing, energetic man trained in the theatre, was vastly different from the reserved, autocratic Rudolf Bing, and Gentele's arrival was eagerly awaited. In creating his team, Gentele asked a new friend, Schuyler Chapin, to be second-in-command. Chapin, involved in the music world for many years, had recently left his job as vice president in charge of the Masterwork Series at Columbia Records to move to Lincoln Center, where he had worked closely with Leonard Bernstein.

Most opera houses plan on works and artists at least two or three seasons ahead, to insure the availability of performers, directors and designers. Some companies are capable of calling one or two months in advance to try to secure my services, but most managements are quite reasonable. *Norma's* phenomenal success put me on the Met's scheduling list and in those days I could accommodate them.

In June 1970, Joan and I took *Norma* to Covent Garden, and I also took my mother. She was not really well, but had recovered enough to get around and I wanted to show her Europe. We even went to Italy for a visit and she had a wonderful time, falling under the same Mediterranean spell as her daughter had.

I filled out the 1969–70 season with *Norma's* while anticipating with delight my next Met role—Rosina in Rossini's *Il Barbiere di Siviglia.*

As you may have gathered by now, Gioacchino Rossini is especially dear to me. The son of a trumpet player and a soprano, Rossini was born in a musical trunk, so to speak, in 1792, and grew up in the theatre. He was an incredibly attractive and musically gifted youth, and his father and uncle thought of turning him into a castrato, but Mama wouldn't hear of it and saved him from the knife. He called himself a "lazybones," but by fifteen was an accomplished singer, could play the violin, horn and harpsichord and had become an accompanist and conductor.

Between 1808 and 1828, this "lazybones" wrote forty operas, at first *opere buffe*, in which he used animated ensembles and finales and unusual rhythms, restored the orchestra to its rightful place of prominence and put the singer at the service of music. In 1812, he wrote *The Touchstone* and used his crescendo effect for the first time. Don Basilio's aria, *"La Calunnia,"* in the *Barber* is a prime example of it, as the orchestra vividly describes the rapid spread of slander by increasing in sound and speed. Whether Rossini actually created the form is a matter of contention, but certainly no one used it to better effect. In 1813, he wrote *Tancredi*, his first *opera seria*, and one of my favorites.

During his productive period, Rossini fell in love with and married the soprano Isabella Colbran, and moved with her to Paris, where he was nicknamed "Monsieur Crescendo." There he wrote *Le Siège de Corinthe* or *L'Assedio di Corinto*, and became part of Parisian high life. Did any other singer ever have so many great operas written for her as Colbran? I think not. Tiring of Colbran, Rossini shipped her off to stay with his widowed father and, after she died in 1845, married a courtesan type named Olympe Pélissier. Olympe coddled Rossini rather than pushed him, as Isabella had. After a brief trip to Italy, he returned in 1855 to spend the rest of his days in Paris, where until his death in 1868 his reputation as a wit and an epicure flourished, and he occasionally penned salon pieces but never operas. It's mind-boggling to think that he stopped writing operas at thirty-seven and lived another forty years. Musicologists and psychologists are still trying to figure it out. One theory is that he suffered great depression and wasn't cured until five years before his death. I can't help wondering what a little Lithium might have helped produce.

My generation knew very little of Rossini except for *Il Barbiere* and, of course, the overture to his last opera, *William Tell*, the rousing call which signaled the arrival of "The Lone Ranger" on the radio waves.

Rossini was twenty-three years old when he wrote *Il Barbiere*. The opera, based on a satirical play by Beaumarchais, took him thirteen days to complete.

In the opera, Rosina is the ward of Dr. Bartolo, who keeps her imprisoned in his house. Count Almaviva catches a glimpse of her, enlists the aid of the local factotum, the barber Figaro, and, disguising himself as a poor student, seeks to win the lovely girl. After much intrigue and comedy during the course of two sparkling, melodious acts, boy does get girl, proving that love conquers all, but a bribe here and there helps.

Rosina was written for a mezzo coloratura, but over the years has been sung by sopranos, too. Honestly, sopranos are never satisfied; as if they didn't have ninety percent of the operatic leads already, they have to poach one of the few big mezzo ones, too—and they can't keep their hands off Carmen, either! I simply adore the role of Rosina. Delicious to sing *and* to act, the Rossini "bounce" so evident in Rosina's character also enlivens Isabella in *L'Italiana in Algeri*. They're like the Dolly Sisters of *bel canto*.

*Il Barbiere* opened in 1971 and marked my first Met primadonna starring role. I was joined by a fine cast: Sherrill Milnes as Figaro, Fernando Corena as Dr. Bartolo and Giorgio Tozzi as the music master, Don Basilio. *Il Barbiere* truly was a romp, and even as I delighted in creating my first Met Rosina, I looked forward to my next. It became one of the roles most associated with me and I'm aching to do it once more before putting "her" away.

Short of making a Met debut, the juiciest plum is having the opening night of a season, and before he departed, Bing had arranged for me and Jimmy McCracken to begin the 1972 season in

Wagner's *Tannhäuser*—I was still flirting with the soprano roles. Despite the fact that Elisabeth would be my first real venture into the Wagnerian repertoire, and therefore very exciting, I had mixed feelings about the production, a tired old warhorse of shabby sets and frayed costumes and not a very glittering vehicle for the opening.

Enter Mr. Gentele.

The Swedish director came for preliminary meetings during the winter of 1971, and we got along splendidly; indeed, his enthusiasm for my work was very high and, after we talked together, I knew my Met career would be on the express lane. Here was a general manager speaking seriously of mounting not only *bel canto* works, but baroque and nineteenth-century French operas as well. The future looked so promising, it was almost scary, and when Gentele announced a switch in the opening-night selection, I was even happier.

Gentele had accepted the *Tannhäuser* and the rest of the repertoire bequeathed by the departing director because, like all incoming directors, he found himself presented with a schedule that had been planned two or three seasons ahead. Then he discovered that the *Tannhäuser* production was one of the seediest in the house and, indeed, its selection for the opening had already been dubbed "Bing's Revenge." He immediately set about remedying the situation, bearing in mind that a substitute choice had to suit his stars: Jimmy, me and the baritone Tom Krause.

If a mezzo said her prayers before she went to bed, they might end ". . . and please, God, give me *Carmen* for opening night at the Met." My prayers were answered, and Jimmy, Tom and I quickly agreed to do the Bizet. There were still snags, though. The latest Met production of *Carmen* had been a disaster, so Gentele had to go to the Board to get money for a new production. He got it, and also assigned himself as director. That man was gutsy!

Gentele threw himself into the project, and at the same time threw out the accepted *Carmen*, returning to the original concept which had premiered at the Opéra-Comique in Paris on March 3, 1875. Spoken dialogue had been employed then, and it was only later that musical recitative had been substituted by Bizet's friend Ernest Guiraud, which was the version of *Carmen* currently heard around the world. When Gentele engaged the services of Leonard Bernstein as conductor and Josef Svoboda as lighting and set designer, I felt certain the outcome would be an unmitigated triumph. We were all up for the occasion, and only one ominous note would have marred the general exhilaration, had we known about it. Tom Krause's wife Jan read cards and, while casting the deck, "saw something awful." She told her husband that a catastrophe was in the cards for Carmen. Though I'm pretty down-to-earth, I have a healthy respect for the supernatural—Carmen herself reads the cards—and Mrs. Krause's prediction would have concerned me. Fortunately, I didn't find out about it until some months later.

During the winter, spring and early summer of 1972, Gentele commuted from Sweden to New York, spending much time putting *Carmen* together. During the preliminary sessions, the work was discussed and re-discussed, analyzed and re-analyzed, and when there were unresolved points, Gentele answered, "We'll work things out in rehearsal." A former actor himself, he knew that artists and directors flourish in a give-and-take situation; he never said, "You have to do this" or "You have to do that." Rarely had I been involved in such a splendid pre-production period, and it thrilled me to be part of the operatic "dream" of Goeran Gentele.

His dream became his memorial. On July 18, 1972, while vacationing in Sardinia, Goeran Gentele was killed in an automobile accident.

The sudden death of this vital man turned our Metropolitan

dream world into a nightmare. What was to have been a monumental opening to a new, glorious era was now the abandoned husk of an idea, conceived, assigned and designed but not yet executed. The driving force, the man who promised to "work things out in rehearsal," was gone; however, we had to go on.

Schuyler Chapin was appointed acting general manager and rumors came thick and fast as to who was going to take over the direction of *Carmen*. Jerome Robbins was mentioned and then it was thought Bernstein himself would do the staging, in collaboration with the designer, Josef Svoboda. For a time, one guess was as good as another. Then I received a phone call from Schuyler,

"Jackie, we've got a director, his name is Bodo Igesz."

"Bodo who?" I answered.

That was my introduction to the thirty-seven-year-old Dutch-born stage director of the Met. Bodo had taken over productions from other directors, but had never before had his own new production at the Met. He had been working with Gentele on the *Carmen* and, in many instances, knew what the late director had had in mind, but even as we pooled our knowledge of the Gentele concept, there were great unknown patches for all of us. Bodo came on board and there were more changes and shifts. Donald Gramm replaced James Morris as Zuniga, and after Teresa Stratas was ordered by her doctor not to sing for three months, Adriana Maliponte was engaged as Micaëla. By August 30, we were well into rehearsals; however, neither Miss Maliponte nor Tom Krause had been able to join us!

I was troubled about a number of other things in the *Carmen*, as well. To begin with, I didn't think the spoken dialogue would work. I thought English-speaking audiences were comfortable with the Guiraud recitatives but would not be with French dialogue, but I finally had to yield to Lenny and Gentele. As it turned out, I was categorically wrong. Next came my misery over the *mise-en-scène*. With all due respect to Svoboda, the sets didn't thrill me; they were stark and modern, and I would have preferred them realistic. Once more, I was overruled. My biggest worry was over the wall-to-wall, ceiling-to-ceiling carpeting Svoboda had slapped on the set. You don't have to work for an audio engineering firm to know that material *absorbs* sound. I called in Henry and Ronald Wilford, among others, to listen, and was satisfied only when they assured me all was all right.

I let the carpet stay, with one alteration. In the name of interior decoration, the prompter's box had been eliminated. I wanted it put back.

The prompter's box is a small compartment usually placed in the middle of the footlights and covered on three sides. The prompter inside is visible only to the participants onstage and his job is to cue the singers by giving them the first words—sometimes the prompter gets carried away and you can hear the cues in the topmost row of the balcony. In Europe, the prompter's box is *de rigueur*; La Scala even has two of them, one for soloists and one for the chorus. There are many artists so tied to the prompter they never take their eyes off him, but I'm from the American school and usually don't need one. Nevertheless, I don't think you can do opera in a repertory company without one. He or she is absolutely indispensable in an emergency and even without an emergency it's nice to know the prompter's there, just in case. That person in the box holds the production together during a performance, and I didn't intend to let them sweep him under Svoboda's carpet. Chalk the box up as a victory for me—it went back.

I won another victory as well, and it's a good thing I did, or I might not be here to be telling you about it. Jimmy McCracken's a pussycat, but when he gets into a part, look out! When we started rehearsing the final scene, in which Don José stabs Carmen as she tries to go past him into the bullfight arena, I heard a click and saw a real switchblade in Jimmy's hand! I instantly stopped the proceedings and announced,

"There's no way you're going to get me on that stage if Jimmy McCracken has a real knife."

Jimmy was disarmed and I lived to die again. Later, during a performance, the chorus didn't hold him back and he took hold of me and threw me down on the stage as I'd *never* been thrown before. Fortunately, I'd lost the battle of the carpet, so my fall was cushioned.

His intensity onstage backfired at *Carmen's* jam-packed dress rehearsal, too. At one point, Don José starts getting passionate with Carmen and wants to make love to her. Jimmy was getting into position, and at the same time trying to get his sword off so he could embrace me. The scabbard wouldn't loosen and he kept yanking, tugging and pulling as he declaimed, *"Ah, que je t'aime, Carmen, que je t'aime!"* It was irresistible and, in an audible English *ad lib*, I answered his impassioned declaration of love with, "Sure, as soon as you take the sword off!"

Jimmy McCracken is great to work with. He gives so much and cares so much that you have to love him. I admire him, too, because he walked away from the Met when they treated him like a second-class citizen by denying him television roles and giving the plums to other tenors.

Opening night came not on the traditional Monday, but on Tuesday, September 19, 1972. Why? Because Monday was Yom Kippur. There wasn't one portent missing in this production!

My dressing room was a midtown Botanical Garden and among the bouquets were the following notes:

[Attached to a stuffed cow] Merde for tonight. I love you and this is *no* bull. Zuniga [Donald Gramm]

Can't be there. Losing my head as I know the audience will tonight over you. Love Beverly Sills [who was singing *Maria Stuarda* across the plaza]

Marion and I send our best for tonight. I would have loved to kill a kosher bull for you tonight. God bless. Marion and Bob Merrill

Thinking of you. Merde and lots of love. Marit [Gentele's wife, who telegraphed from Sweden]

and

Jackie, you are a wonder. Be as wonderful tonight. Love, Lenny

*Carmen*, the "original" version of *Carmen Jones*, is the story of the soldier Don José who falls in love with the gypsy Carmen; gives up his good girlfriend, Micaëla; deserts the army to become a smuggler; and, when the object of his passionate affection turns her attentions to the bullfighter Escamillo, kills her. In our *Carmen*, Don José became a force to be reckoned with rather than a simple country boy falling under the spell of a hot-blooded temptress, and when the curtain rose to the strains of the Fate motif and a single shaft of light fell on Don José, the audience knew something special was coming. Oh, and was it ever special!

For my own part, I had learned a great deal from the 1968 production of *Carmen* I had done for Sarah Caldwell in Boston. My Carmen was not a cardboard Theda Bara vamp, nor a spitcurled, moist-lipped Rita Hayworth. She was an earthy, humorous, passionate gypsy. I even played my own castanets! Traditionally, the operatic gypsy pretends to be using the castanets while a percussionist in the orchestra does the actual clicks and clacks, or else plays them herself, but to a fake rhythm. Early on, however, Lenny Bernstein told me I should learn to play them myself as written in the score, and it made a difference. Alvin Ailey choreographed the *Carmen*, and, though no La Argentina, thanks to Alvin I was even commended for my *dancing*.

The entire production was dazzling, from start to finish. David Walker's costumes—he called them "clothes"—were a Goyaesque blend of browns and blacks, and in the last act I wore a magnificent white lace gown. I was indeed the "Bride of Death," accepting my fate, as Lenny put it, "dressed to the nines."

That night, the critics were ecstatic, the public was ecstatic and all of us associated with the opera were ecstatic. The tragic and terrible circumstances leading up to that moment were not forgotten. We all wanted this *Carmen* to be special for Goeran Gentele, and it was.

After the performance, Jim Nabors and Farol and Bud Seretean gave a party in the Terrace Room of the Plaza Hotel. Though I don't like parties, this one was special. The Terrace Room filled with friends is an experience everyone should have! I didn't get there until late, however. The *Carmen* curtain came down at 11:50, and between well-wishers, taking off makeup, showering and putting on makeup, it was 1:30 a.m. before I arrived. I got not a single bite at the party, and at six a.m. my friend Barbara Kraft made scrambled eggs for me at home. (We had a houseful, but our house was large and was able to accommodate Barb and her daughter Jennifer and all my family.)

The next day, I could have gone into a Rip Van Winkle snooze and, in fact, did sleep most of the day. When I woke, it was to phone call after phone call, and in the days that followed came letter after letter, one of which I'll share.

Dearest Marilyn,

You were magnificent. Of course I was not surprised. I hope you enjoyed the "grunt" that oozed out of the audience at the end of your first aria—it was a for-real reaction and I was proud to be a part of that happy group.

With all great admiration,

Lena Horne

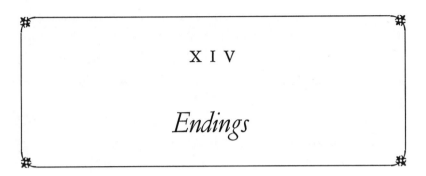

X I V

*Endings*

"Three cheers for Carmen!"
Virgil Thomson in a letter to Schuyler Chapin

*Carmen* put me squarely before the public. With this production, one critic wrote, I "dispelled the benign shadow of Joan Sutherland" and emerged as a star in my own right. Other than my appearance in *Il Barbiere*, I had only been linked with Joan in the eyes of New York's audiences, and one cannot make a grand career as a second banana. *Carmen* changed everything. Now I was such a big deal, I could make my *own* decisions, because I knew everything!

The 1972–73 season marked the Fiftieth Anniversary of the New Jersey Symphony. Henry was scheduled to make his own Met debut conducting *La Bohème* and, after Bernstein's half-dozen performances of *Carmen*, would take up the baton for that production, too. Michael Tilson Thomas was supposed to have taken over, but had pulled out and Schuyler had asked Henry to do it instead. Professionally, both of us were doing very well—why, according to the *Ladies' Home Journal* of September 1972, the Lewises were among America's twenty-five most influential couples, along with Martha and John Mitchell, Jean and Walter Kerr and Masters and Johnson!

On October 10, 1972, the clue for 30 down in the *New York Times* Crossword Puzzle was, "Miss Horne's milieu."

Answer: O

       P

       E

       R

       A

I had arrived.


Had Goeran Gentele lived, things might have turned out differently for me and the Met. His theatre experience was vast and his ingratiating personality made people want to work for him. The sweetest personality in the world, however, could have soured under the kind of financial problems brewing in the Met. Gentele had come from a state-supported arts program, the kind I had experienced in Gelsenkirchen, and whether he could have handled the difficulties intrinsic to the privately endowed institution any better can only be a matter of speculation.

Shortly thereafter, Schuyler Chapin was appointed permanent General Manager and I had another strong ally in the main office, but, as it turned out, he was never in a secure enough position with the Board of Trustees to get their wholehearted approval. In three years, he was ousted.

During the Seventies, I sang eight roles at the Metropolitan: Adalgisa, Rosina and Carmen, followed by Orfeo in Gluck's *Orfeo ed Euridice*, Isabella in Rossini's *L'Italiana in Algeri*, Fidès in Mey-

erbeer's *Le Prophète,* Amneris in Verdi's *Aïda* and the Princess
Eboli in his *Don Carlo.* It wasn't a bad track record, really, but I
had to travel all over the world to do Malcolm Graeme, Arsace,
Tancredi, Orlando and Rinaldo in operas which would have
brought credit to the New York house. Maybe Gentele would have
been able to produce them—who knows now?

The current production of *Orfeo ed Euridice* had come about at
the end of the Bing years, and had been a complete and utter failure. Putting it on the roster for the new administration had surely
been a cruel jest on Sir Rudolf's part. Goeran Gentele was committed to present *Orfeo,* but yours truly, knowing it was such a
miserable piece of work, should never have agreed to appear in it.
I was a *star,* though; I could do anything; I could single-handedly
lift this production out of the muck through the power of my glorious voice. See what happens when you start to believe your own
press?

On October 31, 1972, Mme. Marilyn Horne came a cropper,
along with the rest of *Orfeo ed Euridice.* Harold Schonberg wrote
in *The New York Times* that when I went out to get Euridice, I
"looked for all the world like a Brooklyn matron off to a P.T.A.
meeting." That was kind compared to some of the other cracks.
Charles Mackerras, the musical director of Sadler's Wells in London, made his debut in that production, and though his musical
contributions were well received, it was faint praise for poor Charlie. He was stuck with an ill-conceived mishmash, in which the
chorus sang from the orchestra pit while the corps de ballet danced
the action on stage. Good taste prevents me from going into more
details of this disaster, but I can tell you that Euridice was better
off in Hell than I was on that stage. Appearing in that fiasco was
one of the great moments of conceit in my life, and I learned a
valuable lesson from it.

Rossini's *L'Italiana in Algeri, (The Italian Girl in Algiers)*—a

Gentele choice for me—was a different story, however. It's an *opera buffa* about a shipwrecked young lady named Isabella who is washed up on the Algerian shore, where she immediately sings *"Cruda sorte"* ("Cruel fate"), a bravura aria which has shipwrecked many a singer. Isabella is looking for her missing boyfriend, Lindoro, now the slave of Mustafà, Bey of Algiers. Meanwhile, Mustafà is tired of his wife, Elvira, and wants to turn her over to Lindoro while he finds an Italian girl for himself. A group of pirates comes upon Isabella as well as another survivor, Taddeo, a rejected elderly suitor of Isabella's who has accompanied her on the search for Lindoro. They go before the Bey, and in one of those swift I-see-you—I-know-who-you-are scenes, Lindoro and Isabella recognize each other, but each is involved with another. The Bey wants his Italian girl and Lindoro must take Elvira. In Act II, all the unraveled threads are picked up, straightened out and stretched into a lovely finale. Isabella and Lindoro are united, thanks in good part to Isabella's assertiveness; Mustafà realizes the Italian girl is too much for him to handle, goes back to Elvira, forgives the young Italian couple and bids them *bon voyage* back to Italy.

Isabella is warm and loving, and at the same time a combination of Joan of Arc, Florence Nightingale and Susan B. Anthony. She knows exactly what she wants and makes sure she gets it, and that's how I played the role.

At the opening on November 10, 1973, Luigi Alva was Lindoro; Fernando Corena, Mustafà; and Theodor Uppman, Taddeo. Jean-Pierre Ponnelle made his debut as designer and director, and devised a terrific entrance for me. I was to come in backward and then turn around to face the audience. When he said backward, I thought he was crazy, but as it turned out, the plan worked, and it became one of my favorite entrances ever.

I don't know where he got the idea, but someone later told me that Maurice Schwartz of the Yiddish Theatre in New York always entered backward, whether in *A Ganze Mishuga* or *The Merchant of Venice*. A crowd would gather around him at the rear of the stage, and as the crowd parted, he would back toward the footlights gesticulating wildly till he reached the edge of the apron, then swiftly turn to acknowledge thunderous applause.

For my money, *L'Italiana* was as wonderful as *Orfeo* had been awful, but the reviews weren't totally laudatory. For my singing, yes, but for my acting, no, and the *Times* said the production was "vulgar." The public came, however, and, vulgar or no, liked it. If nothing else, the production provided the first opportunity anyone had had in over fifty years to hear this comic masterpiece at the Metropolitan. Since then, it's had two revivals with me and another is on the way.

Oh, if only some of that Rossini sparkle could have been transported over to 273 Elmwynd Drive in Orange, New Jersey!

I was still leading the life of the New Jersey suburban housewife on the one hand, and opera diva on the other. I did my own shopping and cooking and mothering and was just as involved in those station-wagon pickups as any average American woman. Fame didn't provide any diplomatic immunity in my everyday life; one afternoon I might be singing for United Nations Day at the UN, the next I could be car-pooling. Like other women of the day, I seemed to spend ninety percent of my time behind the wheel. Once, there was a little incident in the car which gave me yet another nickname, one used *only* by intimates.

I had driven over to South Orange Village and was circling around looking for a parking space. It was one of those "you're never going to get a space" days and I *kept* circling. I own a Mercedes sports coupe, and love that car; it's small and heavy, so I can whiz around with impunity. Suddenly, I spotted an opening and whooshed in. I had just shifted into park and was about to turn off the ignition when I looked in the rearview mirror and saw a huge Cadillac behind me, obviously waiting for the space I'd usurped. Not seeing it before was no excuse; I couldn't keep the space, and was shifting into reverse when the driver of the Cadillac got out and stormed over to the side of my Mercedes. He was huge and he was mad. I rolled down the window to explain, but he wasn't waiting for statements. He leaned over and growled slowly, loudly and nastily,

"You little . . . fat . . . Fuck!"

*"Fat!"* I answered back. *"Fat!"* That did it. I turned the ignition off, got out of the car and walked off as the big bruiser waved his fists at me.

"Go ahead, hit me, go ahead, hit me!!" I taunted him. He didn't, but the air was out of my tires when I returned. There was no way I would have given that creep the space, even though he had been there first, not after he called me . . . fat. The nickname, by the way, is "LFF." Nico condensed the phrase and calls me "Little." With his Greek accent, it comes out "Leetela."

It was about that time that Henry took an apartment in New York City. It was "our" pied-à-terre, it said in the papers, but in reality by May of 1974 he was spending the week in the city and coming home weekends to be with Angela. We hadn't been so distanced and angry since the time we had gone to a marriage counselor in California when Angela had been only about a year old. Then we were *screaming* at each other; now we were withdrawn, sullen, silent. Our beautiful home in New Jersey became a sylvan fortress occupied by two armed camps, his and mine. Naturally, we tried to protect Angela, and confined our battles to the hours when she was either asleep or away. Again, a big house helped. To this day, Angela doesn't believe me when I tell her how long her dad and I were estranged, because she didn't see it.

There were other troubles besides the ones at home. Mother's health continued to deteriorate. After the London *Norma* trip, there had been more surgery and more chemotherapy treatments in California. Early in April 1973, she came East again and joined me for the Met opening at Wolf Trap near Washington, but before that, she had made a "grand tour" of her youth, visiting relatives and friends in and around Bradford. She knew she was dying and wanted to say her farewells.

The Washington visit was agony for her, but she never stopped. In constant pain, she willed herself to keep going. She *had* to see everything and her courage would not yield. I watched her climb stair after stair after stair, wincing with each step, yet even in agony Berneice Horne kept her stride!

That spring, I was plagued by a chest infection, aggravated, I'm sure, by my mental state. My marriage was going and so was my mother. When the Met tour reached Dallas that May, I flew to Long Beach and stayed with Mother for a few days. We knew time was running out—a month, maybe two. The plan called for me to leave Long Beach on Monday, sing Tuesday in Minneapolis, return to New Jersey, sing a benefit for cancer research in Toronto on Sunday, then cancel everything and return to stay with Mother until the end.

On Friday, Gloria called. Mother was in a coma. I agonized over the situation because, though Dick, Gloria and Jay and his wife, Linda, were all nearby, no one other than a nurse was at the hospital. I made three phone calls to the Coast, begging my siblings to stay with her in shifts. I would cancel the Toronto benefit and arrive there on Saturday. They felt that because Mother was in a coma, there was no need for them to be there around the clock. "But what if she wakes up?" I cried. "Someone who loves her should be there."

While preparing to leave for Long Beach on Saturday morning, I received the phone call from Gloria. Mother had died. Alone.

Now that she was gone, the immediate need to go to Long Beach was over. I would do the Toronto benefit and then leave for the funeral.

How did I do it? I *had* to. The next evening, I walked onto the stage of the O'Keefe Auditorium and told the audience, "Ladies and gentlemen, this recital is dedicated to my mother, Berneice Horne, who died yesterday of cancer."

I went on and sang a program which included "Songs My Mother Taught Me." Berneice Horne *did* teach me, and I could think of no greater tribute.

Henry and I made one last desperate attempt to reconcile by going on a cruise with our friends Bud and Farol Seretean. I wasn't keen on the idea. Almost every vacation Henry and I had taken together had been a horror; in fact, I'd sworn not to go with him again. Henry didn't want to vacation, either, without Angela—she was at camp—but I optimistically hoped we might come to an understanding away from New Jersey, New York and work. In a way, we did. After a Stygian voyage, Henry returned immediately and I came home later with Farol. I told Henry there would be no more parties, no more socializing. I didn't want to put our friends through the strain of being with us anymore. Our marriage was finished.

Our professional lives, however, were still entwined. Henry was conducting the performances of *L'Italiana* at the Metropolitan, and the next months were sheer agony for me. I was onstage going through the motions, prancing before the public, trying to get a voice up and out over choked-back tears and emotions that were tearing me apart, and there he'd be in the pit waving his arms. I should have been singing Canio in *Pagliacci*; I could have brought down the house with *"Vesti la giubba."* Isabella probably saved me from a breakdown, because I had to keep going.

At first, we said nothing to anyone about our separation and kept our ends up—so well, in fact, that we fooled a lot of people. One evening during a performance, exhausted from singing and the strain of looking at Henry, I was in my dressing room between acts. I had twenty minutes to compose myself and was trying to relax when there was a knock on the door. Judy Blegen came rushing into the room, threw her arms around me and began sobbing.

"Jackie, you've got to help me. My marriage is falling apart. You're the only one I can talk to!" cried the soprano, and I spent the rest of my intermission comforting her and took her home for the night.

In October 1974, the dissolution of our marriage was officially announced. After fourteen years, we were finished—fourteen years, and of those I would say the first five were really happy, and the rest had been a slow dance to the killing ground.

Before, during and after the official announcement, my main concern was Angela. How could I tell her we were no longer a family? I was in psychotherapy at the time and recall going over this subject again and again, putting off the terrible duty of breaking up my child's world. For the first time in my professional life, I was refusing and canceling engagements right and left in order to be with Angela. I was supposed to do Rossini's *Stabat Mater* with Riccardo Muti—for the Pope!—but I just didn't have it. When I spoke to Ronald Wilford and told him I couldn't leave my daughter, he came through as he always does, and said, "Jackie, your personal life comes first!" The time came when we could no longer avoid telling Angela the truth. She wasn't an imbecile, and although she'd accepted her father's absence without question, sooner or later she was going to find out. I didn't want it to be from someone else or the newspapers or television, but I didn't know how to tell her.

One weekend, I was scheduled to sing a concert in New Orleans and decided to take Angela along with me. My plan was to talk with her myself on the trip and then be with her for the weekend. I didn't want to tell her, then leave her alone. Off we went to New Orleans, where my resolution wavered and I fell apart; I could barely look at Angela without tears welling up. I knew I couldn't speak to her calmly, so I called my shrink and cried over the phone, "What am I going to do? What am I going to do?" The analyst was wonderfully firm. "You must be strong," she said, "for your daughter's sake. She's at the age where *you* are her female role model. What you do, she will emulate, and you must now present to Angela a woman of great dignity and strength, someone she can look up to."

That did it. For Angela, I could be brave. For Angela, I had to be strong.

I took her with me to the concert, as I had so many times before, and she remained in the dressing room doing her homework while I performed. The door was ajar and she could hear what was going on even as she worked. I finished, took my bows and went into the dressing room, closing the door behind me. Angela looked up, smiled and said, "Gee, Mom, that sounded good." You have to understand that Angela is very reluctant to praise. She's my most demanding critic, and when she compliments me, I know that either I've been fabulous or she wants something. She didn't want anything that evening, though. I think she sensed a special moment was coming.

It was after that weekend that I knew she had to be told—but not just by me. Directly after our return, Henry spoke with her and then I spoke with her. She refused to believe us at first, but finally accepted it. The Lewises were a family no more.

I had wanted Henry to stay at all costs; he felt he *had* to leave, and I had to accept his decision. Never in my wildest dreams could I have imagined going through what my daughter was going through. Bentz and Berneice Horne had been a permanent entity,

XIV: *Endings*

just what I had wanted to be with Henry, but the time was out of joint, and the promise of a full, rich life together could not be fulfilled. Henry and I had to accept that fact, and so did Angela. Later, when I spoke to the analyst and told her how composed I'd been, she said, "You must have had a role model yourself, a woman in your past who was strong and dignified at all cost." I thought about it and, of course, I *had* had a model, the woman whose quiet strength anchored my life: my mother.

When we returned to New Jersey, I withdrew from other engagements to remain home with my daughter. I couldn't pull her out of school or leave her in the care of others. There was an *Orfeo* scheduled in Chicago, but when I called the late Carol Fox of the Chicago Lyric Opera and told her why I couldn't make it, she was so kind and understanding that I could have hugged her.

My next major assignment was a revival of Ambroise Thomas' *Mignon* in Dallas, Texas. I had had certain reservations about the event anyway, because Sarah Caldwell was scheduled to conduct and direct. Sarah Caldwell isn't high on my list of people to work with. Though there were many admirable touches and effects, her Boston *Carmen* had been chaos, and I'd made up my mind not to appear there again. Miss Caldwell's flair does not include preparation, and we had been so under-rehearsed, we hadn't even made it through the final scene until the actual performance. Thank heavens, Henry had been in the pit, so we'd been musically secure. All I needed in my present state was to be in Sarah Caldwell's hands.

Another sad event was connected with this *Mignon*. Larry Kelly, the founding and guiding light of the Dallas Opera, was mortally ill with cancer at the home of a friend. Even my sympathy for Larry, however, couldn't move me. I couldn't face working. Henry had walked out, I was on my own and terribly afraid I couldn't handle it. I know now that my inability to perform was a combination of my desire to be with Angela and my own depression.

*213*

On a Friday, I called Ronald, told him to cancel the *Mignon* and spent the weekend with Angela. On Monday, I went to the Met for a rehearsal and bumped into Matthew Epstein, then working for Columbia Artists Management.

"Jackie," he said, stopping me in the wings, "I hear you canceled *Mignon*. It's a mistake. You should do it."

"Pushy kid," I thought to myself, but I listened and Matthew put the pressure on. "It's only three weeks away, don't abandon it. It's good for you as well as Dallas. My God, it's been mounted for you! Come on, reconsider." Matthew is not easy to dissuade once he sets his mind on something, and he'd obviously set his mind on *Mignon*. He sincerely believed I should go to Dallas and he convinced me, too.

I called Ronald from the Met and said, "Ronald, call Nicola Rescigno and tell him I've reconsidered the *Mignon*. I'll do it."

By the time I arrived in Dallas, Larry Kelly was dead. The production was a testament to life, however, my life, and a new one began in Dallas.

# X V

## New Beginnings

AMBROISE THOMAS' opera *Mignon* is based on Goethe's *Wilhelm Meister* and premiered in Paris at the Opéra-Comique on November 17, 1866, with Célestine Galli-Marié playing the title role. Mignon, a child of noble birth, has been stolen by gypsies as a little girl, and in the course of the opera is reunited with her father, Lothario, who has been dazedly wandering the land as a minstrel. At the end, Lothario's sense returns and he gives his blessing to the union of Mignon and the young student Wilhelm.

All my fears about Sarah Caldwell materialized on the first day in Dallas when she brought out her score and opened it to a resounding *crack* as the spine of the book bore its first pressure. Until that moment, the inside of that book had obviously not seen the light of day. Sometimes I wonder if Sarah wouldn't be at her best if she just got somebody's old barn and a bunch of kids and five hundred dollars and said, "Okay, let's put on an opera."

As fate would have it, however, Miss Caldwell's questionable *modus operandi* had to take a back seat in my attentions, because someone else materialized in Dallas—someone I'd met once before, very briefly, in the foyer of La Scala. When I heard that Nicola Zaccaria would be singing Lothario, I said to myself, "Well, he probably doesn't have any voice left, but he'll bring great authority to the role." I was convinced Zaccaria, a La Scala fixture for years, must be in his sixties. I remembered thinking at La Scala what an attractive man he was, but I'd still been attached to Henry then, both emotionally and musically. I *saw* when men were attractive, but that was all.

As fate would have it, only two members of the *Mignon* cast were staying at the Sheraton Hotel, and of course they had to be me and Signore Nicola Zaccaria. Every evening after rehearsals, he'd come over and respectfully ask me to join him for dinner, and I would respectfully say I was getting some newspapers and going to bed. I was, too. I'd buy papers and magazines in the lobby, go up to my room and read, study and cry until I fell asleep. One night, we were both at the hotel newsstand at the same time, and he repeated his offer. I smiled and shook my head.

"No, no," I answered. *"Tante grazie, ma no, lei è 'troppo' simpatico"* ("No, thank you very much, but no, you're just too *simpatico*"). Zaccaria spoke Italian, Greek, French and German, but not English. My onstage Italian was pretty good, but offstage I wasn't as secure and wanted Zaccaria to know that I liked him but that he was too threatening. Zaccaria understood me and, bowing politely, turned and walked away to the elevators. I watched him as he walked through the lobby. An extremely graceful man, he moved well in youthful, vigorous strides. This man wasn't any sixty, not by a long shot. Actually, I found out, he was fifty-one, ten years older than I. Like it or not, I was attracted to the handsome basso and, I thought, he to me.

*Mignon* orchestra rehearsals were held in an auditorium at Southern Methodist University, and one afternoon I had arrived early and was waiting for the rest of the cast when Zaccaria came into the hall. Always impeccably dressed, he looked especially handsome that day. He carried a large white carton like the ones used by bakeries and, smiling broadly, motioned for me to come over,

*"Vieni, signora, e guarda, questa pasticceria greca, magnifica, per piacere."*

He had brought Greek pastries and was offering some to me. I put down my score and went over to his side. He opened the box and put it on a table, and as I leaned over to take a look, Nicola Zaccaria took me in his arms, pulled me toward him and kissed me passionately! The last time I had gotten kissed like that was eighteen years ago in *Cenerentola*!

Nico swears I only went for him because of the pastries, but I'm not so sure, because that afternoon I did something wild in Dallas —I fell head over heels in love, madly, passionately in love like a teen-ager. For one week, a forty-year-old, world-famous singer couldn't sleep or eat—I even lost ten pounds. If anyone had told me I'd be wooed and won over baklava in Dallas, I'd have laughed in his face. I guess that's what made it so wonderful, it was so unexpected. With Henry, my feelings had grown out of a long, long friendship, but with Nico it was BAM! and in the twinkling of an eye the scorned wife became the lovesick mezzo. My self-esteem as a woman was at an all-time low when Nico came along. He not only made me feel like a woman again, but more like one than I'd ever felt before. Perhaps I was ready now to *be* a woman.

And to think I almost had canceled!

After *Mignon*, I returned to New Jersey, and I could have flown without a plane. In *Mignon*, Zaccaria and I played father and daughter, but when the curtain fell, we were more like Romeo and Juliet. Nico made that stay in Dallas glorious, and I was literally a new woman when I got back. The new woman was greeted by the same old child, however, and I had to cool my ardor, at least for a while. There was no way I could tell my daughter I'd fallen for another man, especially a daughter who adored her father and still hoped her parents would reconcile. I immediately began to set myself on an independent path.

I contacted my lawyer, Mark Larner, and my accountant, Charles Hess, and with their help, made myself a totally separate financial entity from Henry Lewis, who had already set the process in motion. As each detail of my life started to iron out, I came to realize how totally dependent I had been upon my husband. No wonder he had wanted out. Living proof of the "Cinderella complex," I had wanted my man to take care of me and truly believed he was more capable than I. Now it seems asinine to me. What's so terrible about making your own decisions? The worst that can happen is—you can be wrong! When I married Henry, however, I came to it trailing chains wrought from nineteenth-century feminine attitudes. I didn't trust my feelings, my gut reactions and judgments, and it had something to do with my wanting to present myself to the world as a less intelligent person than I actually was. More than once, my parents had cautioned me, "It's okay to go out and become famous, Jackie, but don't change. Don't get too big for your britches." What they'd been really saying was: "Don't get too far away from us." As a result, I'd trusted Henry's judgments more than my own. To keep from getting "too big for my britches," I'd held back, hiding behind an arras woven of feminine doubts and fears. I might still be cowering there had not Henry called it quits.

Henry Lewis walked out the door and I woke up!

\* \* \*

As years go, 1975 was pretty good. I won a Grammy nomination for a recording of French and Spanish songs done with Marty Katz, and was singing regularly with the Met. As a matter of fact, I was part of that organization's three-week tour of Japan that began on May 25. Henry Lewis went, too, and we took Angela with us. Henry and I were getting on much better since the separation and, though it was strictly professional, Angela was thrilled that we were all together again. Joan Sutherland, Luciano Pavarotti, Franco Corelli and Jimmy McCracken were among the visiting Met all-stars. Joan sang Violetta in *La Traviata* and I sang Carmen.

During the first intermission of one *Carmen* performance, the principals—Jimmy McCracken, Adriana Maliponte, Guillermo Sarabia, Henry Lewis and I—climbed what felt like three million stairs for an audience with the Crown Prince. Japanese royalty doesn't go backstage, so it was arranged for the teen-age heir apparent to greet us in a private room. They never told us the private room was on top of Mount Fuji! All of us were winded from running around onstage, and by the time we reached the Prince, all we could do was stand there and pant. Protocol is protocol, though, and His Royal Highness had to be properly acknowledged.

In the fall, I arrived in Houston to appear in Handel's *Rinaldo*. David Gockley's company has a history of innovative productions and I like working there. In fact, if I were asked to name the up-and-coming men in the managerial field of opera, there's a young man named Jack Mastroiani connected with the Houston Grand Opera who would be high on the list—he'd be Castor to Matthew Epstein's Pollux, since, in my opinion, those two are the shining stars.

Around this time, I had the opportunity to help another operatic star, this time a performing artist. After my fateful Dallas engagement, I stopped in to see Charlie Riecker, one of my great friends in the Met management, to chat about things in general including the scheduled revival of Meyerbeer's *Le Prophète*. Naturally, we talked shop, and Charlie bemoaned the fact that Birgit Nilsson had dropped out of *Tosca* so she could prepare for Sieglinde. He desperately needed a star to put in the glamorous role of Puccini's heroine.

Truth to tell, Tosca's a part I'd adore to do, but it's out of my league. However, I did have a suggestion. While in Dallas, I'd seen the incredible Magda Olivero do a fabulous Tosca. He was a little skeptical; nevertheless, he called in Schuyler Chapin. Olivero, an Italian superstar, was in her sixties and, though she'd never appeared at the Met, had a cult following in America. She'd sung in places like New Jersey and Dallas, and every time she'd sung, her performances had been sold out. Advanced years or not, Olivero was fantastic, so good she practically gave acting and singing lessons while onstage. You could learn more from an Olivero performance than from reading most books on those very subjects. And that's what I told Schuyler and Charlie.

The upshot of our talk was, Magda Olivero made her long-overdue Metropolitan debut as Tosca at the age of sixty-five, in completely sold-out performances before wildly enthusiastic audiences. What a thrill that gave me!

The Met *Prophète* was preceded by my appearance in *Aïda*, with Leontyne Price, in the winter of 1976. The Met's production was lavish, stylized and quite lovely, but Amneris was not greeted with hosannahs. I don't have great success in Verdi roles, partly because I don't want to fight to be heard over the orchestra. I can't and won't pour out big sound all night, and it's suicide for me to try. Caruso once sang in a *Lucia* with the baritone Titta Ruffo. Ruffo put out like a cannon and Caruso tried to keep up with him, with the result that he lost his voice for the evening. The tenor swore he'd never sing with Ruffo again.

Amneris is a great part, however, one of the meatiest in the mezzo repertoire, and when I was asked to do it again at the Salzburg Festival under Herbert von Karajan's direction in 1979, I agreed. I was convinced this would be a great *Aïda* because Von Karajan had done a lovely chamber version of *Die Walküre*, and Mirella Freni and Jose Carreras, artists of delicacy and fine tuning, would be singing Aïda and Radames. Von Karajan would certainly apply a lyrical touch to the normally brassy *Aïda*.

When I got to Salzburg, however, and took one look at the size of the augmented chorus, it was clear I was in for the big-band sound. Von Karajan had quadrupled the sound, which is disaster for Amneris, who hasn't got the high notes to sail out over the orchestra. There are two B flats in the whole part and the rest are all A's and G's. Vocally, the Egyptian princess simply doesn't go into orbit the way her Ethiopian counterpart does, unless she has a huge voice. I don't!

Sure enough, when we started with the orchestra, the sound blasted from the pit like a hundred cannon. Von Karajan might just as well have taken out a gun and shot me in the throat. That Salzburg *Aïda* ranks as one of my monumental failures. Indeed, I'd be inconsolable about the Salzburg fiasco except that I also had one of my finest triumphs there.

I was scheduled to give a recital during that same trip. Marty Katz was along, as were Nico and my friends Mimi and Merritt Cohen. The reviews for my Amneris had been less than great; I certainly was not the darling of the Austrian music world. Everything seemed grim and, overcome by the Teutonic rather than bucolic atmosphere in Salzburg, I had a real mad on, and it was only a question of time before my ire exploded. The evening after the opening *Aïda*, we returned to the parking lot, where, with great difficulty, we finally located the car. The lot was pitch-black; not one miserable little bulb illuminated the vast arena of waiting automobiles. We found the car, but could not find the exit and circled and circled until, completely by accident, we arrived at the egress. There was an automatic toll machine there which none of us could figure out, and an emergency button which Merritt pressed, and still nothing happened.

"The hell with it," I said. "It's getting late. Just lift up the barrier and let's get out of here." Nico got out and tried to push up the long wooden arm blocking our way out. Before you could say *Götterdämmerung*, an attendant roared up on a motorcycle and began shouting in German. Nico dropped the barrier he was struggling to raise, turned and yelled back, "Nazi!" Merritt and Mimi were nearly dying; they didn't know whether to laugh or cry. I got out of the car, stormed over to the parking-lot attendant and let him have it.

"I am *Frau Kammersängerin* Horne," I trumpeted in German in a voice that easily could have carried over a Karajan orchestra, "and we cannot get out of this place. *Open that gate!*" Immediately, the attendant leaped from his cycle seat, rushed over to Nico and raised the barrier for us. This guy knew how to take orders, period.

By the time the recital night came, I'd just about had it with Salzburg. As Marty and I stood offstage waiting to go on, all the pent-up fury over *Aïda* turned to resolution and, just as we stepped out, I said over my shoulder, "Okay, Marty, let's go get 'em!" I never talk like that before a concert—usually it's "good luck," *"merde"* or "oy vay."

We walked on to a polite smattering of applause and I opened the program with Orlando's aria *"Nel profondo cieco mondo,"* which is all black notes! Polite applause give way to pandemonium, and at the end of the recital I had to sing eight encores. Jimmy Levine was out there and I threw him a kiss during the fifth encore. Matthew was in the second row and kept nodding his head in approval as I returned to sing more numbers. After the eighth encore, he shook his head no, and I knew he was right. If Matthew hadn't been there, I might have sung all night. I had redeemed myself in the ears of the Salzburg public, and, fortunately, some friends were witness to one of the greatest recitals I ever gave or (*auf wieder-sehen*, modesty) *the* finest ever given! That evening more than made up for Von Karajan's *Aïda*, and I'm delighted my great accompanist and friend, Marty, could share in that triumph.

Later that year, in Dallas, I sang an Amneris to critical acclaim, helped considerably by the fact that the decibel level of the orchestra was within the range of the human ear and the tempi established by conductor Nicola Rescigno were consistent, not idiosyncratic. Given the proper setting, I can do Amneris damn well.

*Le Prophète*, too, should have been a resounding success. A grand opera in the great French tradition, it has everything going for it, given a good production. The central role of Fidès, mother of the hero, Jean, was associated with four great artists who had sung in most of the fifty-six performances given at the Met up to 1928, the year it left the repertoire. Of the four mezzos, Marianne Brandt, Ernestine Schumann-Heink, Margarete Matzenauer and Louise Homer, I was most drawn to the wonderful Schumann-Heink, whose long, illustrious Met career ended on March 11, 1932, when she sang Erda in *Siegfried* at the age of seventy!

Schumann-Heink has been described as "a great natural phenomenon, like Niagara Falls." Her fame went beyond the opera house, making her truly a "household word." Every Christmas, she sang *"Stille Nacht"*—"Silent Night"—over the radio, and it was said that Christmas wasn't Christmas without Schumann-Heink. During the First World War, when anti-German sentiment was so high that sauerkraut became "victory cabbage," Schumann-Heink's popularity didn't slip a notch. In fact, she gained in the public's affection because of her personal dilemma: she had had many children, along with three husbands, and her sons were in the

German *and* American armies. Caruso adored her and called her *"Nonna"* (Grandmother). Mme. Schumann-Heink was also noted for her ample proportions and once, while appearing in concert with a symphony orchestra, made a spectacular rehearsal entrance. Unable to thread her way down the narrow aisle between the string sections, she smacked, banged and barreled her way down to the front, leaving a trail of displaced chairs and musicians. When at last she reached the podium, the concerned conductor surveyed the wreckage, leaned over and said most gently,

"Perhaps, Mme. Schumann-Heink, you should come in sideways?"

"But, Maestrrrro," replied the contralto, "I haf no zidevays!"

My friend Lamont Johnson, a fine director, wants to do a television feature film on the life of this wonderful woman, with me in the lead. I'd love to do it.

Actually, I should have '"sidestepped" my Fidès. The truth is, I should have canceled the first performance, because I had a terrible case of bronchitis. I could overcome my condition in a role like Rosina, but it was sheer stupidity, while ill, for me to try to take over a blockbuster like Fidès, which is dramatic and laced with *bel canto* flourishes. Fidès is a role that should not be approached in anything less than perfect health. If I had had any sense, I would have followed the advice Dr. Kriso had given me in Vienna all those years ago, but I felt the responsibility of a new production which had just about been created for *my* benefit, and I felt I had to come through. Even more, I had waited and prayed for this role and the maturity to do it, and couldn't let it go. I wanted desperately to do it, and do it right, maybe for the first time. When we'd seen the old orchestral scores for the first time, we were shocked to discover that all the excruciatingly difficult vocal flourishes had been cut out. We immediately restored them—but that didn't help my performance any when I came down with bronchitis.

After the opening, rumors that I was in vocal difficulty began to circulate. Then I got another cold and could barely get through the run. I should have stopped then, but I couldn't—I wouldn't let myself. I was actually booed at the Met, *booed!* Finally, I had no choice: I canceled everything for five weeks and just rested. By the end of those five weeks, I finally felt better, and then I *really* began to sing Fidès. Indeed, Francis Robinson said that my Fidès "did not suffer by comparison with Schumann-Heink and Matzenauer," but I will never shake the memory of those boos out of my mind. Francis, a very special man, one who truly knew, loved and promoted opera, died not long ago, and just before the end sent me a gift through the mail, a lovely autographed picture of Schumann-Heink on the arm of one of her husbands. On his deathbed, Francis Robinson remembered.

Did I learn my lesson? Did I turn from Verdi and Meyerbeer to embrace *bel canto* and only *bel canto?* If I may jump ahead for a moment, the next role I sang at the Metropolitan provides the answer, Princess Eboli in Verdi's *Don Carlo.* Look, I never said I was above reproach. On opening night, February 5, 1979, the verdict was: Verdi, *sì,* Horne, no. Though my Veil Song was well received, I took it from some critics, principally because I had committed the unpardonable operatic sin—I had transposed! Forget sloth, envy, greed, gluttony and the rest, the prime transgression in the eyes of some is fiddling with the key. Yet I had only been following the instructions of the composer himself. Many transpositions in opera are accepted fare. No one ever speaks about *"Che gelida manina," "Di quella pira"* and the like. Why is that? They say blondes have more fun, but I think tenors have more keys.

Verdi himself had transposed Princess Eboli down a full tone and a half, and that's the way it had been published, in the French and Italian editions. The role is low, except for the Veil Song and Eboli's big aria in the third act, *"O don fatale,"* where the highs come on like thunder. In the aria, the Princess Eboli curses her "fatal and cruel gift" of beauty, rising to emotional and vocal heights at the end. Anyone who takes the trouble to check the Paris score will catch on immediately to what Verdi was doing. The lady who sang Eboli in Paris obviously "warmed up" all night and then let 'er rip in *"O don fatale."*

I wish my critics would take the trouble to do the kind of re-search and analysis I do in preparing my roles. *"O don fatale"* was always sung in the lower key at the Met until the 1950s. Oh, well, as the American poet Julia Moore wrote, "Between me and my critics, I leave you to decide."

In August 1978, Marty and I went Down Under for a recital tour. Nico came along, too, and when we arrived at the airport in Sydney, I was given a handwritten note:

> Welcome to our country, we're thrilled you're here. Can't wait to see you.
>
> Joan

Because we left to tour immediately, our meeting had to wait. The recital odyssey was both arduous and rewarding. Australia is a funny combination of modern and old—some of the buildings are modern and most of the plumbing is old. In Melbourne, we stayed on the thirteenth floor of the new Hilton Hotel, which didn't bother me, but convinced my superstitious Greek friend we were in for a run of bad luck.

We unpacked, settled in and very late that evening I turned on the television, hoping to catch a Laurence Olivier movie I'd seen listed. I never got to the film, however, because all of a sudden something whizzed by the front of the set so fast that all I saw was four scurrying little gray legs and a long tail! I put it together, jumped up on top of the bed, grabbed the phone and called the front desk.

"This is V.I.P. Horne," I said, identifying myself just in case. "You send someone up here *fast*, there's a *rat* in this room."

Nico came in to see what the screaming was about and, after my breathless explanation, began to look for the creature in his bare feet. I was so upset, I called Marty's room and he started laughing! Some bellboys appeared and began looking for the mouse, and, sure enough, out it came, scooting across the floor and dashing under furniture. The bellboys chased around the suite and cornered the thing, but it slipped away under a radiator.

"Sorry, Madame," said one. "He's eluded us. We'll try again tomorrow."

"Fine," I answered, "you try again tomorrow for *whomever* is staying in this room, because it won't be *me*."

At three a.m., Nico and I marched through the corridors in our pajamas, followed by an entourage of bellboys laden with luggage.

From mice to mobs. The next day, returning to the hotel from a rehearsal, we ran into a street demonstration. The Prime Minister was staying at our hotel and protesters had tied up the streets. Nico, Marty and I were in a limousine provided by the Australian Broadcasting Company, a stretch vehicle about as long as a block, very fancy. The driver inched his way through the crowd until it became impossible to move without running over Aussies! I had a performance that evening and, while I'm sympathetic to most good causes, needed to get my rest—*ergo*, needed to get to my room. Spotting a policeman nearby, I opened the window to ask for his assistance. Some demonstrators shouted, "Look at the rich folks in their fancy car!" and other phrases of a similar nature, put far less politely. I leaned out of the window and beckoned to one of the hecklers. He looked at his friends, shrugged his shoulders and swaggered over.

"Do you speak English?" I asked him sweetly.

"Yeah," he answered.

"Good," I said, raising my voice. "Up yours!"

The crowd roared, parted like the Red Sea and let us pass.

Sometimes, talking tough is the only way to get results. I talked tough, sang well and had a marvelous time.

We returned to Sydney and checked into our hotel. Joan was appearing as Norma in the great gull-winged opera house and my recital was in the Concert Hall—both events were sold out. After our performance, Marty and I and Nico went to stand in the wings of the opera house for the last act. It was typical Sutherland—stupendous. When the opera finished, we went backstage and found that Joan, along with a close friend, Chester Corone, had prepared and was about to preside over a dinner in our honor. Imagine, she'd just sung the most demanding role in opera and now she was catering a dinner! We did three concerts in Sydney. All were sold out, but we did manage to get tickets to one for Dame Joan.

We left Sydney on September 1 and, after an all-night flight, arrived in Los Angeles on the 2nd. My brother Dick picked me up at the airport. Usually, Dick was so busy he had no time to spare, and we had to be content with phone calls or catch-as-catch-can dinners as I shuttled through Los Angeles to the East Coast. This was Labor Day weekend, however, and Dick was free. We drove to his house, where I spent Sunday and Monday. The weather was beautiful, and Dick, Joanne and I sat out by the pool from morning to dusk on both days, laughing, talking and reminiscing. It was the first opportunity I'd had in years really to enjoy my brother's company.

On September 24, 1978, I was in Canada to perform *Mignon.* That evening, on impulse, I called Dick just to say "hi" and we had a long conversation. The next morning, I had gone out early and returned to the hotel suite to prepare a late breakfast. The television was on in the living room and I heard in the distance a bulletin about a plane crash in San Diego. "Nico," I called out, "did you hear that? Another of those damn little planes caused a major accident." We sat down to eat, and not long after, the opera house called, telling me to call Mrs. Horne. I was supposed to phone Jay's wife, Linda, but, not knowing which Mrs. Horne, called Joanne. When she answered, she asked if I had heard about the plane accident. "Yes," I said. "Isn't it awful, was anyone hurt?" There was a pause. "Jackie, there are no survivors, and Dick was on that plane." I screamed. The horror of that moment has been dulled by time, but it will never, ever leave me.

The next evening, I sang *Mignon* in a fog. I couldn't believe it, I *wouldn't* believe it. In fact, for years after, I would not accept Dick's death. Joanne even warned me. "I accept it, Jackie," she said, "but you won't, and you've got to."

I remember seeking consolation in music and finding it in Mahler's "Resurrection" Symphony. Those words, "You will rise again, oh my dust, oh my dust," provided the link for me. I clung to that uplifting quality in Mahler and it sustained me.

For four years, I refused to accept Dick's death and then finally, most curiously, I came to grips with his passing. In October 1982, I began using hypnosis as a method to lose weight and the hypnotist introduced me to something called "Frozen Glove Therapy." While in a self-hypnotic state, the subject dons a glove, and as I drew it over my hand in the introductory session, the hypnotist told me to imagine I had a boxing glove on and to "feel" the silken warmth of the inside of the glove. I followed her directions and found myself weeping uncontrollably, tears pouring down my face.

"What's the matter?" asked the hypnotist.

"I'm remembering," I answered. "I'm remembering."

The only time in my life I had ever had boxing gloves on was in Bradford when I was a kid. Dick had let me wear his and pretended to box with me. In my hypnotized state, I returned to that incident and, in doing so, was finally able to fully grieve for my brother.

I sold the New Jersey house in 1977 and with Angela moved into a duplex apartment near Lincoln Center. It took me a while to put 273 Elmwynd Drive on the market. For three years, I was in no shape to make any moves and clung to the comforting familiarity of my home and friends. Henry Lewis had left "to find himself," but the upshot was that we *each* found ourselves. What a ridiculous expression, "to find oneself"—as if you could "lose" yourself—but I did do a lot of thinking in that old manse in New Jersey, and when the time came, I was ready to move on.

That "moving-on" continued to take me all over the country and the world. Besides appearances in *Italiana* and *Barbiere* at the Met, I performed in cities such as Houston and Dallas and, of course, in Italy. I consider Italy my musical home and, between operas, recitals and recordings, spend a healthy part of the year there. In fact, I may be better known there than I am in America. My treatment in Parma is an example. Parma is a town that eats opera singers for lunch. Stories of Parma's inhumanity to vocalists fill books—it's the place where a tenor sang his aria three times because the audience kept calling him back. At the end of the third round, the tenor stepped forward to say, "Please, please, I can do it no more," and someone yelled from the balcony, "You'll do it till you do it right!" A baritone in our company was so bad, the porters in his hotel *refused* to carry his bags. Imagine my delight, then, when I discovered that, on one of my more recent visits, the opera house had *paid* my hotel bill for me and Marty—an unheard-of procedure!

I enjoy singing in Italy. Though it's more difficult dealing with La Scala than any other opera house, there's a flair and style in

Milan, even when they're engaged in skulduggery. An incredible expenditure of energy and a hearty dose of subterfuge go into any deal. You have to be on your toes!

In 1980, I was singing *Il Barbiere* in Macerata, a walled city off the Adriatic coast near Ancona, where operas are given in a restored amphitheatre during a summer festival. They're trying to create another Spoleto. I received word that representatives of La Scala wanted to speak to me and, sure enough, five of them came to my hotel room one afternoon. When they asked me what I wanted to sing at La Scala, my answer was direct:

"I want an opening night in a big, new production!"

"*Sì, sì, Signora*," said the La Scala quintet, nodding their heads in unison. "Of course, of course, but if we do this for you, would you do something for us?" Of course I would, and they asked me to do a revival of *L'Italiana*, which I'd done four times at La Scala.

"Okay, okay," I said. "I'll do it, but only in conjunction with another new production."

"Well," declared one gentleman, "1982 is the two-thousandth anniversary of Virgil's birth and we were thinking of doing *Les Troyens* [*The Trojans*]. Would you like to sing both Cassandra and Dido?"

Berlioz' epic opera is so long it's usually given on two separate occasions—Part One and Part Two—and each part contains a mezzo plum. La Scala planned to combine the two sections on the same evening, and was offering me the opportunity to sing both the daughter of Priam and Hecuba, who is cursed with the gift of prophecy, and the Queen of Carthage, who has a tragic love affair with Aeneas.

"Fine," I answered, "but I really only want to do one role. I don't like seeing the same person die twice in one evening, so, if you please, I want to do Dido."

"Certainly," agreed the quintet, nodding their heads and rubbing their hands. "And, Signora, how would you like to sing a recital for us, too?"

"Sure," I replied. "I'll do it, and not only that, I'll do it as a benefit for the Casa Verdi!" The La Scala group nearly keeled over at that offer. The Casa Verdi, established by the great composer, provides shelter for musical senior citizens, and I was proud to donate my services.

Within the week, a contract arrived for *L'Italiana* and the recital. After a long time, when I did not send it back, I received a call telling me that the Virgil project had fallen through. *Les Troyens* had been axed.

"Okay, okay," said Little Mary Sunshine, "I'll live without *The Trojans*. I'll do the recital and *L'Italiana*, and we'll figure out something else in place of the Berlioz." I still hadn't signed any contracts, but wasn't concerned.

Marty, Nico and I went to Milan, and on June 15, 1981, I gave the recital which was not only released as a recording but also taped for television. I'm especially proud of that recital because it included American songs, and all for a worthy cause. I was really thin then, too.

Before the recital, Marty and I were rehearsing in the opera house. The heat was so unbearable that everyone had cleared out for the noon break, leaving the offices empty. Nico took the opportunity to do some judicious sleuthing. He'd been with La Scala for twenty-eight years and, having worked with them, was very suspicious of the Virgil episode.

He was sitting in an administrative office, waiting for me and Marty, when he saw the 1981–82 schedule, and whose name should lead all the rest but Hector Berlioz and his opera *Les Troyens*?

I called my agent in Italy, Luigi Oldani, and told him the story. Oldani called the administrators and cried, "You cannot do this to *La Signora* Horne; you must always tell the straight story in such an instance. If there were problems in the scheduling, you should have come to her and said so." Obviously, La Scala had reneged on their promise to me in order to suit someone else. I didn't know who they were planning to have sing Dido, but the idea that they had tried to put one over on me didn't sit well. I had Nico talk with them on the phone, and by the time the conversation was over, La Scala was ready to mount a *Rinaldo*, televise *L'Italiana* and throw in a gala. I think they'd have thrown in the island of Ischia, too, just to placate me.

This may all seem dreadfully temperamental and ego-oriented, but you must understand one thing about the opera world today: amidst all that glorious sound, there is a competition so fierce and managements so devious that you *must* look out for yourself. Too many careers have collapsed because of bad management, bad advice or simple naïveté.

In addition, I do get a certain satisfaction from all this wheeling and dealing, because *I* can handle it. In the old days, I relied on Henry. I did my own thinking, but I followed my husband's lead, and the times I took matters into my own hands were few and far between. After we were divorced, I took an active interest in my own financial affairs. I recommend the same procedure to all other women, single or married. Sure, I make mistakes. As an opera singer performing in other countries, for instance, I've been stung many times by fluctuations in foreign currencies, but I find it challenging to work out these problems—aided by my lawyer and accountant, of course. You see, I'm not just an opera singer. I'm in the business of singing.

In January 1984, I'll be returning to the Metropolitan for its hundredth-anniversary season in a production of Handel's *Rinaldo*. The occasion will also mark my thirtieth year in opera and coincides with my fiftieth birthday. Originally, the performance was scheduled for January 16, my birth date exactly, but alas, the date has been shifted to the 19th, so I'll already be into the second half of my own century when I bring Handel to the Met for the first time! It just goes to show that you have to persevere. The idea that I made my Met debut before Handel did is staggering. I guess one of the things that has kept me going all these years is my incredible tenacity. Still, you can't hold on forever, and I have a deal with Marty Katz. He's promised to let me know when I'm no longer singing the way he and I know I want to sing. If I go on too long, blame Marty.

In the meantime, I'll be performing in roles I've done for years and in new ones as well. Adding to my repertoire keeps those juices flowing, and I'm working on such diverse characters as Roussel's Padmavati, Saint-Saëns' Dalila, Handel's Orlando and more of my beloved Rossini. I may be nearing fifty, but I have no intention of standing still. My Spring 1983 schedule will give you an idea of what I'm going through:

| | | |
|---|---|---|
| February 20, 23, 26 and March 1 | Hamburg Opera (*Semiramide*) | Hamburg, West Germany |
| March 6 | Teatro Fenice (Recital) | Venice, Italy |
| March 12 (rehearsal March 11) | Orchestre Philharmonique de Monte Carlo | Monte Carlo, Monaco |
| March 29, 30 and 31 | CBS Masterworks recording—Christmas Album with Mormon Tabernacle Choir | Salt Lake City, Utah |
| April 11 | Théâtre Musicale de Châtelet (Recital) | Paris, France |
| April 13 | Opéra Municipal de Lyon (Recital) | Lyon, France |
| April 16 | Recital | Bari, Italy |
| April 19 | Recital | Naples, Italy |

| | | |
|---|---|---|
| April 22 | Avignon Théâtre Municipal (Recital) | Avignon, France |
| April 24 | Le Grand Théâtre de Genève (Recital) | Geneva, Switzerland |
| April 28 | Hamburg Opera (Recital) | Hamburg, West Germany |
| May 2 | Teatro alla Scala (Recital) | Milan, Italy |
| May 9 & 12 (rehearsal beginning May 6) | Berlin Opera (*Semiramide*) | Berlin, West Germany |
| May 22 (rehearsal beginning May 16) | Carnegie Hall (*Tancredi*) | New York, New York |
| May 26 | Graduation (Angela) | Hotchkiss School, Lakeville, Connecticut |
| May 27 | Recital | Dallas, Texas |
| June 5, 8, 11, 14, 17 | Teatro Fenice (*Tancredi*) | Venice, Italy |
| June 22, 24, 26, 28, 30 | Erato recording of French arias | Monte Carlo, Monaco |
| July 1, 2 and 3 | Pathé-Marconi Recording of *Padmavati* | Toulouse, France |
| July 9 | Ravinia Festival | Chicago, Illinois |
| July 31 | Blossom Festival | Cleveland, Ohio |
| August 6 | Tanglewood Festival | Stockbridge, Massachusetts |
| August 13 | Saratoga Festival | Saratoga, New York |

You'll notice that I'm keeping up my recitals. I've always enjoyed singing "solo" and look forward to a continuing concert career. Over the years, I've tried to balance my appearances on the concert and opera stages and consider it imperative to do so. I've always had the feeling that in opera I *go out* to the audience, while in recital I *bring* the audience to me.

Once, singers could specialize in *Lieder* and make their names outside of opera, but today the concert singer is a *rara avis*. Recitals are given by opera stars, their programs packed with arias that really don't belong there. I sing arias in my recitals, too, but it would be a shame to lose the great songs of Schubert, Schumann, Debussy and Wolf. They were written for *bel canto* singing and embody the inspiring melodic line. Because opera stars are the only ones who can draw the crowds, though, we may be reaching the end of the line of great song interpreters. If a singer does too much refined recital work, there are operatic consequences. Constant vocalizing in a "drawing-room setting" is no good for a performer interested in combining an operatic and recital career, because it's such a delicate art: you can hold yourself back in recital and get away with it. The answer is balance, which is what I strive for now: some concerts, some operas; some arias, some *Lieder*.

After singing? Well, I've said I'd like to do some acting and teaching, but I don't feel pressured to plan my second career yet—my first is still booming! Ernestine Schumann-Heink made it to seventy. Why not Marilyn Berneice Horne? We'll leave it to Marty.

Right now, I'm looking backward and forward with equal pleasure, though I must admit it is *different* singing at this age. Ten, twenty and thirty years ago, I walked out on stages, sang to the best of my ability, accepted my kudos or knocks and went home—there was plenty of time. Now, with "time's winged chariot" drawing near, I've gone from reflex to reflection.

At one rehearsal for the 1982 *Norma* in San Francisco, I was late leaving the theatre. No one was around as I crossed the stage to the exit. I've taken that familiar walk over and over again, but this time I paused. The house was dark, except for the naked rehearsal bulb glowing starkly on stage. I looked out at the empty auditorium, into the orchestra, up to the sweeping curve of the balcony and farther up to the topmost reaches. In this theatre, in 1960, I had made my triumphant return to the United States in *Wozzeck*, and here I was reunited with Joan Sutherland in *Norma*, yet it was only one of many stages I'd been on, only one of many houses I called home. I came to all those houses to share that gift God gave me and in quest of that one beauty He put me here to find. In that, I've been successful, and for that, am grateful.

"*Jedes Ding hat seine Zeit,*" Lehmann said to me. Time, that thief, is passing. Someday, I won't be coming "home." I must absorb everything while I'm still singing and step onto the stages of my many homes, and look out at the familiar surroundings, at the people who have come to hear me, to hear music. I must drink in everything because I want to remember everything . . . everything.

# DISCOGRAPHY
## *and*
# INDEX

# DISCOGRAPHY

*Arias from French Operas.* Vienna Opera Orchestra, Henry Lewis, conductor. (Bizet, Massenet, Saint-Saëns, Thomas). 1968. London OS 26064.

*The Age of Bel Canto.* London Symphony/New Symphony of London. (Solos, duets and trios from operas by Puccini, Handel, Lampugnani, Bononcini, Arne, Sheild, Mozart, Boieldieu, Rossini, Auber, von Weber, Bellini, Donizetti and Bolero by Arditi.) Joan Sutherland, Richard Conrad, Richard Bonynge, conductor. 1964. London OSA 1257.

*The Art of Marilyn Horne.* London OS 26277.

*Bach and Handel Arias.* Vienna Cantata Orchestra, Henry Lewis, conductor. (Bach: "Magnificat in D," "Christmas Oratorio," "St. Matthew Passion," "Bist du bei mir," arr. Smith; Handel: "Messiah," "Rodelinda"). 1969. London OS 26067.

Beethoven, Ludwig von. *Symphony no. 9, "Choral."* Vienna Philharmonic Orchestra. Vienna State Opera Chorus. Joan Sutherland, James King, Martti Talvela, Hans Schmidt-Isserstedt, conductor. 1966. London OSA 1159.

————. *Symphony no. 9.* New York Philharmonic. Margaret Price, Jon Vickers, Matti Salminen, Zubin Mehta, conductor. 1984. RCA Unreleased.

Bellini, Vincenzo. *Norma.* London Symphony Orchestra and Chorus. Joan Sutherland, Yvonne Minton, John Alexander, Richard Cross, Richard Bonynge, conductor. 1965. RCA Victor LM-6166, LSC 6166. Excerpts: RCA Victor LM-2842, LSC-2842. Reissued 1968 as London OSA 1394. Highlights: 1975. London OS 26388.

Bizet, Georges. *Carmen.* Metropolitan Opera Orchestra and Chorus. Adriana Maliponte, James McCracken, Leonard Bernstein, conductor. 1973. DG 2709043. Excerpts: 1975. DG 2530534.

―――. *Carmen Jones, the Opera.* Lyrics by Oscar Hammerstein III. Pearl Bailey, Marvin Hayes, LaVern Hutcherson, Herschel B. Gilbert, conductor. 1954. RCA LSC-3335. RCA Victor LM-1881. (Stereoized version of a mono recording). Reissued as RCA Red Seal ARL 1-0046.

―――. *Marilyn Horne Sings Carmen.* Royal Philharmonic Orchestra and Chorus. Michael Molese, Henry Lewis, conductor. 1970. London 21055.

*Diva!* Arias performed by Marilyn Horne, Montserrat Caballé, Ileana Cotrubas, Renata Scotto, Kiri Te Kanawa, Frederica von Stade. 1981. CBS M3X 79343.

Donizetti, Gaetano. *Anna Bolena.* Vienna Opera Orchestra. Vienna State Opera Chorus. Elena Souliotis, Nicolai Ghiaurov, John Alexander, Silvio Varviso, conductor. 1970. London OSA 1436. Highlights: 1972. London OS 26253.

―――. *Lucrezia Borgia.* National Philharmonic. London Opera Orchestra. Joan Sutherland, Giacomo Aragall, Ingvar Wixell, Richard Bonynge, conductor. 1979. London OSA 13129. Decca.

*Duets from Norma and Semiramide.* London Symphony Orchestra. Joan Sutherland, Richard Bonynge, conductor. London OS 26168.

Gesualdo, Carlo. *1560–1613, Madrigals and Sacred Music.* Robert Craft, conductor. Gesualdo Madrigal Singers. 1957. Columbia ML 5234. Reissued 1974 as Odyssey Y 32886.

Gluck, Christoph Willibald. *Orfeo ed Euridice.* Royal Opera Orchestra and Chorus of Covent Garden. Pilar Lorengar, Helen Donath, Georg Solti, conductor. 1970. London OSA 1285. Highlights: 1972. London OS 26214.

*Great Artists at the Met: Marilyn Horne at the Met.* (Bellini, Rossini, Gluck, Bizet, Meyerbeer, Bertoni. From previously recorded albums 1964, 1965, 1969, 1970, 1976, 1980). 1981. RCA Special Products for Met Opera Guild. Met 111-A.

Handel, George Frederick. *Julius Caesar*, Excerpts. New Symphony Orchestra of London. Joan Sutherland, M. Elkins, Monica Sinclair, Richard Conrad, Richard Bonynge, conductor. 1964. London OS 25876.

———. *Airs D'Operas.* I Solisiti Veneti, Claudio Scimone, conductor. 1984. Erato NUM 75047. Digital.

*In Concert at the Met.* Metropolitan Opera Orchestra. Leontyne Price, James Levine, conductor. (The complete concert of March 28, 1982). 1983. RCA CRC2-4609. Digital.

Mahler, Gustav. *Kindertotenlieder*; Wagner, Richard, *Wesendonck Lieder.* Royal Philharmonic, Henry Lewis, conductor. 1970. London OS 26147.

———. *Ruckert Lieder: Songs of a Wayfarer.* Los Angeles Philharmonic, Zubin Mehta, conductor. 1979. London OS 26578.

———. *Symphony no. 2.* Chicago Symphony Orchestra and Chorus. Carol Neblett, Claudio Abbado, conductor. 1977. DG 2707094.

———. *Symphony no. 3.* Chicago Symphony Orchestra and Chorus. Glen Ellyn Children's Chorus. James Levine, conductor. 1976. RCA ARL 2-1757.

Leigh, Mitch. *Man of La Mancha,* Selections. Jim Nabors, Richard Tucker, Jack Gilford, Madeleine Kahn, Paul Weston, conductor. 1972. Columbia S31237.

*Marilyn Horne, French and Spanish Songs.* (Bizet, Debussy, de Falla, Nin). Martin Katz, piano. 1974. London OS 26301.

*Marilyn Horne, German Lieder.* (Schubert, Schumann, Wolf, R. Strauss). Martin Katz, piano. 1974. London OS 26302.

*Marilyn Horne: Live from La Scala.* Martin Katz, piano. 1983. CBS M 37819. LP/Cassette.

*Marilyn Horne dal Vivo al Teatro Regio di Parma.* (Bellini, Bizet, Bongiovanni, Donizetti, Foster, Handel, Meyerbeer, Rossini, Thomas, Verdi). Martin Katz, piano. 1980. GB 11. Diapason record.

*Marilyn Horne's Greatest Hits.* (Arias from *Il Barbiere di Siviglia, Les Huguenots, Carmen, Norma, Orfeo ed Euridice, Mignon, Semiramide*). 1973. London OS 26346.

Massenet, Jules. *La Navarraise.* London Symphony Orchestra. 1976. RCA AGL 1-3793.

*Met Stars in Hollywood.* Eileen Farrell, Sherrill Milnes, Dorothy Kirsten, Robert Merrill, Dale Moore, Ezio Pinza, Eleanor Steber, Risë Stevens, Jan Peerce, Lily Pons, Cesare Siepi. 1981. Met 205. Metropolitan Opera Guild.

Meyerbeer, Giacomo. *Le Prophète.* Royal Philharmonic, Ambrosian Chorus. Renata Scotto, James McCracken, Jerome Hines, Henry Lewis, conductor. CBS M4 34340.

Mozart, Wolfgang Amadeus. *Don Giovanni.* English Chamber Orchestra. Joan Sutherland, Pilar Lorengar, Gabriel Bacquier, Werner Krenn, Donald Gramm, Richard Bonynge, conductor. 1970. London OSA 1434. Highlights: London 26215.

———. *Requiem.* Vienna Philharmonic. Elly Ameling, Ugo Benelli, C. Franc, István Kertesz, conductor. 1966. London OSA 1157.

*Our Garden of Hymns.* Tennessee Ernie Ford, Jack Fascinato, conductor. 1967. Capitol ST 2845.

Ponchielli, Amilcare. *La Gioconda.* Academie St. Cecilia. Renata Tebaldi, Carlo Bergonzi, Robert Merrill, Lamberto Gardelli, conductor. 1968. London OSA 1388. Highlights: 1970. London OS 26162.

*Presenting Marilyn Horne.* Royal Opera House Orchestra, Covent Garden, Henry Lewis, conductor. (Operatic arias from *Semiramide, Le Prophète, La Figlia di Reggimento, La Clemenza di Tito, L'Italiana in Algeri, Les Huguenots, La Cenerentola*). London OS 25910.

Puccini, Giacomo. *Il Trittico.* London Philharmonic/New Philharmonic Orchestra. Ambrosian Opera Chorus. Desborough School Choir. Renata Scotto, Ileana Cotrubas, Lorin Maazel, conductor. 1977. CBS M34505.

Ravel, Maurice. *Sheherazade*; de Falla, Manuel, *El Amor Brujo.* New York Philharmonic/Orchestra National de France, Leonard Bernstein, conductor. 1978. CBS M35102.

Respighi, Ottorino. *Laud to the Nativity.* Los Angeles Philharmonic, Alfred Wallenstein, conductor. 1960. Capitol P-8572. SP-8572.

Rossini, Gioacchino. *Marilyn Horne, Arias from Rossini.* Royal Opera Orchestra, Covent Garden, Henry Lewis, conductor. 1966. London OS 25910.

———. *Arias from The Siege of Corinth and La Donna del Lago.*

London 26305.

————. *Giovanna D'Arco and Songs.* Martin Katz, piano. 1982. CBS 1M 37296. Digital 1MT.

————. *Il Barbiere di Siviglia.* La Scala Orchestra and Chorus. Leo Nucci, Enzo Dara, Samuel Ramey, Paolo Barbacini, Riccardo Chailly, conductor. 1982. CBS 13M 37862. Digital.

————. *L'Italiana in Algeri.* I Solisti Veneti. Samuel Ramey, Ernesto Palacio, Domenico Trimarchi, Kathleen Battle, E. Foti, Nicola Zaccaria, Claudio Scimone, conductor. 1981. RCA ARL 3-3855.

————. *Semiramide.* London Symphony Orchestra, Ambrosian Opera Chorus. Joan Sutherland, Joseph Rouleau, M. Serge, Spiro Malas, Richard Bonynge, conductor. 1966. London OSA 1383. Highlights: 1969. London OS 26086.

*Salute to George London.* Victor ARL 1-4667.

*Souvenir of a Golden Era.* (Rossini: *Il Barbiere Di Siviglia, Otello, Tancredi, Semiramide, L'Italiana in Algeri*; Bellini: *Capuleti e di Montecchi*; Beethoven: *Fidelio*; Verdi: *Il Trovatore*; Gounod: *Sapho*; Gluck: *Orphee et Euridice, Alceste*; Meyerbeer: *Le Prophète*). Orchestre Suisse Romande and the Geneva Opera Chorus, Henry Lewis, conductor. 1972. Singly, London OS 25966. Together, London OS 25967.

Stravinsky, Igor. *Four Russian Choruses; Three Souvenirs.* Igor Stravinsky, conductor. 1956. Columbia ML-5107.

Thomas, Ambroise. *Mignon.* Philharmonic Orchestra. Ambrosian Opera Chorus. Frederica von Stade, Ruth Welting, Alain Vanzo, Nicola Zaccaria, Antonio de Almeida, conductor. (Complete/ in French). 1978. CBS M4 34590.

Verdi, Giuseppe. *Il Trovatore.* National Philharmonic Orchestra. Joan Sutherland, Luciano Pavarotti, Ingvar Wixell, Nicolai Ghiaurov, Richard Bonynge, conductor. 1977. London OSA 13124.

————. *Requiem.* Vienna Philharmonic. Vienna State Opera Chorus. Joan Sutherland, Luciano Pavarotti, Martti Talvela, Georg Solti, conductor. 1968. London OSA 1275.

Vivaldi, Antonio. *Orlando Furioso.* I Solisti Veneti. Victoria de los Angeles, Lucia Valentini-Terrani, Dalmacio Gonzales, Lajos Kozma, Sesto Bruscantini, Nicola Zaccaria, Claudio Scimone, conductor. 1978. RCA ARL 3-2869.

# INDEX

*MARILYN HORNE lives in New York City. Her friend and collaborator,* JANE SCOVELL, *lives in Cambridge, Massachusetts. Ms. Scovell is a journalist whose pieces, under the name Jane Appleton, have appeared in* Cosmopolitan, Redbook, Ms., *the* New York Times, *the* Boston Herald, *the* Boston Globe, Travel & Leisure, *and many other publications. She has also taught courses in opera and film at Newton College of the Sacred Heart and lectures for Harvard University's Center for Lifelong Learning.*

GREENLAND

KNUD RASMUSSEN LAND

WASHINGTON LAND

Cape
Constitution

St. George's
Fjord

Sherard Osborn Fjord

Black Horn Cliffs

Cape
Bryant

Hall
Basin

Kennedy Channel

ELLESMERE ISLAND